Victorian Wor

Sixteen Biographies

George Henry Blore

Alpha Editions

This edition published in 2024

ISBN : 9789362923097

Design and Setting By
Alpha Editions
www.alphaedis.com
Email - info@alphaedis.com

As per information held with us this book is in Public Domain.
This book is a reproduction of an important historical work. Alpha Editions uses the best technology to reproduce historical work in the same manner it was first published to preserve its original nature. Any marks or number seen are left intentionally to preserve its true form.

Contents

PREFACE ....- 1 -
INTRODUCTION ....- 3 -
THOMAS CARLYLE ....- 9 -
SIR ROBERT PEEL ....- 24 -
CHARLES JAMES NAPIER ....- 39 -
ANTHONY ASHLEY COOPER ....- 53 -
JOHN LAWRENCE ....- 66 -
JOHN BRIGHT ....- 78 -
CHARLES DICKENS ....- 92 -
ALFRED TENNYSON ....- 106 -
CHARLES KINGSLEY ....- 125 -
GEORGE FREDERICK WATTS ....- 138 -
JOHN COLERIDGE PATTESON ....- 154 -
SIR ROBERT D. B. MORIER, G.C.B., P.C. ....- 171 -
JOSEPH LISTER ....- 191 -
WILLIAM MORRIS ....- 209 -
JOHN RICHARD GREEN ....- 223 -
CECIL RHODES ....- 239 -
FOOTNOTES: ....- 253 -

PREFACE

Some excuse seems to be needed for venturing at this time to publish biographical sketches of the men of the Victorian era. Several have been written by men, like Lord Morley and Lord Bryce, having first-hand knowledge of their subjects, others by the best critics of the next generation, such as Mr. Chesterton and Mr. Clutton-Brock. With their critical ability I am not able to compete; but they often postulate a knowledge of facts which the average reader has forgotten or has never known. Having written these sketches primarily for boys at school I am not ashamed to state well-known facts, nor have I wished to avoid the obvious.

Nor do these sketches aim at obtaining a sensation by the shattering of idols. I have been content to accept the verdicts passed by their contemporaries on these great servants of the public, verdicts which, in general, seem likely to stand the test of time. Boys will come soon enough on books where criticism has fuller play, and revise the judgements of the past. Such a revision is salutary, when it is not unfair or bitter in tone.

At a time when the subject called 'civics' is being more widely introduced into schools, it seems useful to present the facts of individual lives, instances chosen from different professions, as a supplement to the study of principles and institutions. There is a spirit of public service which is best interpreted through concrete examples. If teachers will, from their own knowledge, fill in these outlines and give life to these portraits, the younger generation may find it not uninteresting to 'praise famous men and our fathers that begat us'.

It seems hardly necessary in a book of this kind to give an imposing list of authorities consulted. In some cases I should find it difficult to trace the essay or memoir from which a statement is drawn; but in the main I have depended on the standard Lives of the various men portrayed, from Froude's *Carlyle* and Forster's *Dickens* to Mackail's *Morris* and Michell's *Rhodes*. And, needless to say, I have found the *Dictionary of National Biography* most valuable. If boys were not frightened from the shelves by its bulk, it would render my work superfluous; but, though I often recommend it to them, I find few signs that they consult it as often as they should. It may seem that no due proportion has been observed in the length of the different sketches; but it must be remembered that, while short Lives of Napier and Lawrence have been written by well-known authors, it is more difficult for a boy to satisfy his curiosity about Lister, Patteson, or Green; and of Morier no complete life has yet been published.

I am indebted to Mr. Emery Walker for assistance in the selection of the portraits.

Three of my friends have been kind enough to read parts of the book and to give me advice: the Rev. A. T. P. Williams and Mr. C. E. Robinson, my colleagues here, and Mr. Nowell Smith, Head Master of Sherborne. I owe much also to the good judgement of Mr. Milford's reader. If I venture to thank them for their help, they are in no way responsible for my mistakes. Writing in the intervals of school-mastering I have no doubt been guilty of many, and I shall be grateful if any reader will take the trouble to inform me of those which he detects.

G.H.B.

WINCHESTER,
April 1920.

INTRODUCTION

THE VICTORIAN ERA

We like to fancy, when critics are not at our elbow, that each Age in our history has a character and a physiognomy of its own. The sixteenth century speaks to us of change and adventure in every form, of ships and statecraft, of discovery and desecration, of masterful sovereigns and unscrupulous ministers. We evoke the memory of Henry VIII and Elizabeth, of Wolsey and Thomas Cromwell, of Drake and Raleigh, while the gentler virtues of Thomas More and Philip Sidney seem but rare flowers by the wayside.

The glory of the seventeenth century shines out amid the clash of arms, in battles fought for noble principles, in the lives and deaths of Falkland and Hampden, of Blake, Montrose, and Cromwell. If its nobility is dimmed as we pass from the world of Shakespeare and Milton to that of Dryden and Defoe, yet there is sufficient unity in its central theme to justify the enthusiasm of those who praise it as the heroic age of English history.

Less justice, perhaps, is done when we characterize the eighteenth century as that of elegance and wit; when, heedless of the great names of Chatham, Wolfe, and Clive, we fill the forefront of our picture with clubs and coffee-houses, with the graces of Chesterfield and Horace Walpole, the beauties of Gainsborough and Romney, or the masterpieces of Sheraton and Adam. But each generalization, as we make it, seems more imperfect and unfair; and partly because Carlyle abused it so unmercifully, this century has in the last fifty years received ample justice from many of our ablest writers.

Difficult indeed then it must seem to give adequate expression to the life of a century like the nineteenth, so swift, so restless, so many-sided, so full of familiar personages, and of conflicts which have hardly yet receded to a distance where the historian can judge them aright. The rich luxuriance of movements and of individual characters chokes our path; it is a labyrinth in which one may well lose one's way and fail to see the wood for the trees.

The scientist would be protesting (all this time) that this is a very superficial aspect of the matter. He would recast our framework for us and teach us to follow out the course of our history through the development of mathematics, physics, and biology, to pass from Newton to Harvey, and from Watt to Darwin, and in the relation of these sciences to one another to find the clue to man's steady progress.

The tale thus told is indeed wonderful to read and worthy of the telling; but, to appreciate it fully, it needs a wider and deeper knowledge than many possess. And it tends to leave out one side of our human nature. There are many whose sympathies will always be drawn rather to the influence of man upon man than to the extension of man's power over nature, to the development of character rather than of knowledge. To-day literature must approach science, her all-powerful sister, with humility, and crave indulgence for those who still wish to follow in the track where Plutarch led the way, to read of human infirmity as well as of human power, not to scorn anecdotes or even comparisons which illustrate the qualities by which service can be rendered to the State.

To return to the nineteenth century, some would find a guiding thread in the progress of the Utilitarian School, which based its teaching on the idea of pursuing the greatest happiness of the greatest number, the school which produced philosophers like Bentham and J. S. Mill, and politicians like Cobden and Morley. It was congenial to the English mind to follow a line which seemed to lead with certainty to practical results; and the industrial revolutions caused men at this time to look, perhaps too much, to the material conditions of well-being. Along with the discoveries that revolutionized industry, the eighteenth century had bequeathed something more precious than material wealth. John Wesley, the strongest personal influence of its latter half, had stirred the spirit of conscious philanthropy and the desire to apply Christian principles to the service of all mankind. Howard, Wilberforce, and others directed this spirit into definite channels, and many of their followers tinged with a warm religious glow the principles which, even in agnostics like Mill, lent consistent nobility to a life of service. The efforts which these men made, alone or banded into societies, to enlarge the liberties of Englishmen and to distribute more fairly the good things of life among them, were productive of much benefit to the age.

Under such leadership indeed as that of Bentham and Wilberforce, the Victorian Age might have been expected to follow a steady course of beneficence which would have drawn all the nobler spirits of the new generation into its main current. Clear, logical, and persuasive, the Utilitarians seemed likely to command success in Parliament, in the pulpit, and in the press. But the criterion of happiness, however widely diffused (and that it had not gone far in 1837 Disraeli's *Sybil* will attest), was not enough to satisfy the ardent idealism that blazed in the breasts of men stirred by revolutions and the new birth of Christian zeal. In contrast to the ordered pursuit of reform, the spirit of which the Utilitarians hoped to embody in societies and Acts of Parliament, were the rebellious impulses of men filled with a prophetic spirit, walking in obedience to an inward voice, eager to cry aloud their message to a generation wrapped in prosperity and self-contentment. They formed no single school and followed no single line. In a few cases we may observe the relation of master and pupil, as between Carlyle and Ruskin; in more we can see a small band of friends like the Pre-Raphaelite Brotherhood, the leaders of the Oxford Movement, or the scientific circle of

Darwin and Hooker, working in fellowship for a common end. But individuality is their note. They sprang often from surroundings most alien to their genius; they wandered far from the courses which their birth seemed to prescribe; the spirit caught them and they went forth to the fray.

The time in which they grew up was calculated to mould characters of strength. Self-control and self-denial had been needed in the protracted wars with France. Self-reliance had been learnt in the hard school of adversity. Imagination was quickened by the heroism of the struggle which had ended in the final victory of our arms. And to the generations born in the early days of the nineteenth century lay open fields wider than were offered to human activity in any other age of the world's history. Now at last the full fruits of sixteenth-century discovery were to be reaped. It was possible for Gordon, by the personal ascendancy which he owed to his single-minded faith, to create legends and to work miracles in Asia and in Africa; for Richard Burton to gain an intimate knowledge of Islam in its holiest shrines; for Livingstone, Hannington, and other martyrs to the Faith to breathe their last in the tropics; for Franklin, dying, as Scott died nearly seventy years later, in the cause of Science, to hallow the polar regions for the Anglo-Saxon race. Darkest Africa was to remain impenetrable yet awhile. Only towards the end of the century, when Stanley's work was finished, could Rhodes and Kitchener conspire to clasp hands across its deserts and its swamps: but on the other side of the globe a new island-empire had been already created by the energy of Wakefield, and developed by the wisdom of Parkes and Grey. In distant lands, on stricken fields less famous but no less perilous, Wellington's men were applying the lessons which they had learnt in the Peninsula. On distant seas Nelson's ships were carrying explorers equipped for the more peaceful task of scientific observation. In this century the highest mountains, the deepest seas, the widest stretches of desert were to reveal their secrets to the adventurers who held the whole world for their playground or field of conquest.

And not only in the great expansion of empire abroad but in the growth of knowledge at home and the application of it to civil life, there was a field to employ all the vigour of a race capable of rising to its opportunities. There is no need to remind this generation of such names as Stephenson and Herschel, Darwin and Huxley, Faraday and Kelvin; they are in no danger of being forgotten to-day. The men of letters take relatively a less conspicuous place in the evolution of the Age; but the force which they put into their writings, the wealth of their material, the variety of their lives, and the contrasts of their work, endow the annals of the nineteenth century with an absorbing interest. While Tennyson for the most part stayed in his English homes, singing the beauties of his native land, Browning was a sojourner in Italian palaces and villas, studying men of many races and many times, exploring the subtleties of the human heart. The pen of Dickens portrayed all classes of society except, perhaps, that which Thackeray made his peculiar field. The historians, too, furnish singular contrasts: the vehement pugnacity of Freeman is a foil to the serene studiousness of Acton; the erratic career of Froude to the concentration of Stubbs. The influence exercised on their contemporaries by recluses such as Newman or Darwin may be compared with the more worldly activities of Huxley and Samuel Wilberforce. Often we see equally diverse elements in following the course of a single life. In Matthew Arnold we wonder at the poet of 'The Strayed Reveller' coexisting with the zealous inspector of schools; in William Morris we find it hard to reconcile the creative craftsman with the fervent apostle of social discontent. Perhaps the most notable case of this diversity is the long pilgrimage of Gladstone which led him from the camp of the 'stern, unbending Tories' to the leadership of Radicals and Home Rulers. There is an interest in tracing through these metamorphoses the essential unity of a man's character. On the other hand, one cannot but admire the steadfastness with which Darwin and Lister, Tennyson and Watts, pursued the even tenor of their way.

Again we may notice the strange irony of fortune which drew Carlyle from his native moorlands to spend fifty years in a London suburb, while his disciple Ruskin, born and bred in London, and finding fit audience in the universities of the South, closed his long life in seclusion amid the Cumbrian fells. So two statesmen, who were at one time very closely allied, present a similarly striking contrast in the manner of their lives. Till the age of forty Joseph Chamberlain limited himself to municipal work in Birmingham, and yet he rose in later life to imperial views wider than any statesman's of his day. Charles Dilke, on the other hand, could be an expert on 'Greater Britain' at thirty and yet devote his old age to elaborating the details of Local Government and framing programmes of social reform for the working classes of our towns. Accidents these may be, but they lend to Victorian biography the charm of a fanciful arabesque or mosaic of varied pattern and hue.

Eccentrics, too, there were in fact among the literary men of the day, even as there are in the fiction of Dickens, of Peacock, of George Meredith. There was Borrow, who, as an old man, was tramping solitarily in the fields of Norfolk, as earlier he wandered alone in wild Wales or wilder Spain. There was FitzGerald, who remained all his life constant to one corner of East Anglia, and who yet, by the precious thread of his correspondence, maintained contact with the great world of Victorian letters to which he belonged.

Some wandered as far afield as Asia or the South Seas; some buried themselves in the secluded courts of Oxford and Cambridge and became mythical figures in academic lore. Not many were to be found within hail of

London or Edinburgh in these forceful days. Brougham, the most omniscient of reviewers, with the most ill-balanced of minds, belongs more properly to the preceding age, though he lived to 1868; and it is from this age that the novelists probably drew their eccentric types. But between eccentricity and vigorous originality who shall draw the dividing line?

Men like these it is hard to label and to classify. Their individuality is so patent that any general statement is at once open to attack. The most that we can do is to indicate one or two points in which the true Victorians had a certain resemblance to one another, and were unlike their successors of our own day. They were more evidently in earnest, less conscious of themselves, more indifferent to ridicule, more absorbed in their work. To many of them full work and the cares of office seemed a necessity of life. It was a typical Victorian who, after sixteen years of public service, writing a family letter, says, 'I feel that the interest of business and the excitement of responsibility are indispensable to me, and I believe that I am never happier than when I have more to think of and to do than I can manage in a given period'. Idleness and insouciance had few temptations for them, cynicism was abhorrent to them. Even Thackeray was perpetually 'caught out' when he assumed the cynic's pose. Charlotte Brontë, most loyal of his admirers and critics, speaks of the 'deep feelings for his kind' which he cherished in his large heart, and again of the 'sentiment, jealously hidden but genuine, which extracts the venom from that formidable Thackeray'. Large-hearted and generous to one another, they were ready to face adventure, eager to fight for an ideal, however impracticable it seemed. This was as true of Tennyson, Browning, Matthew Arnold, and all the *genus irritabile vatum*, as of the politicians and the men of action. They made many mistakes; they were combative, often difficult to deal with. Some of them were deficient in judgement, others in the saving gift of humour; but they were rarely petty or ungenerous, or failed from faint-heartedness or indecision. Vehemence and impatience can do harm to the best causes, and the lives of men like the Napiers and the Lawrences, like Thomas Arnold and Charles Kingsley, like John Bright and Robert Lowe, are marred by conflicts which might have been avoided by more studied gentleness or more philosophic calm. But the time seemed short in which they could redress the evils which offended them. They saw around them a world which seemed to be lapped in comfort or swathed in the dead wrappings of the past, and would not listen to reasoned appeals; and it would be futile to deny that, by lifting their voices to a pitch which offends fastidious critics, Carlyle and Ruskin did sometimes obtain a hearing and kindle a passion which Matthew Arnold could never stir by his scholarly exhortations to 'sweetness and light'.

But it would be a mistake to infer from such clamour and contention that the Victorians did not enjoy their fair share of happiness in this world. The opposite would be nearer the truth: happiness was given to them in good, even in overflowing measure. Any one familiar with Trevelyan's biography of Macaulay will remember with what fullness and intensity he enjoyed his life; and the same fact is noted by Dr. Mozley in his Essay on that most representative Victorian, Thomas Arnold. The lives of Delane, the famous editor of *The Times*, of the statesman Palmerston, of the painter Millais, and of many other men in many professions, might be quoted to support this view. In some cases this was due to their strong family affections, in others to their genius for friendship. A good conscience, a good temper, a good digestion, are all factors of importance. But perhaps the best insurance against moodiness and melancholy was that strenuous activity which made them forget themselves, that energetic will-power which was the driving force in so many movements of the day.

How many of the changes of last century were due to general tendencies, how far the single will of this man or that has seriously affected its history, it is impossible to estimate. To many it seems that the rôle of the individual is played out. The spirit of the coming era is that of organized fellowship and associated effort. The State is to prescribe for all, and the units are, somehow, to be marshalled into their places by a higher collective will. Under the shadow of socialism the more ambitious may be tempted to quit the field of public service at home and to look to enterprises abroad—to resign poor England to a mechanical bureaucracy, a soulless uniformity where one man is as good as another. But it is difficult to believe that society can dispense with leaders, or afford to forget the lessons which may be learnt from the study of such noble lives. The Victorians had a robuster faith. Their faith and their achievements may help to banish such doubts to-day. As one of the few survivors of that Victorian era has lately said: 'Only those whose minds are numbed by the suspicion that all times are tolerably alike, and men and women much of a muchness, will deny that it was a generation of intrepid efforts forward.' Some fell in mid-combat: some survived to witness the eventual victory of their cause. For all might be claimed the funeral honours which Browning claimed for his Grammarian. They aimed high; they 'threw themselves on God': the mountain-tops are their appropriate resting-place.

THOMAS CARLYLE

1795-1881

1795. Born at Ecclefechan, Dumfriesshire, December 4.

1809. Enters Edinburgh University.

1814-18. Schoolmaster at Annan and Kirkcaldy. Friendship with Edward Irving.

1819-21. Reading law and literature at Edinburgh and Mainhill.

1821. First meeting with Jane Welsh at Haddington.

1822-3. Tutorship in Buller family.

1824-5. German literature, Goethe, *Life of Schiller*.

1826. October 17, marriage; residence at Comely Bank, Edinburgh.

1827. Jeffrey's friendship; articles for *Edinburgh Review*.

1828-34. Craigenputtock, with intervals in London and Edinburgh; poverty; solitude; profound study; *Sartor Resartus* written; reading for *French Revolution*.

1834. Cheyne Row, Chelsea, permanent home.

1834. Begins to read for, 1841 to write, *Cromwell*.

1834-6. *French Revolution* written; finished January 12, 1837.

1837-40. Four courses of lectures in London. (German literature, *Heroes*.)

1844. Changes plan of, 1845 finishes writing, *Cromwell*.

1846-51. Studies Ireland and modern questions; *Latter-Day Pamphlets*, 1849.

1851. Choice of Frederick the Great of Prussia for next subject.

1857. Two vols. printed; 1865, rest finished and published.

1865. Lord Rector of Edinburgh University.

1866. Death of Mrs. Carlyle, April 21.

1867-9. Prepares Memorials of his wife; friendship with Froude.

1870. Loses the use of his right hand.

1874. Refuses offer of Baronetcy or G.C.B.

1881. Death at Chelsea, February 5; burial at Ecclefechan.

THOMAS CARLYLE
PROPHET

North-west of Carlisle (from which town the Carlyle family in all probability first took their name), a little way along the border, the river Annan comes down its green valley from the lowland hills to lose itself in the wide sands of the Solway Firth. At the foot of these hills is the village of Ecclefechan, some eight miles inland. Here in the wide irregular street, down the side of which flows a little beck, stands the grey cottage, built by the stonemason James Carlyle, where he lived with his second wife, Margaret Aitken; and here on December 4, 1795, the eldest of nine children, their son Thomas was born. There is little to redeem the place from insignificance; the houses are mostly mean, the position of the village is tame and commonplace. But if a visitor will mount the hills that lie to the north, turn southward and look over the wide expanse of land and water to the Cumbrian mountains, then, should he be fortunate enough to see the landscape in stormy and unsettled weather, he may realize why the land was so dear to its most famous son that he could return to it from year to year throughout his life and could there at all times soothe his most unquiet moods. Through all his years in London he remained a lowland Scot and was most at home in Annandale. With this district his fame is still bound up, as that of Walter Scott with the Tweed, or that of Wordsworth with the Lakes.

In this humble household Thomas Carlyle first learnt what is meant by work, by truthfulness, and by reverence, lessons which he never forgot. He learnt to revere authority, to revere worth, and to revere something yet higher and more mysterious—the Unseen. In *Sartor Resartus* he describes how his hero was impressed by his parents' observance of religious duties. 'The highest whom I knew on earth I here saw bowed down with awe unspeakable before a Higher in Heaven; such things especially in infancy, reach inwards to the very core of your being.' His father was a man of unusual force of character and gifted with a wonderful power of speech, flashing out in picturesque metaphor, in biting satire, in humorous comment upon life. He had, too, the

Scotch genius for valuing education; and it was he who decided that Tom, whose character he had observed, should have every chance that schooling could give him. His mother was a most affectionate, single-hearted, and religious woman; labouring for her family, content with her lot, her trust for her son unfailing, her only fear for him lest in his new learning he might fall away from the old Biblical faith which she held so firmly herself.

Reading with his father or mother, lending a hand at housework when needed, nourishing himself on the simple oatmeal and milk which throughout life remained his favourite food, submitting himself instinctively to the stern discipline of the home, he passed, happily on the whole, through his childhood and soon outstripped his comrades in the village school. His success there led to his going in his tenth year to the grammar school at Annan; and before he reached his fourteenth year he trudged off on foot to Edinburgh to begin his studies at the university.

Instead of young men caught up by express trains and deposited, by the aid of cabmen and porters, in a few hours in the sheltered courts of Oxford and Cambridge, we must imagine a party of boys, of fourteen or fifteen years old, trudging on foot twenty miles a day for five days across bleak country, sleeping at rough inns, and on their arrival searching for an attic in some bleak tenement in a noisy street. Here they were to live almost entirely on the baskets of home produce sent through the carriers at intervals by their thrifty parents. It was and is a Spartan discipline, and it turns out men who have shown their grit and independence in all lands where the British flag is flown.

The earliest successes which Carlyle won, both at Annan and at Edinburgh, were in mathematics. His classical studies received little help from his professors, and his literary gifts were developed mostly by his own reading, and stimulated from time to time by talks with fellow students. Perhaps it was for his ultimate good that he was not brought under influences which might have guided him into more methodical courses and tamed his rugged originality. The universities cannot often be proved to have fostered kindly their poets and original men of letters; at least we may say that Edinburgh was a more kindly Alma Mater to Carlyle than Oxford and Cambridge proved to Shelley and Byron. His native genius, and the qualities which he inherited from his parents, were not starved in alien soil, but put out vigorous growth. From such letters to his friends as have survived, we can see what a power Carlyle had already developed of forcibly expressing his ideas and establishing an influence over others.

He left the university at the age of nineteen, and the next twelve years of his life were of a most unsettled character. He made nearly as many false starts in life as Goldsmith or Coleridge, though he redeemed them nobly by his persistence in after years. In 1814 his family still regarded the ministry as his vocation, and Carlyle was himself quite undecided about it. To promote this idea the profession of schoolmaster was taken up for the time. He continued in it for more than six years, first at Annan and then at Kirkcaldy; but he was soon finding it uncongenial and rebelling against it. A few years later he tried reading law with no greater contentment; and in order to support himself he was reduced to teaching private pupils. The chief friend of this period was Edward Irving, the gifted preacher who afterwards, in London, came to tragic shipwreck. He was a native of Annan, five years older than Carlyle, and he had spent some time in preaching and preparing for the ministry. He was one of the few people who profoundly influenced Carlyle's life. At Kirkcaldy he was his constant companion, shared his tastes, lent him books, and kindled his powers of insight and judgement in many a country walk. Carlyle has left us records of this time in his *Reminiscences*, how he read the twelve volumes of Irving's *Gibbon* in twelve days, how he tramped through the Trossachs on foot, how in summer twilights he paced the long stretches of sand at Irving's side.

It was Irving who in 1822 commended him to the Buller family, with whom he continued as tutor for two years. Charles Buller, the eldest son, was a boy of rare gifts and promise, worthy of such a teacher; and but for his untimely death in 1848 he might have won a foremost place in politics. The family proved valuable friends to Carlyle in after-life, besides enabling him at this time to live in comfort, with leisure for his own studies and some spare money to help his family. But for this aid, his brother Alexander would have fared ill with the farming, and John could never have afforded the training for the medical profession.

Again, it was Irving who first took him to Haddington in 1821 and introduced him to Jane Baillie Welsh, his future wife. Irving's sincerity and sympathy, his earnest enthusiasm joined with the power of genuine laughter (always to Carlyle a mark of a true rich nature), made him through all these years a thoroughly congenial companion. He really understood Carlyle as few outside his family did, and he never grew impatient at Carlyle's difficulty in settling to a profession. 'Your mind,' he wrote, 'unfortunately for its present peace, has taken in so wide a range of study as to be almost incapable of professional trammels; and it has nourished so uncommon and so unyielding a character, as first unfits you for, and then disgusts you with, any accommodations which for so cultivated and so fertile a mind would easily procure favour and patronage.' Well might Carlyle in later days find a hero in tough old Samuel Johnson, whose sufferings were due to similar causes. The other source which kept the fire in him aglow through these difficult years was the confidence and affection of his whole family, and the welcome which he always found at home. Disappointed though they were at his failure, as yet, to settle to a profession and to earn a steady income, for all that 'Tom' was to be a great man; and when he could find time to spend some months at Mainhill, or later at Scotsbrig,[1] a room could always be found for him, hours of peace and solitude could be enjoyed, the most wholesome food, and the most cordial affection, were there rendered as loyal ungrudging tribute. But new ties were soon to be knit and a new chapter to be opened in his life.

John Welsh of Haddington, who died before Carlyle met his future wife, was a surgeon and a man of remarkable gifts; and his daughter could trace her descent to such famous Scotsmen as Wallace and John Knox. Her own mental powers were great, and her vivacity and charming manners caused her to shine in society wherever she was. She had an unquestioned supremacy among the ladies of Haddington and many had been the suitors for her hand. When Irving had given her lessons there, love had sprung up between tutor and pupil, but this budding romance ended tragically in 1822. Before meeting her he had been engaged to another lady; and when a new appointment gave him a sure income, he was held to his bond and was forced to crush down his passion and to take farewell of Miss Welsh. At what date Carlyle conceived the hope of making her his wife it is difficult to say. Her beauty and wit seem to have done their work quickly in his case; but she was not one to give her affections readily, for all the intellectual sympathy which united them. In 1823 she was contemplating marriage, but had made no promise; in 1824 she had accepted the idea of marrying him, but in 1825 she still scouted the conditions in which he proposed to live. His position was precarious, his projects visionary, and his immediate desire was to settle on a lonely farm, where he could devote himself to study, if she would do the household drudgery. Because his mother whom he loved and honoured was content to lead this life, he seemed to think that his wife could do the same; but her nature and her rearing were not those of the Carlyles and their Annandale neighbours. It involved a complete renunciation of the comforts of life and the social position which she enjoyed; and much though she admired his talents and enjoyed his company, she was not in that passion of love which could lift her to such heights of self-sacrifice.

By this time we can begin to discern in his letters the outline of his character—his passionate absorption in study, his moodiness, his fits of despondency, his intense irritability; his incapacity to master his own tongue and temper. In happy moments he shows great tenderness of feeling for those whom he loves or pities; but this alternates with inconsiderate clamour and loud complaints deafening the ears of all about him, provoked often by slight and even imaginary grievances. It is the artistic nature run riot, and that in one who preached silence and stoicism as the chief virtues—an inconsistency which has amused and disgusted generations of readers. It was impossible for him to do his work with the regular method, the equable temper, of a Southey or a Scott. In dealing with history he must image the past to himself most vividly before he could expound his subject; and that effort and strain cost him sleepless nights and days of concentrated thought. Nor was he an easier companion when his work was finished and he could take his ease. Then life seemed empty and profitless; and in its emptiness his voice echoed all the louder. The ill was within him, and outward circumstances were powerless to affect his nature.

At this time he was chiefly occupied in reading German literature and spreading the knowledge of it among his countrymen. After Coleridge he was the first of our literary men to appreciate the poets and mystics of Germany, and he did more even than Coleridge to make Englishmen familiar with them. He acquired at this time a knowledge of French and Italian literature too; but the philosophy of Kant and the writings of Goethe and Schiller roused him to greater enthusiasm. From Kant he learnt that the guiding principle of conduct was not happiness, but the 'categorical imperative' of duty; from Goethe he drew such hopefulness as gleams occasionally through his despondent utterances on the progress of the human race. He translated Goethe's novel, *Wilhelm Meister*, in 1823, and followed it up with the *Life of Schiller*. There was no considerable sale for either of these books till his lectures in London and his established fame roused a demand for all he had written. In these days he was practising for the profession of a man of letters, and was largely influenced by personal ambition and the desire to earn an income which would make him independent; he was not yet fired with a mission, or kindled to white heat.

His long courtship was rewarded in October 1826. When the marriage took place the bride was twenty-five years old and the bridegroom thirty. Men of letters have not the reputation of making ideal husbands, and the qualities to which this is due were possessed by Carlyle in exaggerated measure. It was a perilous enterprise for any one to live with him, most of all for such a woman, delicately bred, nervous, and highly strung. She was aware of this, and was prepared for a large measure of self-denial; but she could not have foreseen how severe she would find the trial. The morbid sensitiveness of Carlyle to his own pains and troubles, so often imaginary, joined with his inconsiderate blindness to his wife's real sufferings, led to many heart-burnings. If she contributed to them, in some degree, by her wilfulness, jealous temper, and sharpness of tongue, ill-health and solitude may well excuse her.

His own confessions, made after her death, are coloured by sorrow and deep affection: no doubt he paints his own conduct in hues darker than the truth demands. Shallow critics have sneered at the picture of the philosopher whose life was so much at variance with his creed, and too much has, perhaps, been written about the subject. If reference must be made to such a well-worn tale, it is best to let Carlyle's own account stand as he wished it to stand. His moral worth has been vindicated in a hundred ways, not least by his humility and honesty about himself, and can bear the test of time.

For the first two years of married life Carlyle's scheme of living on a farm was kept at bay by his wife, and their home was at Edinburgh. Carlyle refers to this as the happiest period of his life, though he did not refrain from loud laments upon occasions. The good genius of the household was Jeffrey, the famous editor of the *Edinburgh Review*, who was distantly related to Mrs. Carlyle. He made friends with the newly-married pair, opened a path for them into the society of the capital, and enabled Carlyle to spread the knowledge of German authors in the *Review* and to make his bow before a wider public. The prospects of the little household seemed brighter, but, by generously making over all her money to her mother, his wife had crippled its resources; and Carlyle was of so difficult a humour that neither Jeffrey nor any one else could guide his steps for long. Living was precarious; society made demands even on a modest household, and in 1828 he at length had his way and persuaded his wife to remove to Craigenputtock. It was in the loneliness of the moors that Carlyle was to come to his full stature and to develop his astonishing genius.

Craigenputtock was a farm belonging to his wife's family, lying seventy feet above the sea, sixteen miles from Dumfries, among desolate moors and bogs, and fully six miles from the nearest village. 'The house is gaunt and hungry-looking. It stands with the scanty fields attached as an island in a sea of morass. The landscape is unredeemed either by grace or grandeur, mere undulating hills of grass and heather with peat bogs in the hollows between them.' So Froude describes the home where the Carlyles were to spend six years, the wife in domestic labours, in solitude, in growing ill-health, the husband in omnivorous reading, in digesting the knowledge that he gathered, in transmuting it and marking it with the peculiar stamp of his genius. There was no true companionship over the work. As the moorland gave the fresh air and stillness required, so the wife might nourish the physical frame with wholesome digestible food and save him from external cares; the rest must be done by lonely communing with himself. He needed no Fleet Street taverns or literary salons to encourage him. Goethe, with whom he exchanged letters and compliments at times, said with rare insight that he 'had in himself an originating principle of conviction, out of which he could develop the force that lay in him unassisted by other men'.

Few were the interruptions from without. His fame was not yet established. In any case pilgrims would have to undertake a very rough journey, and the fashion of such pilgrimages had hardly begun. But in 1833 from distant America came one disciple, afterwards to be known as the famous author Ralph Waldo Emerson; and he has left us in his *English Traits* a vivid record of his impression of two or three famous men of letters whom he saw. He describes Carlyle as 'tall and gaunt, with a cliff-like brow, self-possessed, and holding his extraordinary powers of conversation in easy command; clinging to his northern accent with evident relish; full of lively anecdote, and with a streaming humour, which floated everything he looked upon'.[2]

Much of his time was given to reading about the French Revolution, which was to be the subject of his greatest literary triumph. But the characteristic work of this period is *Sartor Resartus* ('The tailor patched anew'), in which Carlyle, under a thin German disguise, reveals himself to the world, with his views on the customs and ways of society and his contempt for all the pretensions and absurdities which they involved. In many places it is extravagant and fantastic, as when 'the most remarkable incident in modern history' proves to be George Fox the Quaker making a suit of leather to render himself independent of tailors; in others it rises to the highest pitch of poetry, as in the sympathetic lament over the hardships of manual labour. 'Venerable to me is the hard Hand; crooked, coarse; wherein notwithstanding lies a cunning virtue, indefeasibly royal, as of the Sceptre of this Planet. Venerable, too, is the rugged face, all weather-tanned, besoiled, with its rude intelligence; for it is the face of a Man living manlike. O, but the more venerable for thy rudeness, and even because we must pity as well as love thee! Hardly-entreated Brother! For us was thy back so bent, for us were thy straight limbs and fingers so deformed; thou wert our Conscript on whom the lot fell, and fighting our battles wert so marred.' It is through such passages that Carlyle has won his way to the hearts of many who care little for history, or for German literature.

The book evidently contains much that is autobiographical, and helps us to understand Carlyle's childhood and youth; but it is so mixed up with fantasy and humour that it is difficult to separate fiction from fact. Its chief aim seems to be the overthrow of cant, the ridiculing of empty conventions, and the preaching of sincerity and independence. But not yet was Carlyle's generation prepared to listen to such sermons. Jeffrey was bewildered by the tone and offended at the style; publisher after publisher refused it; and when at length it was launched upon the world piecemeal in *Fraser's Magazine*, the reading public either ignored it or abused it in the roundest terms. During all this time Carlyle was anxiously looking for some surer means of livelihood, and had not yet decided that literature was to be his profession. He had hopes at different times of professorships in Edinburgh and St. Andrews, and of the editorship of various reviews; but these all came to nothing. For some posts he was not suited; for others his application could find no support. He even thought of going to America, where Emerson and other admirers would have welcomed him. But the disappointments in Scotland decided him to make one more effort in London before accepting defeat, and in 1834 he found a house at Chelsea and prepared to quit his hermitage among the moors.

Cheyne Row, Chelsea, was to be his new home, a quiet street running northward from the riverside in a quarter of London not then invaded by industrialism. The house, No. 24, with its little garden, has been made into a Carlyle museum, and may still be seen on the east side of the street facing a few survivors of the sturdy old pollarded lime-trees standing there 'like giants in Tawtie wigs'. His bust, by Boehm, is in the garden on the Embankment not a hundred yards away. With this district are connected other names famous in literature and art, but its presiding genius is the 'Sage of Chelsea', who spent the last forty-seven years of his life in it; and there, in a double-walled room, in spite of trivial disturbances from without, in spite of far more serious fits of dejection and discontent within, he composed his three greatest historical books. At the outset his prospects were not bright, and at the end of 1834 he confessed 'it is now twenty-three months since I earned a penny by the craft of literature'. There was need of much faith; and it was fortunate for him that he had at his side one who believed in his genius and who was well qualified to judge. He must have been thinking of this when he wrote of Mahomet in *Heroes* and of the prophet's gratitude to his first wife Kadijah: 'She believed in me when none else would believe. In the whole world I had but one friend and she was that!' In the same place he quoted the German writer Novalis: 'It is certain my conviction gains infinitely, the moment another soul will believe in it.'

So fortified, he worked through the days of poverty and gloom, with groans and outbursts of fury, kindling to white heat as he imaged to himself the men and events of the French Revolution, and throwing them on to paper in lurid pictures of flame. One terrible misadventure chilled his spirit in 1835, when the manuscript of the first volume was lent to J. S. Mill, and was accidentally burnt; but, after a short fit of despair, he set manfully to work to repair the loss, and the new version was finished in January, 1837. This book marked an epoch in the writing of history. Hitherto few had realized what potent force there was in the original documents lying stored in libraries and record offices. They were 'live shells' buried in the dust of a neglected magazine; and in the hands of Carlyle they came to life again and worked havoc among the traditional judgements of history. This book was also the turning point in his career. Dickens, Thackeray, and others hailed it with enthusiasm; gradually it made its way with the public at large; and as in the following years Carlyle, prompted by some friends, gave successful courses of lectures,[3] his position among men of letters became assured, and he had no more need to worry over money. Living in London he became known to a wider circle, and his marvellous powers of conversation brought visitors and invitations in larger measure than he desired. The new friends whom he valued most were Mr.

and Lady Harriet Baring,[4] and he was often their guest in London, in Surrey, in Scotland, and later at The Grange in Hampshire. But he remained faithful to his older and more humble friends, while he also made himself accessible to young men of letters who seemed anxious to learn, and who did not offend one or other of his many prejudices. Such were Sterling, Ruskin, Tennyson, and James Anthony Froude.

Despite these successes Carlyle's letters at this time are full of the usual discontents. London life and society stimulated him for the time, but he paid dearly for it. Late dinners and prolonged bouts of talk, in which he put forth all his powers, were followed by dyspepsia and lassitude next day; and the neighbours, who kept dogs or cocks which were accused of disturbing his slumbers, were the mark for many plaints and lamentations. He could not in any circumstances be entirely happy. Work was so exciting with the imagination on fire, that it kept him awake at night; idleness was still more fatal in its effects. And so, after a few years of relative calm, in 1839 we find his active brain struggling to create a true picture of Oliver Cromwell and to expound the meaning of the Great Civil War.

It was to be no easy task. For nearly five years he was to wrestle with the subject, trying in vain to give it adequate shape and form, and then to scrap the labours of years and to start again on a new plan; but in the end he was to win another signal victory. While the *French Revolution* may be the higher artistic triumph, *Cromwell* is more important for one who wishes to understand the life-work of Carlyle and all for which he stood. The emptiness of political theories and institutions, the enduring value of character, are lessons which no one has preached more forcibly. In his opinion the success of the English revolution, the blow to tyranny and misgovernment in Church and State, was not due to eloquent members of the Long Parliament, but to plain God-fearing men, who, if they quoted scripture, did so not from hypocrisy but because it was the language in which they habitually thought. Nor could they build up a new England till they had found a leader. It was the ages which had faith to recognize their worthiest man and to accept his guidance which had achieved great things in the world, not those which prated of democracy and progress. To make his countrymen, in this age of fluent political talk, see the true moral quality of the men of the seventeenth century—this it was which occupied seven years of Carlyle's life and filled his thoughts. It was indeed a labour of Hercules. Much of the material was lost beyond repair, much buried in voluminous folios and State papers, much obscured by the cant and prejudice of eighteenth-century authors. To recall the past, Carlyle needed such help as geography would give him, and he spent many days in visiting Dunbar, Worcester, and other sites. To Naseby he went in 1842, in company with Dr. Arnold, and 'plucked two gowans and a cowslip from the burial heaps of the slain'. A more important task was to recover authentic utterances of Cromwell and his fellow workers, and to put these in the place of the second-hand judgements of political partisans; and this involved laborious researches in libraries. Above all, he had to interpret these records in a new spirit, exercising true insight and sympathy, to put life into the dry bones and to present his readers with the living image of a man. He combined in unique fashion the laborious research of a student with the moral fervour of a prophet.

Despite the strain of these labours Carlyle showed few signs of his fifty years. The family were of tough stock; and the years which he had spent in moorland air had increased the capital of health on which he could draw. The flight of time was chiefly marked by his growing antipathy to the political movements of the day, and by a growing despondency about the future. People might buy his books; but he looked in vain for evidence that they paid heed to the lessons which he preached. The year of revolutions, 1848, followed by the setting up of the French Empire and the collapse of the Roman Republic, produced nothing but disappointment, and he became louder and more bitter in his judgements on democracy. 1849 saw the birth of the *Latter-Day Pamphlets* in which he outraged Mill and the Radicals by his scornful words about Negro Emancipation, and by the savage delight with which he shattered their idols. He loved to expose what seemed to him the sophistries involved in the conventional praise of liberty. Of old the mediaeval serf or the negro slave had some one who was responsible for him, some one interested in his physical well-being. The new conditions too often meant nothing but liberty to starve, liberty to be idle, liberty to slip back into the worst indulgences, while those who might have governed stood by regardless and lent no help. Such from an extreme point of view appeared the policy of *laisser-faire*; and he was neither moderate nor impartial in stating his case. 'An idle white gentleman is not pleasant to me;... but what say you to an idle black gentleman, with his rum bottle in his hand,... no breeches on his body, pumpkin at discretion, and the fruitfullest region of the earth going back to jungle round him?' In a similar vein he dealt with stump oratory, prison reform, and other subjects, tilting in reckless fashion at the shields of the reforming Radicals of the day; nor was he less outspoken when he met in person the champions of these views. A letter to his wife in 1847 tells of a visit to the Brights at Rochdale; how 'John and I discorded in our views not a little', and how 'I shook peaceable Brightdom as with a passing earthquake'. From books he could learn: to human teachers he proved refractory. Had he been more willing to listen to others, his judgements on contemporary events might have been more valuable. All his life he was, as George Meredith says, 'Titanic rather than Olympian, a heaver of rocks, not a shaper'; and this fever of denunciation grew with advancing years. But with these spurts of volcanic energy alternate moods of the deepest depression. His journal for 1850 says, 'This seems really the Nadir of my fortunes; and in hope, desire, or outlook, so far as common mortals reckon such, I never was more bankrupt. Lonely, shut up within my contemptible and yet *not* deliberately ignoble self, perhaps there never was, in modern literary or other history, a more solitary soul, *capable* of any friendship or honest relation to others.' By this time he was feeling the need of another task, and in 1851 he chose Frederick the Great of Prussia for the subject of his next book.

To this generation apology seems to be needed for an English author who lavishes so much admiration on Prussian men and institutions. But Carlyle, whose chief heroes had been men of intense religious convictions, like Luther, Knox, and Cromwell, could find no hero after his heart in English history subsequent to the Civil War. Eloquent Pitts and Burkes, jobbing Walpoles and Pelhams, were to him types of politicians who had brought England to her present plight. German literature had always kept its influence over him and had directed his attention to German history; Frederick, without religion as he was, seemed at any rate sincere, recognized facts, and showed practical capacity for ruling (essential elements in the Carlylean hero), and the subject would be new to his readers. The labour involved was stupendous; it was to fill his life and the lives of his helpers for thirteen years. Of these helpers the chief credit is due to Joseph Neuberg, who piloted him over German railways, libraries, and battle-fields in the search for picturesque detail, and to Henry Larkin, who toiled in London to trace references in scores of authors, and who finally crowned the work by laborious indexing, which made Carlyle's labyrinth accessible to his readers. There were masses of material hidden away and unsifted; and, as in the case of Cromwell, only a man of original genius could penetrate this inert mass with shafts of light and make the past live again. The task grew as he continued his researches. He groped his way back to the beginning of the Hohenzollerns, and sketched the portraits of the old Electors in a style unequalled for vividness and humour. He drew a full-length portrait of Frederick William, most famous of drill-sergeants, and he studied the campaigns of his son with a thoroughness which has been a model to soldiers and civilians ever since. We have the record of two tours which he made in Germany to view the scene of operations;[5] and it is amazing how exact a picture he could bring away from a short visit to each separate battle-field. His diligence, accuracy, and wide grasp of the subject satisfied the severest judges; and the book won him a success as complete and enduring in Germany as in England and America.

When this was finished, Carlyle was on the verge of seventy and his work was done; though the evening of his life was long, his strength was exhausted. His wife lived just long enough to see the seal set upon his fame, and to hear of his election to be Lord Rector of Edinburgh University. But in April 1866, while he was in Scotland for his installation, which she was too weak to attend, he heard the news of her sudden death from heart failure in London;

and after this he was a broken man. By reading her journal he learnt, too late, how much his own inconsiderate temper had added to her trials, and his remorse was bitter and lasting. He shut himself off from all his friends except Froude, who was to be his literary executor, and gave himself to collecting and annotating the memorials which she had left. Each letter is followed by some words of tender recollection or some cry of self-reproach. He has erected to her the most singular of literary monuments, morbid perhaps, but inspired by a feeling which was in his case natural and sincere.

About 1870 he began to lose the use of his right hand and he found it impossible to compose by dictation. Of the last years of his life there is little to narrate. The offer of a baronetcy or the G.C.B. from Mr. Disraeli in 1874 pleased him for the moment, but he resolutely refused external honours. He took daily walks with Froude, daily drives when he became too weak to go on foot. Towards the end the Bible and Shakespeare were his most habitual reading. He had long ceased to be a member of any church, but his belief in God and in God's working in history was the very foundation of his being, and the lessons of the Bible were to him inexhaustible and ever new. Death came to him peacefully in February, 1881; and as he had expressed a definite wish, he was buried at Ecclefechan, though a public funeral in the Abbey was offered and its acceptance would have met with the approval of his countrymen.

The very wealth of records makes it difficult to judge his character fairly. Few men have so laid bare the thoughts and feelings of their hearts. It is easy to blame the unmanly laments which he utters over his health, his solitude, and his sufferings, real or imaginary; few imaginative writers have the every-day virtues. His egotism, too, is difficult to defend. If, as he himself admits, he invariably took an undue share of talk, often in fact monopolizing it, wherever he was, we must remember that the brilliance of his gifts was admitted by all; less pardonable is his habit of disparaging other men, and especially other men of letters. His pen-pictures of Mill, Wordsworth, Coleridge, and others, are wonderfully vivid but too often sour in flavour; his sketch of Charles Lamb is an outrage on that generous and kindly soul. Too often he was unconscious of the pain given by such random words. When he was brought to book, he was honourable enough to recant. Fearing on one occasion to have offended even the serene loyalty of Emerson, he cries out protestingly, 'Has not the man Emerson, from old years, been a Human Friend to me? Can I ever forget, or think otherwise than lovingly of the man Emerson?'

But whatever offence Carlyle committed with his ungovernable tongue or pen, he had rare virtues in conduct. His generosity was as unassuming as it was persistent; and it began at home. Long before he was free from anxieties about money for himself, he was helping two of his brothers to make a career, one in agriculture, and the other in medicine. In his latter days he regularly gave away large sums in such a way that no one knew the source from which they came. His letters show a deep tenderness of affection for his mother, his wife, and others of the family; and the humble Annandale home was always in his thoughts. His charity embraced even those whose claim on him was but indirect. When his wife was dead, he could remember to celebrate her birthday by sending a present to her old nurse. He was scrupulous in money-dealing and frugal in all matters of personal comfort; in his innermost thoughts he was always pure-hearted and sincere; for nothing on earth would he traffic in his independence or in adherence to the truth.

His style has not largely influenced other historians; and this is as well, since imitations of it easily fall into mere obscurity and extravagance. But his historical method has been of great value, the patient study of original authorities, the copious references quoted, the careful indexing, all being proof how anxious he was that the subject should be presented clearly and veraciously, rather than that the books should shine as literary performances. How far the principles which he valued and taught have spread it is difficult to say. Party politicians still appeal to the sacred name of liberty without inquiring what true liberty means; publicists still speak as if the material gains of modern life, cheap food and machine-made products, meant nothing but advance in the history of the human race; but there are others who look to the spiritual factors and wish to enlarge the bounds of political economy.

The writings of Carlyle, and of Ruskin, on whom fell the prophet's mantle, certainly made their influence felt in later books devoted to that once 'dismal' science. Few can be quite indifferent to the man or to his message. Those who demand moderation, clearness, and Attic simplicity, will be repelled by his extravagances or by his mysticism. Others will be attracted by his glowing imagination and by his fiery eloquence, and will reserve for him a foremost place in their affections. These will echo the words which Emerson was heard to say on his death-bed, when his eyes fell on a portrait of the familiar rugged features, '*That* is the man, my man'.

SIR ROBERT PEEL
From the painting by J. Linnell in the National Portrait Gallery

SIR ROBERT PEEL

1788-1850

1788. Born near Bury, Lancashire, July 5.

1801-4. Harrow School.

1805. Christ Church, Oxford.

1809. M.P. for Cashel, Ireland.

1811. Under-Secretary for the Colonies.

1812-18. Chief Secretary for Ireland.

1817. M.P. for Oxford University.

1819. President of Bullion Committee.

1820. Marriage to Julia, daughter of General Sir John Floyd.

1822-7. Home Secretary in Lord Liverpool's Government.

1827. Canning's short ministry and death.

1828-30. Home Secretary and leader in Commons under the Duke of Wellington.

1829. Catholic Emancipation carried.

1832. Lord Grey's Reform Bill carried.

1834-5. Prime Minister; Tamworth manifesto.

1839. 'Bedchamber Plot': Peel fails to form ministry.

1841-6. Prime Minister a second time.

1844. Peel's Bank Act.

1846. Corn Laws repealed. Peel, defeated on Irish Coercion Bill, resigns.

1850. Accident, June 29, and death, July 2.

SIR ROBERT PEEL
STATESMAN

In the years that lay between the Treaty of Utrecht and the close of the Napoleonic wars British politics were largely dominated by Walpole and the two Pitts: their great figures only stand out in stronger relief because their place was filled for a time by such weak ministers as Newcastle and Bute, as Grafton and North. In the nineteenth century there were many gifted statesmen who held the position of first minister of the Crown. Disraeli and Palmerston by shrewdness and force of character, Canning and Derby by brilliant oratorical gifts, Russell and Aberdeen by earnest devotion to public service, were all commanding figures in their day, whose claims to the chieftainship of a party and of a government were generally admitted. Gladstone, the most versatile genius of them all, had abilities second to none; but his place in history will for long be a subject of acute controversy. He stands too close to our own time to be fairly judged. Of the others no one had the same combination of gifts as Sir Robert Peel, no one had in the same measure that particular knowledge, judgement, and ability which characterize the *statesman*. His career was the most fruitful, his work the most enduring: he has left his mark in English history to a degree which no one of his rivals can equal.

The Peel family can be traced back to the misty days of Danish inroads. Its original home in England is disputed between Yorkshire and Lancashire; but as early as the days of Elizabeth the branch from which our statesman was descended is certainly to be found at Blackburn, and its members lived for generations as sturdy yeomen of that district. The first of them known to strike out an independent line was his grandfather, Robert Peel, who with his brother-in-law, Mr. Haworth, started the first firm for calico-printing in Lancashire about the year 1760, ceasing the practice of sending the material to be printed in France. This grandfather was a type of the men who were making the new England, leading the way in the creation of industries that were to transform the North and Midlands. The business prospered and he moved from Blackburn to Burton-on-Trent, where he built three new mills. His third son, named Robert, was also gifted with resource. Beginning as a member of the family firm, he soon came to be its chief director, and added another branch at Tamworth, where later he built the house of Drayton Manor, the family seat in the nineteenth century. He was a Tory and a staunch follower of the younger Pitt, who rewarded his services with a baronetcy in 1800. He too was a typical man of his age and class, an age of material progress and expansion, a class full of self-confidence and animated by a spirit of stubborn resistance to so-called un-English ideas. His eldest son, the third Robert and the second baronet, is our subject. It is impossible to grasp the springs of his conduct unless we know what traditions he inherited from his forbears.

Peel's education was begun at home with a specific purpose. Though his father had every reason to be satisfied with his own success, for his son he cherished a yet higher ambition and one which he did not conceal. He said openly that he intended him to be Prime Minister of his country. The knowledge of this provoked many jests among the boy's friends and caused him no slight embarrassment. It conspired with the shyness and reserve, which were innate in him, to win him from the outset a reputation for pride and aloofness. If he had not been forced to mix with those of his own age, and if he had not resolutely set himself to overcome this feeling, he might have grown into a student and a recluse. Both at school and college he did 'attend to his book': at Harrow he roused the greatest hopes. His brilliant schoolfellow, Lord Byron, while claiming to excel him in general information and history, admits that Peel was greatly his superior as a scholar. The working of their minds, now and afterwards, was curiously different. Bagehot[6] illustrates the contrast by a striking metaphor: Byron's mind, he says, worked by momentary eruptions of volcanic force from within and then relapsed into inactivity. Peel on the other hand steadily accumulated knowledge and opinions, his mind receiving impressions from outward experience like the alluvial soil deposited by a river in its course. But this is to anticipate. At Oxford Peel was the first man to win a 'Double First' (i.e. a first class both in classics and mathematics), in which distinction Gladstone alone, among our Prime Ministers, equalled him. But he also found time during the term to indulge in cricket, in rowing, and in riding, while in the vacation he developed a more marked taste for shooting, and thus freed himself from the charge of being a mere bookworm. He was good-looking, rather a dandy in his dress, stiff in his manner, regular in his habits, conforming to the Oxford standards of excellence and as yet showing few signs of independence of character.

Peel went into Parliament early, after the fashion of the day. He was twenty-one when, in 1809, a seat was offered him at Cashel in Ireland. The system of 'rotten boroughs' had many faults—our text-books of history do not spare it—but it may claim to have offered an easy way into Parliament for some men of brilliant talents. Peel's family connexions and his own training marked out the path for him. It was difficult for the young Oxford prizeman not to follow Lord Chancellor Eldon, that stout survival of the high old Tories: it was impossible for his father's son not to sit behind the successors of Pitt. We shall see how far his own reasoning powers and clear vision led him from this path; but the early influences were never quite effaced. His first patron was Lord Liverpool, to whom he became private secretary in the following year. This nobleman, described by Disraeli in a famous passage as an 'arch-mediocrity' was Prime Minister for fifteen years. He owed his long tenure of office largely to the tolerance with which he allowed his abler lieutenants to usurp his power: perhaps he owed it still more to the victories which

Wellington was then winning abroad and which secured the confidence of the country; but at least he seems to have been a good judge of men. In 1811 he promoted Peel to be Under-Secretary for the Colonies, and in 1812 to be Chief Secretary for Ireland. His abilities must have made a great impression to win him such promotion: he must have had plenty of self-confidence to undertake such duties, for he was only twenty-four years old. We are accustomed to-day to under-secretaries of forty or forty-five; but we must remember that the younger Pitt led the House of Commons at twenty-four and was Prime Minister at twenty-five.

At Dublin Castle Peel was not expected to deal with the great political questions which convulsed Parliament at different periods of the century. He had to administer the law. It was routine work of a tedious and difficult kind; it involved the close study of facts—not in order to make a showy speech or to win a case for the moment, but in order to frame practical measures which would stand the test of time. Peel eschewed the usual recreations of Dublin society, and flung himself into his work whole-heartedly. In Roman history we see how Caesar was trained in the details of administration as quaestor, aedile, praetor, consul, while Pompeius passed in a lordly progress from one high command to another; how Caesar voluntarily exiled himself from Rome for ten years to conquer and develop Gaul, while Cicero bewailed himself over a few months' absence from the Forum. Of these three famous men only one proved himself able to guide the ship of state in stormy waters. Analogy must not be too closely pressed; but we see that, while Canning for all his ability established no durable influence, and his oratory burnt itself out after a brief blaze, while Wellington's fame paled year after year from his inability to control the course of civil strife, Peel's light burnt brighter every decade, as he rose from office to office and faced one difficult situation after another with coolness and success. He stayed at his post in Dublin for six years: he worked at the details of his office—education, agriculture, and police—and brought in many practical reforms. His beneficial activity is still better seen in the years 1821 to 1827 when he was Home Secretary. To-day he is chiefly remembered as the eponymous hero of our police; but in many other ways his tenure of the latter office is a landmark in departmental work. It may be that he originated little himself: that Romilly was the pioneer in the humanizing of law, that Horner taught him the doctrines of sound finance, that Huskisson led the way in freeing trade from the shackles with which it had been bound. But Peel in all these cases lent generous support and made their cause his own. He had a cool head and a warm heart, a knowledge of Parliament and an influence in Parliament already unrivalled. He saw what could be done, and how it could be done, and so he was able to push through successfully the reforms which his colleagues initiated. The value of his work in this sphere has never been seriously contested.

The point on which Peel's enemies fastened in judging his career was the number of times that he changed his convictions, abandoned his party, and carried through a measure which he himself had formerly opposed. To understand his claim to be called a great statesman it is particularly necessary to study these changes.

The first instance was the Reform of the Currency. Early in the French wars the London banks had been in difficulties. The Government was forced to borrow large sums from the Bank of England in order to give subsidies to our allies, and was unable to pay its debts. The Bank could not at the same time meet the demands of the Government and the claims of its private customers. Since a panic might at any moment cause an unprecedented run on its reserves, Pitt suspended cash payments till six months after the conclusion of peace. The Bank was thus allowed to circulate notes without being obliged to pay full cash value for them immediately on demand, and the purchasing power of these notes tended to vary far more than that of a metal currency. Also foreigners refused to accept a pound note in the place of a pound sterling; foreign payments had to be made in specie, and the gold was rapidly drained abroad. When the war was over, Horner and other economists began to draw attention to the bad effect of this on foreign trade and to the varying price of commodities at home, due to the want of a fixed currency. As Pitt had allowed the system of inconvertible paper, the Tories generally applauded and were ready to perpetuate it. The elder Sir Robert Peel had been always a firm supporter of these views and his son began by accepting them. He continued to acquiesce in them till his attention was definitely turned to the subject. In 1819 he was asked to be a member of a committee of very eminent men, including Canning and Mackintosh, which was to investigate the question, and he was elected chairman of it. But, though his verdict was taken for granted by his party, his mind was so constituted that he could not shut it against evidence. He listened to arguments, and judged them fairly; and, being by nature unable to palter with the truth, once he was convinced of it, he threw in all his weight with the reformers and reported in favour of a return to cash payments. History has vindicated his judgement, and he himself crowned his financial work by the famous Bank Act of 1844, passed when he was Prime Minister.

The second question on which Peel's conduct surprised his colleagues was that of Catholic Emancipation. Since 1793 Roman Catholic electors had the parliamentary vote; but, since no Roman Catholic could sit in Parliament, they had hitherto been content to cast their votes for the more tolerant of the Protestant candidates. Pitt had failed to induce George III to grant the Catholics civil equality, and George IV, despite his liberal professions, took up the same attitude as his father on succeeding to the throne. But the majority of the Whigs, and some even of the Tories, such as Castlereagh and

Canning, were prepared to make concessions; and since 1820 the Irish agitation led by O'Connell had been gaining in strength. Peel had several reasons for being on the other side. His early training by his father, his friendship with Eldon and Wellington, his attachment to the Established Church, all had influence upon him. He saw clearly that Disestablishment would follow closely in Ireland on the granting of the Catholic demands; and since 1817, when he became Member for Oxford University, he felt bound to resist this. In taking this line he was no better and no worse than any other Tory member of the day; and in later times many politicians have allowed their traditions and prejudices to blind them to the existence of an Irish problem.

For all that, Peel ought earlier to have recognized the facts, to have looked ahead and formed a policy. As Chief Secretary for Ireland he had unrivalled opportunities for studying the whole question; but he did not let it penetrate beneath the surface of his mind. He had continued to bring up the same arguments on the few occasions when he spoke at Westminster, and had buried himself in administrative work. He seems to have hoped that he could evade it. If the Whigs got a majority and introduced an Emancipation Bill, he would have satisfied his constituents by formally opposing the measure and would not have gone beyond this. As he saw it gradually coming, he satisfied his own conscience by retiring from Lord Liverpool's Government and by refusing to join Canning, when he became Prime Minister in 1827. As a private member he would only be responsible for his own vote, and would not feel that he was settling the question for others. But Canning died after holding office only a month, and a Government was formed by Wellington in which Peel returned to office as Home Secretary and became leader of the House of Commons. Now he had to pay the penalty for his lack of foresight, and to deal with the tide of feeling which had been rising for some years on both sides of the Irish Channel. At least he could see facts which were before his eyes.

In 1828, before he had been twelve months in office, his decision was aided by a definite event. A by-election had to be fought in Clare, Mr. Fitzgerald seeking re-election on joining the Government. Against him came forward no less a person than Daniel O'Connell himself, the most eloquent and most popular of the Catholic leaders; and, although under the existing laws his candidature was void, he received an overwhelming majority. The bewilderment of the Tories was ludicrous. Fitzgerald himself wrote, 'The proceedings of yesterday were those of madmen; but the country is mad.' Peel took a careful view of the situation and decided on his course. He certainly laid himself open to the charge of giving way before a breach of the law, and the charge was pressed by the angry Tories. But his judgement was clearly based on a complete survey of all the facts. A single event was the candle which lit up the scene, but by the light of it he surveyed the whole room. He still held to his view about the dangers of Disestablishment ahead, but he maintained that a crisis had arisen involving graver dangers at the moment, and that the statesman must choose the lesser of two evils. There is no doubt that the situation was critical. The Duke of Wellington and Lord Anglesey (a Waterloo veteran, who was Lord Lieutenant of Ireland) both had fears of mutiny in the army; and civil war was to be expected, if O'Connell was not admitted to the House of Commons. Peel's personal consistency was one matter; the public welfare was another and a weightier. His first idea was to retire from office and to lend unofficial support to a measure which he could not advocate in principle. But the only hope of breaking down the old Tory opposition lay in the influence of the Tory ministers; no Whig Government could prevail in the temper of that time; and Wellington appealed in the strongest terms to Peel to remain in office and to lead the House. Peel yielded from motives of public policy and made himself responsible for a measure of Catholic Emancipation, which he had been pledged to resist.

It was a surrender—an undisguised surrender—and Peel did not, as on the Bullion Committee, profess to have changed his mind. But it was an honest surrender carried out in the light of day; and, before Parliament met, Peel announced his decision to resign his seat at Oxford and to give his constituents the chance of expressing their opinion of his conduct. The verdict was not long in doubt: the University, which in 1865 rejected another of its brilliant sons, gave a majority of one hundred and forty-six against him, and his political connexion with Oxford was severed. The verdict of posterity has been more liberal. The chief fault laid to Peel's charge is that he should for so many years have ignored all signs of the danger which was approaching, and not have made up his mind in time. He could see the crisis clearly, when it came, and could put the national interest above everything else: he could not look far enough ahead.

It was a similar want of foresight that led to the fall of the Tory Government in 1830. The Reform movement, so long delayed by the great wars, had been gathering force again. Events in France, where Charles X was driven from the throne and Louis Philippe proclaimed as Citizen-king, gave it additional impetus. The famous lawyer Brougham was thundering against the Government in Parliament, while throughout the country the platforms from which Radical orators declaimed were surrounded by eager throngs. The history of the movement cannot be told here. Its chief actors were the Whigs, who on Wellington's resignation formed a Government under Earl Grey at the end of 1830. Peel was fighting a losing fight and he did not show his usual judgement or cool temper. He opposed the Reform Bill to the last: he was haranguing violently against it when Black Rod arrived to summon the

Commons to the presence of the King. William IV came down in person, at the instance of the Whig ministers, to dissolve Parliament and so to stay all proceedings by which, in the as yet unreformed Parliament, the Bill might have been defeated. In the General Election of 1831 the Whigs carried all before them, and in July, when Lord Grey carried the second reading, he could command a majority of 136. Even then it took three months of stubborn fighting to vanquish the Tory opposition in the House of Commons. When the Peers rejected the Bill, the question was raised whether a Tory Government could be formed; but Peel, however he might dislike the Bill, could recognize facts, and his refusal to co-operate in defying public opinion was decisive. Lord Grey returned to office fortified by the King's promise to make any number of new peers, if required; and the influence of Wellington was effective in dissuading the Upper House from further futile resistance. Again Peel had shown his good sense in accepting the situation. So far as he was concerned, there was no talk of repeal. He explicitly said that he regarded the question as 'finally and irrevocably disposed of', and he set to work to adapt his policy to the new situation.

It might well seem a desperate one for the Tories. Here were three hundred new members, most of whom had just received their seats from the Whigs against the direct opposition of their rivals. Gratitude and self-interest impelled them to support the Whig party; and its leaders, who had for nearly fifty years been out in the cold shade of opposition, might count on a long spell of power, especially as the Canningites, stronger in talents than in numbers, joined them at this juncture. Brougham had gone to the House of Lords, but three future Prime Ministers—Stanley (afterwards Lord Derby), Lord John Russell, and Palmerston—were in the House of Commons serving under Lord Althorp, who, though gifted with no oratorical talent, by his good sense and still more by his high character, commanded general respect. On the other side there was only one figure of the first rank, and that was Peel. Till 1832 he had not grown to his full stature: the Reformed Parliament gave him his chance and drew forth all his powers. It represented a new force in politics. No longer were the members sent to Westminster by a few great land-holders, by the small market towns, and by the agricultural labourers. The great industrial districts, Lancashire, Yorkshire, and the Midlands, were there in the persons of well-to-do citizens, experienced in business and serious in temper; and Peel, who was himself sprung from a notable family of this kind, was eminently the man to lead these classes and to win their confidence. It was also a gain to him to stand alone. His judgement was ripened, his confidence firm; and he could dominate his party, while the able and ambitious leaders on the other side too often clashed with one another. Above all, in the years 1832 to 1834, he showed that he had patience. Instead of snatching at occasions to ally himself with O'Connell, who was in opposition to every Government, and to embarrass the Whigs in a factious party-spirit, he showed a marked respect for principle. He supported or opposed the Whig bills purely on their merits, and gradually trained his party to be ready for the inevitable reaction when it should come.

By 1834 the tendencies to disruption in the victorious party were clearly showing themselves. First Stanley, on grounds of policy, and then Lord Grey, for personal reasons never quite cleared up, resigned office. Soon after, Lord Althorp left the House of Commons on succeeding to his father's earldom, and a little later Melbourne, the new Premier, was unexpectedly dismissed by the King. At the time Peel, expecting no immediate crisis, was abroad, in Rome; and we have interesting details of his slow journey home to meet the urgent call of Wellington, who was carrying on the administration provisionally. The changes of the last few years were shown by the fact that the Tories felt bound to choose their Premier from the Lower House. It was Wellington who recommended Peel for the place which, under the old conditions, he might have been expected to take himself. On his return, Peel accepted the task of forming a ministry, and, conscious of the numerical weakness of his own party, he made overtures to some of the Whigs. But Stanley and Graham[7] refused to join him, and he had to fall back on the Tories of Wellington's last Government. Before going to the country he laid down his principles in the famous Tamworth Manifesto.[8] This manifesto is important for its acceptance of the changes permanently made by the Reform Bill, and for the clear exposition of his attitude towards the important Church questions which were imminent. It is an excellent document for any one to study who wishes to understand the evolution of the old Tories into the modern Conservative party.

Peel's first administration was not destined to last long. The Liberal wave was not spent, and the Tories had little to hope for, at this moment, from a General Election. As so often happened afterwards, when the two English parties were evenly balanced, the Irish votes turned the scale. Peel had been forced into this position by the King: his own judgement would have led him to wait some years. He fought dexterously for four months, helped in some measure by Stanley, who had left the Whigs when they threatened the Established Church in Ireland; but it was this question which in the end upset him. Lord John Russell, in alliance with O'Connell, proposed the disendowment of that Church and defeated Peel by thirty-three votes. It was a question of principle, though it was raised in a factious way, and subsequent history showed that the mover, after his tactical victory of the moment, could not effect any practical solution. Peel was driven to resign. But in this short period, so far from losing credit, he had won the confidence of his party and the respect of his opponents; he had put some useful measures on the Statute Book; and he had shown the country that a new spirit, practical and enlightened, was growing up in the Tory party, and that there was a minister capable of utilizing it for the general good.

In the Greville papers and other literature of the time we get many references to the predominant place which he held in the esteem of the House of Commons. An entry in Greville's journal for February 1834 shows Peel's unique power. 'No matter how unruly the House, how impatient or fatigued, the moment he rises, all is silence, and he is sure of being heard with profound attention and respect.' Lady Lyttelton,[9] who met him later at Windsor, shows us another aspect. His readiness and presence of mind come out in the most trivial matters. When Queen Victoria suddenly, one evening, issued her command that all who could dance were to dance, the more elderly guests were much embarrassed. Such an order was not to Peel's taste. 'He was, in fact, to a close observer, evidently both shy and cross'; but he was 'much the best figure of all, so mincing with his legs and feet, his countenance full of the funniest attempt to look unconcerned and "matter of course".' Another time when games were improvised in the royal circle, Lady Lyttelton was 'much struck with the quickness and watchful cautious characteristic sagacity which Sir Robert showed in learning and playing a new round game'. And to the ladies-in-waiting he commended himself by his quiet courtesy. 'Sir Robert Peel', we read, 'was in his most conversable mood and so very agreeable. I never enjoyed an evening more.'

Perhaps the best description to show how personally he impressed his contemporaries at this time is given by Lord Dalling and Bulwer in his memoir. Sir Robert Peel, he tells us, was 'tall and powerfully built, his body somewhat bulky for his limbs, his head small and well-formed, his features regular. His countenance was not what would be generally called expressive, but it was capable of taking the expression he wished to give it, humour, sarcasm, persuasion, and command, being its alternate characteristics. The character of the man was seen more... in the whole person than in the face. He did not stoop, but he bent rather forwards; his mode of walking was peculiar, and rather like that of a cat, but of a cat that was well acquainted with the ground it was moving over; the step showed no doubt or apprehension, it could hardly be called stealthy, but it glided on firmly and cautiously, without haste, or swagger, or unevenness.... The oftener you heard him speak, the more his speaking gained upon you.... He never seemed occupied with himself. His effort was evidently directed to convince you, not that he was *eloquent*, but that he was *right*.... He seemed rather to aim at gaining the doubtful, than mortifying or crushing the hostile.' These qualities appealed especially to the practical men of business whom the Reform Bill had brought into politics. They were suited to the temper of the day, and his speaking won the favour of the best judges in the House of Commons. Though he disappointed ardent crusaders like Lord Shaftesbury by his apparent coldness and calculating caution, he impressed his fellow members as pre-eminently honest and as anxious to advance in the most effective manner those causes which his judgement approved. He was not the man to lead a forlorn hope, but rather the sagacious commander who directed his troops through a practicable breach.

He was to be in opposition for another six years; but during these years the Whigs were in constant difficulties, and, as Greville notes, it was often obvious that Peel was leading the House from the front Opposition bench. Had he imitated Russell's conduct in 1834 and devoted his chief energies to overthrowing the Whigs, he could have found many an occasion. Sedition in Canada and Jamaica, rivalry with France in the Levant and with Russia in the Farther East, financial troubles and deficits, the spread of Chartist doctrine, all combined to embarrass a Government which had no single will and no concentrated resolution. The accession of Queen Victoria, in 1837, made no change for the moment. But Wellington's famous remark that the Tories would have no chance with a Queen because Peel had no manners and he had no small talk, is only quoted now because of the falsity of the prediction; both politicians soon came to form a better estimate of her judgement and public spirit. It was some years before this could be fairly tested. The Tories, while improving their position, failed to gain an absolute majority in the elections, and Peel's want of tact in insisting on the Queen changing all the ladies of her household delayed his triumph from 1839 to 1841. Meanwhile he spent his energies in training his party and organizing their resources. He studied measures and he studied men, and he gradually gathered round him a body of loyal followers who believed in their chief and were ready to help him in administrative reform when the time should come. Among his most devoted adherents was Mr. Gladstone, at this time more famous as a churchman than as a financier; and even Mr. Disraeli, for all his eccentricities, accepted Peel's leadership without question. Few could then foresee the very different careers that lay before his two brilliant lieutenants.

By 1841 the power of the Whigs was spent. A vote of want of confidence was carried by Peel, the King dissolved Parliament, and the Tories came back with a majority of ninety in the new House of Commons. Now begins the most famous part of Peel's career, that associated with the Repeal of the Corn Laws, the third of his so-called 'betrayals' of his party. No action of his has been so variously criticized, none caused such bitterness in political circles. There is no space here to discuss the value of Protection or the wisdom of the Anti-Corn-Law League, still less the merits or demerits of a fixed duty as opposed to a 'sliding-scale'. We are concerned with Peel's conduct and must try to answer the questions—What were Peel's earlier views on the subject? What caused him to change these views? Was this change effected honestly, or was he guilty of abandoning his party in order to retain office himself?

The Corn Laws, introThatduced in 1670, re-enacted in 1815, forbade any one to import corn into England till the price of home-grown corn had reached eighty shillings a quarter. It is easy to attack a system based on rigid figures applied to conditions varying widely in every century; but the idea was that the English farmer should be given a decisive advantage over his foreign rivals, and only when the price rose to a prohibitive point might the interest of the consumer be allowed to outweigh that of the producer. The revival of the old law in 1815 met with strong opposition. England had greatly changed; the agricultural area had not been widely increased, but there were many more millions of mouths to feed, thanks to the growth of population in the industrial districts. But while in 1815 the House of Commons represented almost exclusively the land-owning and corn-growing classes, between 1815 and 1840 opposition to their policy had lately been growing and had been organized, outside Parliament, by the famous league of which Richard Cobden was the leading spirit. Peel, though he had been brought up by his father a strong Protectionist and Tory, had been largely influenced by Huskisson, the most remarkable President of the Board of Trade that this country has ever seen, and had shown on many occasions that he grasped the principle of Free Trade as well as any statesman of the day. The Whigs had left the finances of the country in a very bad state, and Peel had to take sweeping measures to restore credit. From 1842 to 1845 he brought in Budgets of a Free Trade character, designed to encourage commerce by remitting taxation, especially on raw material; and he made up the loss thus incurred by the Treasury, by imposing an income-tax. To this policy there were two exceptions, the Corn Laws and the Sugar Duties. On the latter he felt that England, since she had abolished slave-owning, had a duty to her colonies to see that they did not suffer by the competition of sugar produced by slave labour elsewhere. On the former he held that England ought, so far as possible, to produce its own food and to be self-sufficing; and as a practical man he recognized that it was too much to expect of the agricultural interest, so strongly represented in both Houses of Parliament, to pronounce what seemed to be its death-warrant. But through these years he came more and more to see that the interest of a class must give way to the interest of the nation; and his clear intellect was from time to time shaken by the arguments of the Anti-Corn-Law League and its orators. In 1845 he was probably expecting that he would tide over this Parliament, thanks to his Budgets and to good harvests, and that at a general election he would be able to declare for a change of fiscal policy without going back on his pledges to the party. Meanwhile his general attitude had been noted by shrewd observers. Cobden himself in a speech delivered at Birmingham said, 'There can be no doubt that Sir Robert Peel is at heart as good a Free Trader as I am. He has told us so in the House of Commons again and again.'

Among the causes which influenced Peel at the moment two are specially noteworthy as reminding us of the way in which his opinion was changed over Catholic Emancipation. Severe critics say that, to retain office, he surrendered to the agitation of Cobden, as he had surrendered to that of O'Connell. Undoubtedly the increasing size and success of Cobden's meetings, which were on a scale unknown before in political agitation, did cause Peel to consider fully what he had only half considered before: it did help to force open a door in his mind, and to break down a water-tight compartment. But Peel's mind, once opened, saw far more than an agitation and a transfer of votes: it looked at the merits of the question and surveyed the interest of the whole country. He had seen that the fall of a Protestant Church was less serious than the loss of Ireland: he now saw that a shock to the agricultural interest was less serious than general starvation in the country. And as with the Clare election, so with the Irish potato famine in 1845: a definite event arrested his attention and clamoured for instant decision. Peel was as humane a man as has ever presided over the destinies of this country, and the picture of Ireland's sufferings was brought forcibly before his imagination by the reports presented to him and by his own knowledge of the country. His personal consistency could not be put in the balance against national distress.

That the manner in which he made the change did give great offence to his followers, there is no room to doubt. Peel was naturally reserved in manner and in his Cabinet he occupied a position of such unquestioned superiority that he had no need of advice to make up his mind, and was apt to keep matters in his own hand. Whether he was preparing to consult his colleagues or not, the Irish potato famine forced his hand before he had done so. When in November 1845 he made suddenly in the Cabinet a definite proposal to suspend the duties on corn, only three members supported him. Year after year Peel had opposed the motion brought in by Mr. Villiers for repeal: only those who had been studying the situation as closely as Peel and with as clear a vision—and they were few—could understand this sudden declaration of a change of policy. After holding four Cabinet councils in one week, winning over some waverers, but still failing to get a unanimous vote, he expressed a wish to resign. But the Whigs, owing to personal disagreements, could not form a ministry and Queen Victoria asked Peel to retain office: it was evident that he alone could carry through the measure which he believed to be so urgent, and he steeled himself to face the breach with his own party. As Lord John Russell had already pledged the Whigs to repeal, the issue was no longer in doubt; but Peel was not to win the victory without heavy cost. Disraeli, who had been offended at not being given a place in the ministry in 1841, came forward, rallied the agricultural interest, and attacked his leader in a series of bitter speeches, opening old sores, and charging him with having for the second time broken his pledges and betrayed his party. The

Protectionists could not defeat the Government. In the Commons the Whig votes ensured a majority: in the Lords the influence of Wellington triumphed over the resistance of the more obstinate landowners. The Bill passed its third reading by ninety-eight votes.

But Peel knew how uncertain was his position in view of the hostility aroused. At this very time the Irish question was acute, as a Coercion Bill was under consideration, and this gave his enemies their chance. The Protectionist Tories made an unprincipled alliance for the moment with the Irish members; and on the very day when the Repeal of the Corn Laws passed the House of Lords, the ministry was defeated in the Commons. The moment of his fall, when Disraeli and the Protectionists were loudest in their exultation, was the moment of his triumph. It is the climax of his career. In the long debate on Repeal he had refused to notice personal attacks: he now rose superior to all personal rancour. In defeat he bore himself with dignity, and in his last speech as minister he praised Cobden in very generous terms, giving him the chief credit for the benefits which the Bill conferred upon his fellow-countrymen. This speech gave offence to his late colleagues, Aberdeen, Sidney Herbert, and Gladstone, and was interpreted as being designed to mark clearly Peel's breach with the Conservative party. The whole episode is illustrated in an interesting way in the *Life of Gladstone*. Lord Morley[11] reports a long conversation between the two friends and colleagues, where Peel declares his intention to act in future as a private member and to abstain from party politics. Gladstone, while fully allowing that Peel had earned the right to retire after such labours ('you have been Prime Minister in a sense in which no other man has been since Mr. Pitt's time'), pointed out how impossible it would be for him to carry out his intentions. His personal ascendancy in Parliament was too great: men must look to him as a leader. But Peel evidently was at the end of his strength, and had been suffering acutely from pains in the head, due to an old shooting accident but intensified by recent hard work. For the moment repose was essential.

It was Gladstone, Peel's disciple and true successor, who seven years later paid the following tribute to his memory: 'It is easy', he said, 'to enumerate many characteristics of the greatness of Sir Robert Peel. It is easy to speak of his ability, of his sagacity, of his indefatigable industry. But there was something yet more admirable... and that was his sense of public virtue;... when he had to choose between personal ease and enjoyment, or again, on the other hand, between political power and distinction, and what he knew to be the welfare of the nation, his choice was made at once. When his choice was made, no man ever saw him hesitate, no man ever saw him hold back from that which was necessary to give it effect.' Though his own political views changed, Gladstone always paid tribute to the moral influence which

Peel had exercised in political life, purifying its practices and ennobling its traditions.

For the last four years of his life he was in opposition, but he held a place of dignity and independence which few fallen ministers have ever enjoyed. He was the trusted friend and adviser of Queen Victoria and the Prince Consort; he was often consulted in grave matters by the chiefs of the Government; his speeches both in the House and in the country carried greater weight than those of any minister. Despite the bitterness of the Protectionists he seemed still to have a great future before him, and in any national emergency the country would unfailingly have called him to the helm. But on July 29, 1850, when he was just reaching the age of sixty-two, he had a fall from his horse which caused very grave injuries, and he only survived three days.

The interest of Peel's life is almost absorbed by public questions. He was not picturesque like Disraeli; he did not, like Gladstone, live long enough to be in his lifetime a mythical figure; the public did not cherish anecdotes about his sayings or doings, nor did he lend himself to the art of the caricaturist. He was an English gentleman to the backbone, in his tastes, in his conduct, in his nature. His married life was entirely happy, he had a few devoted friends, he avoided general society; he had a genuine fondness for shooting and country life, he was a judicious patron of art, and his collection of Dutch pictures form to-day a very precious part of our National Gallery. Just because of his aloofness, his gravity, the concentration of his energies, he is the best example that we can study if we want to know how an English statesman should train himself to do work of lasting value and how he should bear himself in the hour of trial. Within little more than half a century three famous politicians, Peel, Gladstone, and Chamberlain, have split their parties in two by an abrupt change of policy, and their conduct has been bitterly criticized by those to whom the traditions of party are dear. It is the glory of British politics that these traditions remained honourable so long, and no one of these statesmen broke with them lightly or without regret. For all that, let us be thankful that from time to time statesmen do arise who are capable of responding to a still higher call, of following their own individual consciences and of looking only to what, so far as they can judge, is the highest interest of the nation.

CHARLES JAMES NAPIER

1782-1853

1782.	Born in London, August 10.
1794.	Commission in 33rd Regiment.
1800.	At Shorncliffe with Sir John Moore.
1809.	Wounded and prisoner at Coruña.
1810-11.	Peninsula War: Busaco, Fuentes d'Onoro, &c. Lieut.-Colonel, 1811.
1812-13.	Bermuda and American War.
1815-17.	Military College at Farnham.
1820.	Corfu.
1822-30.	Cephalonia.
1835.	Living quietly in France and England.
1837.	Major-General.
1838.	K.C.B.
1839.	Command in North of England. Chartist agitation.
1841.	Command in India at Poona.
1842-7.	War and organization in Sind.
1849-50.	Commander-in-Chief in India.
1853.	Died at Oaklands, near Portsmouth, August 29.

SIR CHARLES NAPIER, G.C.B.

Soldier

The famous Napier brothers, Charles, George, and William, came of no mean parentage. Their father, Colonel the Hon. George Napier, of a distinguished Scotch family, was remarkable alike for physical strength and mental ability. In the fervour of his admiration his son Charles relates how he could 'take a pewter quart and squeeze it flat in his hand like a bit of paper'. In height 6 feet 3 inches, in person very handsome, he won the admiration of others besides his sons. He had served in the American war, but his later years were passed in organizing work, and he showed conspicuous honesty and ability in dealing with Irish military accounts. One of his reforms was the abolition of all fees in his office, by which he reduced his own salary from £20,000 to £600 per annum, emulating the more famous act of the elder Pitt as Paymaster-general half a century before. Their mother, Lady Sarah Lennox, daughter of the Duke of Richmond, had been a reigning toast in 1760. She had even been courted by George III, and might have been handed down to history as the mother of princes. In her old age she was more proud to be the mother of heroes; and her letters still exist, written in the period of the great wars, to show how a British mother could combine the Spartan ideal with the tenderest personal affection.

SIR CHARLES NAPIER
From the drawing by Edwin Williams in the National Portrait Gallery

Their father's appointment involved residence in Ireland from 1785 onwards, and the boys passed their early years at Celbridge in the neighbourhood of Dublin. Here they were far from the usual amusements and society of the time, but they were fortunate in their home circle and in the character of their servants, and they learnt to cherish the ancient legends of Ireland and to pick up everything that could feed their innate love of adventure and romance. Close to their doors lived an old woman named Molly Dunne, who claimed to be one hundred and thirty-five years of age, and who was ready to fill the children's ears with tales of past tragedies whenever they came to see her. Sir William Napier tells us how she was 'tall, gaunt, and with high sharp lineaments, her eyes fixed in their huge orbs, and her tongue discoursing of bloody times: she was wondrous for the young and fearful for the aged'.

Instead of class feeling and narrow interests the boys developed early a great sympathy for the poor, and a capacity for judging people independently of rank. Charles Napier himself, born in Whitehall, was three years old when they moved to Ireland. He was a sickly child, the one short member of a tall family, but equal to any of them in courage and resolution. His heroism in endurance of pain was put to a severe test when he broke his leg at the age of seventeen. It was twice badly set. He was threatened first by the entire loss of it, next with the prospect of a crooked leg, but he bore cheerfully the most excruciating torture in having it straightened by a series of painful experiments, and in no long time he recovered his activity. In the army he showed his strength of will by rigid abstinence from drinking and gambling, no easy feat in those days; and he learned by his father's example to control all extravagance and to live contentedly on a small allowance. His earliest enthusiasm among books was for Plutarch's *Lives*, the favourite reading of so many great commanders. He had many outdoor tastes: riding, fishing, and shooting, and he was soon familiar with the country-side. There was no need of classes or prizes to stimulate his reading, no need of organized games to provide an outlet for his energies or to fill his leisure time.

The confidence that his father had in the training of his sons is best shown by the early age at which he put them in responsible positions. Charles actually received a commission in the 33rd Regiment at the age of twelve, but he did not see service till he was seventeen. Meanwhile the young ensign continued his schooling from his father's house at Celbridge, to which he and his brother returned every evening, sometimes in the most unconventional manner. Celbridge, like other Irish villages, had its pigs. The Irish pig is longer in the leg and more active than his English cousin, and the Napier boys would be seen careering along at a headlong pace on these strange mounts, with a cheering company of village boys behind them. They were Protestants among older Roman Catholic comrades, but they soon became the leaders in the school, and Charles, despite his youth and small stature, was chosen to command a school volunteer corps at the age of fourteen. At seventeen he joined his regiment at Limerick, and for six or seven years he led the life of a soldier in various garrison towns of southern England, fretting at inaction, learning what he could, and welcoming any chance of increased work and danger. At this time his enthusiasm for soldiering was very variable. In a letter written in 1803 he makes fun of the routine of his profession, as he was set to practise it, and ends up, 'Such is the difference between a hero of the present time and the idea of one formed from reading Plutarch! Yet people wonder I don't like the army!'

But this was a passing mood. When stirring events were taking place, no one was more full of ardour, and when he came under such a general as Sir John Moore he expressed himself in a very different tone. In 1805 Moore was commanding at Hythe, and Charles Napier's letters are aglow with enthusiasm for the great qualities which he showed as an administrator and army reformer. Like Wolseley seventy or eighty years later, Moore had the gift of finding the best among his subalterns and training them in his own excellences. After his own father there was no one who had so much influence as Moore in the making of Charles Napier. In 1808 he sailed for the Peninsula with the rank of major, commanding the 50th Regiment in the colonel's absence; he took an active part in Moore's famous retreat at Coruña, and in the battle was taken prisoner after conduct of the greatest gallantry in leading his regiment under fire. Two months later he was released and again went to the front. In 1810 and 1811 he and his brothers George and William were fighting under Wellington, and were all so frequently wounded that the family fortunes became a subject of common talk. On more than one occasion Wellington himself wrote to Lady Sarah to inform her of the gallantry and misfortunes of her sons. At Busaco Charles had his jaw broken and was forced to retire into hospital at Lisbon. In his haste to rejoin the army, which he did when only half convalescent, he accomplished the feat of riding ninety miles on one horse in a single day; and in the course of his ride met two of his brothers being carried down, wounded, to the base. But in 1811 promotion withdrew Charles Napier from the Peninsula. A short command in Guernsey was followed by another in Bermuda, which involved him in the American war. He had little taste for warfare with men of the same race as himself, and was heartily glad to exchange back to the 50th in 1813, and to return to England. He started out as a volunteer to share in the campaign of Waterloo, but all was over before he could join the army in Flanders, and this part of his soldiering career ended quietly. He had received far more wounds than honours, and might well have been discouraged in the pursuit of his profession.

But here we can put to the test how far Napier's expressions of distaste for the service affected his conduct. He chafed at the inactivity of peace; but instead of abandoning the army for some more profitable career, he used his enforced leisure to prepare for further service and to extend his knowledge of political and military history. He spent the greater part of three years at the Military College, then established at Farnham, varying his professional studies with sallies into the domain of politics, and as a result he developed marked Radical views which he held through life. His note-books show a splendid grasp of principles and a close attention to facts; they range from the enforcing of the death penalty for marauding to the details of cavalry-kit. His Spartan regime became famous in later years; even now he prescribed a strict rule, 'a cloak, a pair of shoes, two flannel shirts, and a piece of soap—these, wrapped up in an oil-skin, must go in the right holster, and a pistol in the left.' He took no opinions at second hand, but studied the best authorities and thought for himself; he was as thorough in self-education as the famous Confederate general 'Stonewall' Jackson, who every evening sat for an hour, facing a blank wall and reviewing in his mind the subjects which he had read during the day.

No opportunity for reaping the fruit of these studies and exercising his great gifts was given him till May 1819. Then he was appointed to the post of inspecting-officer in the Ionian Islands;[12] and in 1822 he was appointed Military Resident in Cephalonia, the largest of these islands, a pile of rugged limestone hills, scantily supplied with water, and ruined by years of neglect and the oppression of Turkish pashas. So began what was certainly the happiest, and perhaps the most fruitful, period in Charles Napier's life. It was not strictly military work, but, without the authority which his military rank gave him and without the despotic methods of martial law, little could have been achieved in the disordered state of the country. The whole episode is a good example of how a well-trained soldier of original mind can, when left to himself, impress his character on a semi-civilized people, and may be compared with the work of Sir Harry Smith in South Africa, or Sir Henry Lawrence in the Punjab. The practical reforms which he initiated in law, in commerce, in agriculture, are too numerous to mention. 'Expect no letters from me', he writes to his mother, 'save about roads. No going home for me: it would be wrong to leave a place where so much good is being done.... My market-place is roofed. My pedestal is a tremendous job, but two months more will finish that also. My roads will not be finished by me.' And again, 'I take no rest myself and give nobody else any.' To his superiors he showed himself somewhat impracticable in temper, and he was certainly exacting to his subordinates, though generous in his praise of those who helped him. He was compassionate to the poor and vigorous in his dealings with the privileged classes; and he gave the islanders an entirely new conception of justice. When he quitted the island after six years of office he left behind him two new market-places, one and a half miles of pier, one hundred miles of road largely blasted out of solid rock, spacious streets, a girls' school, and many other improvements; and he put into the natives a spirit of endeavour which outlived his term of office. One sign of the latter was that, after his departure, some peasants yearly transmitted to him the profits of a small piece of land which he had left uncared for, without disclosing the names of those whose labours had earned it.

During this period, in visits to Corinth and the Morea, he worked out strategic plans for keeping the Turks out of Greece. He also made friends with Lord Byron, who came out in 1823 to help the Greek patriots and to meet his death in the swamps of Missolonghi. Byron conceived the greatest admiration for Napier's talents and believed him to be capable of liberating Greece, if he were given a free hand. But this was not to be. Reasons of State and petty rivalries barred the way to the appointment of a British general, though it might have set the name of Napier in history beside those of Bolivar and Garibaldi; for he would have identified himself heart and soul with such a cause, and, in the opinion of many good judges, would have triumphed over the difficulties of the situation.

From 1830 to 1839 there is little to narrate. The gifts which might have been devoted to commanding a regiment, to training young officers, or to ruling a distant province, were too lightly rated by the Government, and he spent his time quietly in England and France educating his two daughters,[13] interesting himself in politics, and continuing to learn. It was the political crisis in England which called him back to active life. The readjustment of the labour market to meet the use of machinery, and the occurrence of a series of bad harvests had caused widespread discontent, and the Chartist movement was at its height in 1839. Labourers and factory owners were alarmed; the Government was besieged with petitions for military protection at a hundred points, and all the elements of a dangerous explosion were gathered together. At this critical time Charles Napier was offered the command of the troops in the northern district, and amply did he vindicate the choice. By the most careful preparation beforehand, by the most consummate coolness in the moment of danger, he rode the storm. He saw the danger of billeting small detachments of troops in isolated positions; he concentrated them at the important points. He interviewed alarmed magistrates, and he attended, in person and unarmed, a large gathering of Chartists. To all he spoke calmly but resolutely. He made it clear to the rich that he would not order a shot to be fired while peaceful measures were possible; he made it equally clear to the Chartists that he would suppress disorder, if it arose, promptly and mercilessly. With only four thousand troops under his command to control all the industrial districts of the north, Newcastle and Manchester, Sheffield and Nottingham, he did his work effectually without a shot being fired. 'Ars est celare artem': and just because of his success, few observers realized from how great a danger the community had been preserved.

Thus he had proved his versatile talents in regimental service in the Peninsula, in the reclamation of an eastern island from barbarism, and in the control of disorder at home. It was not till he had reached the age of sixty that he was to prove these gifts in the highest sphere, in the handling of an army in the field and in the direction of a campaign. But the offer of a command in India roused his indomitable spirit, the more so as trouble was threatening on the north-west frontier. An ill-judged interference in Afghānistān had in 1841 caused the massacre near Kābul of one British force: other contingents were besieged in Jalālābād and Ghazni, and were in danger of a similar fate, and the prestige of British arms was at its lowest in the valley of the Indus. Lord Ellenborough, the new Viceroy, turned to Charles Napier for advice, and in April 1842 he was given the command in Upper and Lower Sind, the districts comprising the lower Indus valley. It was his first experience of India and his first command in war. He was sixty years old and he had not faced an enemy's army in the field since the age of twenty-five. As he said, 'I go to command in Sind with no orders, no instructions, no precise line of policy given! How many men are in Sind? How many soldiers to command? No one knows!... They tell me I must form and model the staff of the army altogether! Feeling myself but an apprentice in Indian matters, I yet look in vain for a master.' But the years of study and preparation had not been in vain, and responsibility never failed to call out his best qualities. It was not many months before British officers and soldiers, Baluch chiefs and Sindian peasants owned him as a master—such a master of the arts of war and peace as had not been seen on the Indus since the days of Alexander the Great.

First, like a true pupil of Sir John Moore, he set to work thoroughly to drill his army. He experimented in person with British muskets and Marāthā matchlocks, and reassured his soldiers on the superiority of the former. He experimented with rockets to test their efficiency; and, with his usual luck in the matter of wounds, he had the calf of his leg badly torn by one that burst. He would put his hand to any labour and his life to any risk, if so he might stir the activity of others and promote the cause. He convinced himself, by studying the question at first hand, that the Baluch Amīrs, who ruled the country, were not only aliens but oppressors of the native peasantry, not only ill-disposed to British policy, but actively plotting with the hill-tribes beyond the Indus, and at the right moment he struck.

The danger of the situation lay in the great extent of the country, in the difficulty of marching in such heat amid the sand, and in the possibility of the Amīrs escaping from his grasp and taking refuge in fortresses in the heart of the desert, believed to be inaccessible. His first notable exploit was a march northwards one hundred miles into the desert to capture Imāmghar; his last, crowning a memorable sixteen days, was a similar descent upon Omarkot, which lay one hundred miles eastward beyond Mīrpur. These raids involved the organization of a camel corps, the carrying of water across the desert, and the greatest hardships for the troops, all of which Charles Napier shared uncomplainingly in person. Under his leadership British regiments and Bombay sepoys alike did wonders. Who could complain for himself when he saw the spare frame of the old general, his health undermined by fever and watches, his hooked nose and flashing eye turned this way and that, riding daily at their head, prepared to stint himself of all but the barest necessaries and to share every peril? He had begun the campaign in January; the crowning success was won on April 6. Between these dates he fought two pitched battles at Miāni and Dabo, and completely broke the power of the Amīrs.

Miāni (February 17, 1843) was the most glorious day in his life. With 2,400 troops, of whom barely 500 were Europeans, he attacked an army variously estimated between 20,000 and 40,000. Drawn up in a position, which they had themselves chosen, on the raised bank of a dry river bed, the Baluchī seemed to have every advantage on their side. But the British troops, advancing in echelon from the right, led by the 22nd Regiment, and developing an effective musketry fire, fought their way up to the outer slope of the steep bank and held it for three hours. Here the 22nd, with the two regiments of Bombay sepoys on their left, trusting chiefly to the bayonet, but firing occasional volleys, resisted the onslaught of Baluchī swordsmen in overwhelming numbers. During nearly all this time the two lines were less than twenty yards apart, and Napier was conspicuous on horseback riding coolly along the front of the British line. The matchlocks, with which many of the Baluchī were armed, seem to have been ineffective; their national weapon was the sword. The tribesmen were grand fighters but badly led. They attacked in detachments with no concerted action. For all that, the British line frequently staggered under the weight of their courageous rushes, and irregular firing went on across the narrow gap. Napier says, 'I expected death as much from our own men as from the enemy, and I was much singed by our fire—my whiskers twice or thrice so, and my face peppered by fellows who, in their fear, fired over all heads but mine, and nearly scattered my brains'. Not even Scarlett at Balaclava had a more miraculous escape. This exposure of his own person to risk was not due to mere recklessness. In his days at the Royal Military College he had carefully considered the occasions when a commander must expose himself to get the best out of his men; and from Coruña to Dabo he acted consistently on his principles. Early in the battle he had cleverly disposed his troops so as to neutralize in some measure the vast numerical superiority of the enemy; his few guns were well placed and well served. At a critical moment he ordered a charge of cavalry which broke the right of their position and threatened their camp; but the issue had to be decided by hard fighting, and all depended on the morale which was to carry the troops through such a punishing day.

The second battle was fought a month later at Dabo, near Hyderābād. The most redoubtable of the Amīrs, Sher Muhammad, known as 'the Lion of

Mīrpur', had been gathering a force of his own and was only a few miles distant from Miāni when that battle was fought. Napier could have attacked him at once; but, to avoid bloodshed, he was ready to negotiate. 'The Lion' only used the respite to collect more troops, and was soon defying the British with a force of 25,000 men, full of ardour despite their recent defeat. Indeed Napier encouraged their confidence by spreading rumours of the terror prevailing in his own camp. He did not wish to exhaust his men needlessly by long marches in tropical heat; so he played a waiting game, gathering reinforcements and trusting that the enemy would soon give him a chance of fighting. This chance came on March 24, and with a force of 5,000 men and 19 guns Napier took another three hours to win his second battle and to drive Sher Muhammad from his position with the loss of 5,000 killed. The British losses were relatively trifling, amounting to 270, of whom 147 belonged to the sorely tried 22nd Regiment. They were all full of confidence and fought splendidly under the general's eye. 'The Lion' himself escaped northwards, and two months of hard marching and clever strategy were needed to prevent him stirring up trouble among the tribesmen. The climate took toll of the British troops and even the general was for a time prostrated by sunstroke; but the operations were successful and the last nucleus of an army was broken up by Colonel Jacob on June 15. Sher Muhammad ended his days ignominiously at Lahore, then the capital of the Sikhs, having outlived his fame and sunk into idleness and debauchery.

Thus in June 1843 the general could write in his diary: 'We have taught the Baluch that neither his sun nor his desert nor his jungles nor his nullahs can stop us. He will never face us more.' But Charles Napier's own work was far from being finished. He had to bind together the different elements in the province, to reconcile chieftain and peasant Baluch, Hindu, and Sindian, to living together in amity and submitting to British rule; and he had to set up a framework of military and civilian officers to carry on the work. He held firmly the principle that military rule must be temporary. For the moment it was more effective; but it was his business to prepare the new province for regular civil government as soon as was feasible. He showed his ingenuity in the personal interviews which he had with the chieftains; and the ascendancy which he won by his character was marked. Perhaps his qualities were such as could be more easily appreciated by orientals than by his own countrymen, for he was impetuous, self-reliant, and autocratic in no common degree. He was only one of a number of great Englishmen of this century whose direct personal contact with Eastern princes was worth scores of diplomatic letters and paper constitutions. Such men were Henry Lawrence, John Nicholson, and Charles Gordon; in them the power of Great Britain was incarnate in such a form as to strike the imagination and leave an ineffaceable impression. Many of the Amīrs wished to swear allegiance to a governor present in the flesh rather than to the distant queen beyond the sea, so strongly were they impressed by Napier's personal character.

He did not forget his own countrymen, least of all that valued friend 'Thomas Atkins' and his comrade the sepoy. By the erection of spacious barracks he made the soldier's life more pleasant and his health more secure; and in a hundred other ways he showed his care and affection for them. In return few British generals have been so loved by the rank and file. He also gave much thought to material progress, to strengthening the fortress of Hyderābād, to developing the harbour at Karāchi, and, above all, to enriching the peasants by irrigation schemes. It was the story of Cephalonia on a bigger scale; but Napier was now twenty years older, overwhelmed with work, and he could give less attention to details. He did his best to find subordinates after his own heart, men who would 'scorn delights and live laborious days'. 'Does he wear varnished boots?' was a typical question that he put to a friend in Bombay, when a new engineer was commended to him. His own rewards were meagre. The Grand Cross of the Bath and the colonelcy of his favourite regiment, the 22nd, were all the recognition given for a campaign whose difficulties were minimized at home because he had mastered them so triumphantly.

Two other achievements belong to the period of his government of Sind. The campaign against the tribes of the Kachhi Hills, to the north-west of his province, rendered necessary by continued marauding, shows all his old mastery of organization. Any one who has glanced into Indian history knows the danger of these raids and the bitter experience which our Indian army has gained in them. In less than two months (January-March 1845) Napier had led five thousand men safely over burning deserts and through most difficult mountain country, had by careful strategy driven the marauders into a corner, forcing them to surrender with trifling loss, and had made an impression on the hill chieftains which lasted for many a year. This work, though slighted by the directors of the Company, received enthusiastic praise from such good judges of war as Lord Hardinge and the Duke of Wellington. The second emergency arose when the first Sikh war broke out in the Punjab. Napier felt so confident in the loyalty of his newly-pacified province that within six weeks he drew together an army of 15,000 men, and took post at Rohri, ready to co-operate against the Sikhs from the south, while Lord Hardinge advanced from the east. Before he could arrive, the decisive battle had been fought, and all he was asked to do was to assist in a council of war at Lahore. The mistakes made in the campaign had been numerous. No one saw them more clearly than Napier, and no one foretold more accurately the troubles which were to follow. For all that, he wrote in generous admiration of Lord Hardinge the Viceroy and Lord Gough the Commander-in-Chief at a time when criticism and personal bitterness were prevalent in many quarters.

After this he returned to Sind with health shattered and a longing for rest. He continued to work with vigour, but his mind was set on resignation; and the bad relations which had for years existed between him and the directors embittered his last months. No doubt he was impatient and self-willed, inclined to take short cuts through the system of dual control[14] and to justify them by his own single-hearted zeal for the good of the country. But the directors had eyes for all the slight irregularities, which are inevitable in the work of an original man, and failed entirely to estimate the priceless services that he rendered to British rule. In July 1847 he resigned and returned to Europe; but even now the end was not come. 'The tragedy must be re-acted a year or two hence,' he had written in March 1846, seeing clearly that the Sikhs had not been reconciled to British rule. In February 1849 the directors were forced by the national voice to send him out to take supreme military command and to retrieve the disasters with which the second Sikh war began. They were very reluctant to do so, and Napier himself had little wish for further exertions in so thankless a service. But the Duke of Wellington himself appealed to him, the nation spoke through all its organs, and he could not put his own wishes in the scale against the demands of public service.

He made all speed and reached Calcutta early in May, but he found no enemy to fight. The issue had been decided by Lord Gough and the hard fighting of Chiliānwāla. He had been cheated by fortune, as in 1815, and he never knew the joy of battle again. He was accustomed to settle everything as a dictator; he found it difficult to act as part of an administrative machine. He was unfamiliar with the routine of Indian official life, and he was now growing old; he was impatient of forms, impetuous in his likes and dislikes, outspoken in praise and condemnation. His relations with the masterful Viceroy, Lord Dalhousie, were soon clouded; and though he delighted in the friendship of Colin Campbell and many other able soldiers, he was too old to adapt himself to new men and new measures. In 1850 the rumblings of the storm, which was to break seven years later, could already be heard, and Napier had much anxiety over the mutinous spirit rising in the sepoy regiments. He did his best to go to the bottom of the trouble and to establish confidence and friendly relations between British and natives, but he had not time enough to achieve permanent results, and he was often fettered by the regulations of the political service. His predictions were as striking now as in the first Sikh war; but he was not content to predict and to sit idle. He was unwearied in working for the reform of barracks, though his plans were often spoiled by the careless execution of others. He was urgent for a better tone among regimental officers and for more consideration on their part towards their soldiers. If more men in high position had similarly exerted themselves, the mutiny would have been less widespread and less fatal. His resignation was due to a dispute with Lord Dalhousie about the sepoys' pay. Napier acted *ultra vires* in suspending on his own responsibility an order of the Government, because he believed the situation to be critical, while the Viceroy refused to regard this as justified. His departure, in December 1850, was the signal for an outburst of feeling among officers, soldiers, and all who knew him. His return by way of Sind was a triumphal progress.

He had two years to live when he set foot again in England, and most of this was spent at Oaklands near Portsmouth. His health had been ruined in the public service; but he continued to take a keen interest in passing events and to write on military subjects to Colin Campbell and other friends. At the same time he devoted much of his time to his neighbours and his farm. In 1852 he attended as pall-bearer at the Duke of Wellington's funeral; his own was not far distant. His brother, Sir William, describes the last scene thus: 'On the morning of August 29th 1853, at 5 o'clock, he expired like a soldier on a naked camp bedstead, the windows of the room open and the fresh air of Heaven blowing on his manly face—as the last breath escaped, Montagu McMurdo (his son-in-law), with a sudden inspiration, snatched the old colours of the 22nd Regiment, the colour that had been borne at Miāni and Hyderābād, and waved them over the dying hero. Thus Charles Napier passed from the world.'

He was a man who roused enthusiastic devotion and provoked strong resentment. Like Gordon, he was a man who could rule others, but could not be ruled; and his official career left many heart-burnings behind. His equally passionate brother, Sir William, who wrote his life, took up the feud as a legacy and pursued it in print for many years. It is regrettable that such men cannot work without friction; but in all things it was devotion to the public service, and not personal ambition, that carried Charles Napier to such extremes. From his youth he had trained himself to such a pitch of self-denial and ascetic rigour that he could not make allowance for the frailties of the average man. His keen eye and swift brain made him too impatient of the shortcomings of conscientious officials. He was ready to work fifteen hours a day when the need came; he was able to pierce into the heart of a matter while others would be puzzling round the fringes of it. Rarely in his long and laborious career did an emergency arise capable of bringing out all his gifts; and his greatest exploits were performed on scenes unfamiliar to the mass of his fellow countrymen. But a few opinions can be given to show that he was rated at his full value by the foremost men of the day.

Perhaps the most striking testimony comes from one who never saw him; it was written three years after his death, when his brother's biography appeared. It was Carlyle, the biographer of Cromwell and Frederick the Great, the most famous man of letters of the day, who wrote in 1856: 'The fine and noble qualities of the man are very recognizable to me; his piercing, subtle intellect turned all to the practical, giving him just insight into men and into things; his inexhaustible, adroit contrivances; his fiery valour; sharp promptitude to seize the good moment that will not return. A lynx-eyed, fiery man, with the spirit of an old knight in him; more of a hero than any modern I have seen for a long time.' A second tribute comes from one who had known him as an officer and was a supreme judge of military genius. Wellington was not given to extravagant words, but on many occasions he expressed himself in the warmest terms about Napier's talents and services. In 1844, speaking of the Sind campaign in the House of Lords, he said: 'My Lords, I must say that, after giving the fullest consideration to these operations, I have never known any instance of an officer who has shown in a higher degree that he possesses all the qualities and qualifications necessary to enable him to conduct great operations.' In the House of Commons at the same time Sir Robert Peel—the ablest administrative statesman of that generation, who had read for himself some of Napier's masterly dispatches—said: 'No one ever doubted Sir Charles Napier's military powers; but in his other character he does surprise me—he is possessed of extraordinary talent for civil administration.' Again, he speaks of him as 'one of three brothers who have engrafted on the stem of an ancient and honourable lineage that personal nobility which is derived from unblemished private character, from the highest sense of personal honour, and from repeated proofs of valour in the field, which have made their name conspicuous in the records of their country'.

Indifferent as Charles Napier was to ordinary praise or blame, he would have appreciated the words of such men, especially when they associated him with his brothers; but perhaps he would have been more pleased to know how many thousands of his humble fellow countrymen walked to his informal funeral at Portsmouth, and to know that the majority of those who subscribed to his statue in Trafalgar Square were private soldiers in the army that he had served and loved.

LORD SHAFTESBURY
From the painting by G. F. Watts in the National Portrait Gallery

ANTHONY ASHLEY COOPER

SEVENTH EARL OF SHAFTESBURY

1801-85

1801.	Born in Grosvenor Square, London, April 28.
1811.	His father succeeds to the earldom. He himself becomes Lord Ashley.
1813-17.	Harrow.
1819-22.	Christ Church, Oxford.
1826.	M.P. for Woodstock.
1828.	Commissioner of India Board of Control.
1829.	Chairman of Commission for Lunatic Asylums.
1830.	Marries Emily, daughter of fifth Earl Cowper.
1832.	Takes up the cause of the Ten Hours Bill or Factory Act.
1833.	M.P. for Dorset.
1836.	Founds Church Pastoral Aid Society.
1839.	Founds Indigent Blind Visiting Society.
1840.	Takes up cause of Boy Chimney-sweepers.
1842.	Mines and Collieries Bill carried.
1843.	Joins the Ragged School movement.
1847.	Ten Hours Bill finally carried.
1847.	M.P. for Bath.
1848.	Public Health Act. Chairman of Board of Health.
1851.	President of British and Foreign Bible Society.
1851.	Succeeds to the earldom.
1855.	Lord Palmerston twice offers him a seat in the Cabinet.
1872.	Death of Lady Shaftesbury.

1884.   Receives the Freedom of the City of London.

1885.   Dies at Folkestone, October 1.

LORD SHAFTESBURY
Philanthropist

The word 'Philanthropist' has suffered the same fate as many other words in our language. It has become hackneyed and corrupted; it has taken a professional taint; it has almost become a byword. We are apt to think of the philanthropist as an excitable, contentious creature, at the mercy of every fad, an ultra-radical in politics, craving for notoriety, filled with self-confidence, and meddling with other people's business. Anthony Ashley Cooper, the greatest philanthropist of the nineteenth century, was of a different type. By temper he was strongly conservative. He always loved best to be among his own family; he was fond of his home, fond of the old associations of his house. To come out into public life, to take his place in Parliament or on the platform, to be mixed up in the wrangling of politics was naturally distasteful to him. It continually needed a strong effort for him to overcome this distaste and to act up to his sense of duty. It is only when we remember this that we can do justice to his lifelong activity, and to the high principles which bore him up through so many efforts and so many disappointments. For himself he would submit to injustice and be still: for his fellow countrymen and for his religion he would renew the battle to the last day of his life.

His childhood was not happy. His parents had little sympathy with children, his father being absorbed in the cares of public life, his mother given up to society pleasures. He had three sisters older than himself, but no brother or companion, and he was left largely to himself. At the age of seven he went to a preparatory school, where he was made miserable by the many abuses which flourished there; and it was not till he went to Harrow at the age of twelve that he began to enjoy life. He had few of the indulgences which we associate with the early days of those who are born heirs to high position. But, thus thrown back on himself, the boy nurtured strong attachments, for the old housekeeper who first showed him tenderness at home, for the school where he had learnt to be happy, and for the Dorset home, which was to be throughout his life the pole-star of his affections. The village of Wimborne St. Giles lies some eight miles north of Wimborne, in Dorset, on the edge of Cranborne Forest, one of the most beautiful and unspoiled regions in the south of England, which 'as late as 1818 contained twelve thousand deer and as many as six lodges, each of which had its walk and its ranger'. Here he wandered freely in his holidays for many years, giving as yet little promise of an exceptional career; here you may find in outlying cottages those who still treasure his memory and keep his biography among the few books that adorn their shelves.

From Harrow, Lord Ashley went at the age of sixteen to read for two years with a clergyman in Derbyshire; in 1819 he went to Christ Church, Oxford, and three years later succeeded in taking a first class in classics. He had good abilities and a great power of concentration. These were to bear fruit one day in the gathering of statistics, in the marshalling of evidence, and in the presentation of a case which needed the most lucid and most laborious advocacy.

He came down from Oxford in 1822, but did not go into Parliament till 1826, and for the intervening years there is little to chronicle. In those days it was usual enough for a young nobleman to take up politics when he was barely of age, but Lord Ashley needed some other motive than the custom of the day. It is characteristic of his whole life that he responded to a call when there was a need, but was never in a hurry to put himself forward or to aim at high position. We have a few of his own notes from this time which show the extent of his reading, and still more, the depth of his reflections. As with Milton, who spent over five years at Cambridge and then five more in study and retirement at Horton, the long years of self-education were profitable and left their mark on his life. His first strong religious impulse he himself dates back to his school-days at Harrow, when (as is now recorded in a mural tablet on the spot) in walking up the street one day he was shocked by the indignities of a pauper funeral. The drunken bearers, staggering up the hill and swearing over the coffin, so appalled him that the sight remained branded on his memory and he determined to devote his life to the service of the poor. But one such shock would have achieved little, if the decision had not been strengthened by years of thought and resolution. His tendency to self-criticism is seen in the entry in his diary for April, 1826 (his twenty-fifth birthday). He blames himself for indulging in dreams and for having performed so little; but he himself admits that the visions were all of a noble character, and we know what abundant fruit they produced in the sixty years of active effort which were to follow. The man who a year later could write sincerely in his diary, 'Immortality has ceased to be a longing with me. I desire to be useful in my generation,' had been little harmed by a few years of dreaming dreams, and had little need to be afraid of having made a false start in life.

When he entered the House of Commons as member for Woodstock in 1826, Lord Ashley had strong Conservative instincts, a fervid belief in the British constitution, and an unbounded admiration for the Duke of Wellington, whose Peninsula victories had fired his enthusiasm at Harrow. It was to his wing of the Conservative party that Ashley attached himself; and it was the duke who, succeeding to the premiership on the premature death of Canning, gave him his first office, a post on the India Board of Control. The East India Company with its board of directors (abolished in 1858) still ruled India, but was since 1778 subject in many ways to the control of the British Parliament, and the board to which Lord Ashley now belonged exercised some of the functions since committed to the Secretary of State for India. He set himself conscientiously to study the interests of India, but over the work of his department he had little chance of winning distinction. In fact his first prominent speech was on the Reform of Lunatic Asylums, not an easy subject for a new member to handle. He was diffident in manner and almost inaudible. Without the kindly encouragement of friends he might have despaired of future success; but his sincerity in the cause was worth more than many a brilliant speech. The Bill was carried, a new board was constituted, and of this Lord Ashley became chairman in 1829, and continued to hold the office till his death fifty-six years later. This was the first of the burdens that he took upon himself without thought of reward, and so is worthy of special mention, though it never won the fame of his factory legislation. But it shows the character of the man, how ready he was to step into a post which meant work without remuneration, drudgery without fame, prejudice and opposition from all whose interests were concerned in maintaining the abuses of the past.

It was this spirit which led him in 1836 to take up the Church Pastoral Aid Society,[15] in 1839 to found the Indigent Blind Visiting Society, in 1840 to champion the cause of chimney-sweeps, and in all these cases to continue his support for fifty years or more. We are accustomed to-day to 'presidents' and 'patrons' and a whole broadsheet of complimentary titles, to which noblemen give their names and often give little else. Lord Ashley understood such an office differently. He was regular in attendance at meetings, generous in giving money, unflinching in his advocacy of the cause. We shall see this more fully in dealing with the two most famous crusades associated with his name.

Though these growing labours began early to occupy his time, we find the record of his life diversified by other claims and other interests. In 1830 he married Emily, daughter of Lord Cowper, who bore him several children, and who shared all his interests with the fullest sympathy; and henceforth his greatest joys and his deepest sorrows were always associated with his family life. At home his first hobby was astronomy. At the age of twenty-eight he was ardently devoted to it and would spend all his leisure on it for weeks together, till graver duties absorbed his time. But he was no recluse, and all through his life he found pleasure in the society of his friends and in paying them visits in their homes. Many of his early visits were paid to the Iron Duke at Strathfieldsaye; in later life no one entertained him more often than Lord Palmerston, with whom he was connected by marriage. He was the friend and often the guest of Queen Victoria, and in his twenty-eighth year he is even found as a guest at the festive board of George IV. 'Such a round of laughing and pleasure I never enjoyed: if there be a hospitable gentleman on earth it is His Majesty.' And at all times he was ready to mix freely and on terms of social equality with all who shared his sympathies, dukes and dustmen, Cabinet ministers and costermongers.

In the holiday season he delighted to travel. In his journals he sets down the impressions which he felt among the pictures and churches of Italy, and in the mountains of Germany and Switzerland; he loves to record the friendliness of the greetings which he met among the peasantry of various lands. When he talked to them no one could fail to see that he was genuinely interested in them, that he wanted to know their joys and their sorrows, and to enrich his own knowledge by anything that the humblest could tell him. Still more did he delight in Scotland, where he had many friends. He was of the generation immediately under the spell of the 'Wizard of the North', and the whole country was seen through a veil of romantic and historical association. There he went nearly every year, to Edinburgh, to Roslin, to Inveraray, to the Trossachs, and to a hundred other places—and if his heart was stirred with the glories of the past, his eye was quick to 'catch the manners living as they rise'. As he commented caustically at Rome on 'the church lighted up and decorated like a ball-room—the bishop with a stout train of canons, listening to the music precisely like an opera', so at Newbattle he criticizes the coldness of the kirk, 'all is silent save the minister, who discharges the whole ceremony and labours under the weight of his own tautologies'. His bringing up had been in the Anglican church; he was devoted to her liturgy, her congregational worship, her moderation and simplicity combined with reverence and warmth. Although these travels were but interludes in his busy life, they show that it was not for want of other tastes and interests of his own that his life was dedicated to laborious service. He was very human himself, and there were few aspects of humanity which did not attract him.

With his father relations were very difficult. As his interest in social questions grew, his attention was naturally turned on the poor nearest to his own doors, the agricultural labourers of Dorset. Even in those days of low wages Dorset was a notorious example quoted on many a Radical platform: the wages of the farm labourers were frequently as low as seven shillings a week, and the conditions in which they had often to bring up a large family of children were deplorable. If Lord Ashley had not himself felt the shame of their poverty, their bad housing and their other hardships, there were plenty of opponents ready to force them on his notice in revenge for his having exposed their own sores. He was made responsible for abuses which he could not remedy. While his father, a resolute Tory of the old type, still lived, the son was unable to stir. He sedulously tried to avoid all bitterness; but he could not, when publicly challenged, avoid stating his own views about fair wages and fair conditions of living, and his father took offence. For years it was impossible for the son to come under his father's roof. When the old earl died in 1851, his son lost no time in proving his sincerity as a reformer; but meanwhile he had to go into the fray against the manufacturers with his arms tied behind his back and submit to taunts which he little deserved. That he could carry on this struggle for so many years, without embittering the issues, and without open exposure of the family quarrel, shows the strength of character which he had gained by years of religious discipline and self-control.

Politics proper played but a small part in his career. The politicians found early that he was not of the 'available' type—that he would not lend himself to party policy or compromise on any matter which seemed to him of national interest. Such political posts as were offered to him were largely held out as a bait to silence him, and to prevent his bringing forward embarrassing measures which might split the party. Ashley himself found how much easier it was for him to follow a single course when he was an independent member. Reluctantly in 1834 he accepted a post at the Board of Admiralty and worked earnestly in his department; but this ministry only lasted for one year, and he never held office again, though he was often pressed to do so. He was attached to Wellington; but for Peel, now become the Tory leader, he had little love. The two men were very dissimilar in character; and though at times Ashley had friendly communications with Peel, yet in his diary Ashley often complains bitterly of his want of enthusiasm, of what he regarded as Peel's opportunism and subservience to party policy. The one had an instinct for what was practical and knew exactly how far he could combine interests to carry a measure; the other was all on fire for the cause and ready to push it forward against all obstacles, at all costs. Ashley, it is true, had to work through Parliament to attain his chief ends, and many a bitter moment he had to endure in striving towards the goal. But if he was not an adroit or successful politician, he gradually, as the struggle went on, by earnestness and force of character, made for himself in the House a place apart, a place of rare dignity and influence; and with the force of public opinion behind him he was able to triumph over ministers and parties.

It was in 1832 that he first had his attention drawn to the conditions of labour in factories. He never claimed to be the pioneer of the movement, but he was early in the field. The inventions of the latter part of the eighteenth century had transformed the north of England. The demand for labour had given rise to appalling abuses, especially in the matter of child labour. From London workhouses and elsewhere children were poured into the labour market, and by the 'Apprentice System' were bound to serve their masters for long periods and for long hours together. A pretence of voluntary contract was kept up, but fraud and deception were rife in the system and its results were tragic. Mrs. Browning's famous poem, 'The Cry of the Children,' gives a more vivid picture of the children's sufferings than many pages of prose. At the same time we have plenty of first-hand evidence from the great towns of the misery which went along with the wonderful development of national wealth. Speaking in 1873 Lord Shaftesbury said, 'Well can I recollect in the earlier periods of the Factory movement waiting at the factory gates to see the children come out, and a set of dejected cadaverous creatures they were. In Bradford especially the proofs of long and cruel toil were most remarkable. The cripples and distorted forms might be numbered by hundreds perhaps by thousands. A friend of mine collected together a vast number for me; the sight was most piteous, the deformities incredible.' And an eye-witness in Bolton reports in 1792: 'Anything like the squalid misery, the slow, mouldering, putrefying death by which the weak and feeble are perishing here, it never befell my eyes to behold, nor my imagination to conceive.' Some measures of relief were carried by the elder Sir Robert Peel, himself a cotton-spinner; but public opinion was slow to move and was not roused till 1830, when Mr. Sadler,[16] member for Newark, led the first fight for a 'Ten Hours Bill'. When Sadler was unseated in 1832, Lord Ashley offered his help, and so embarked on the greatest of his works performed in the public service. He had the support of a few of the noblest men in England, including Robert Southey and Charles Dickens; but he had against him the vast body of well-to-do people in the country, and inside Parliament many of the most progressive and influential politicians. The factory owners were inspired at once by interest and conviction; the political economy of the day taught them that all restrictions on labour were harmful to the progress of industry and to the prosperity of the country, while the figures in their ledgers taught them what was the most economical method of running their own mills.

Already it was clear that Lord Ashley was no mere sentimentalist out for a momentary sensation. At all times he gave the credit for starting the work to Sadler and his associates; and from the outset he urged his followers to fix on a limited measure first, to concentrate attention on the work of children and young persons, and to avoid general questions involving conflicts between capital and labour. Also he took endless pains to acquaint himself at first hand with the facts. 'In factories,' he said afterwards, 'I examined the mills, the machinery, the homes, and saw the workers and their work in all its details. In collieries I went down into the pits. In London I went into lodging-houses and thieves' haunts, and every filthy place. It gave me a power I could not otherwise have had.' And this was years before 'slumming' became fashionable and figured in the pages of *Punch*; it was no distraction caught up for a week or a month, but a labour of fifty years! We have an account of him as he appeared at this period of his life: 'above the medium height, about 5 feet 6 inches, with a slender and extremely graceful figure... curling dark hair in thick masses, fine brow, features delicately cut, the nose perhaps a trifle too prominent,... light blue eyes deeply set with projecting eyelids, his mouth small and compressed.' His whole face and appearance seems to have had a sculpturesque effect and to have suggested the calm and composure of marble. But under this marble exterior there was burning a flame of sympathy for the poor, a fire of indignation against the system which oppressed them.

In 1833 some progress was made. Lord Althorp, the Whig leader in the Commons, under pressure from Lord Ashley, carried a bill dealing indeed with some of the worst abuses in factories, but applying only to some of the great textile industries. That it still left much to be done can be seen from studying the details of the measure. Children under eleven years of age were not to work more than nine hours a day, and young persons under nineteen not more than twelve hours a day. Adults might still work all day and half the night if the temptation of misery at home and extra wages to be earned was too strong for them. It seems difficult now to believe that this was a great step forward, yet for the moment Ashley found that he could do no more and must accept what the politicians gave him. In 1840, however, he started a fresh campaign on behalf of children not employed in these factories, who were not included in the Act of 1833, and who, not being concentrated in the great centres of industry, escaped the attention of the general public. He obtained a Royal Commission to investigate mines and other works, and to report upon their condition. The Blue Book was published in 1842 and created a sensation unparalleled of its kind. Men read with horror the stories of the mines, of children employed underground for twelve or fourteen hours a day, crouching in low passages, monotonously opening and shutting the trap-doors as the trollies passed to and fro. Alone each child sat in pitchy darkness, unable to stir for more than a few paces, unable to sleep for fear of punishment with the strap in case of neglect, and often surrounded with vermin. Women were employed crawling on hands and knees along these passages, stripped to the waist, stooping under the low roofs, and even so chafing and wounding their backs, as they hauled the coal along the underground rails, or carrying in baskets on their backs, up steps and ladders, loads which varied in weight from a half to one and a half hundredweights. The physical health, the mental education, and the moral character of these poor creatures suffered equally under such a system; and well might those responsible for the existence of such abuses fear to let the Report be published. But copies of it first reached members of Parliament, then the public at large learnt the burden of the tale, and Lord Ashley might now hope for enough support from outside to break down the opposition in the House of Commons and the delays of parliamentary procedure.

'The Mines and Collieries Bill' was brought in before the impression could fade, and on June 7, 1842, Ashley made one of the greatest of his speeches and drove home powerfully the effect of the Report. His mastery of facts was clear enough to satisfy the most dispassionate politician; his sincerity disarmed Richard Cobden, the champion of the Lancashire manufacturers and brought about a reconciliation between them; his eloquence stirred the hearts of Queen Victoria and the Prince Consort, and drew from the latter words of glowing admiration and promises of support. In August the bill finally passed the House of Lords, and a second great blow had been struck. Practices which were poisoning at the source the lives of the younger generation were forbidden by law; above all, it was expressly laid down that, after a few years, no woman or girl should be employed in mines at all. The influence which such a law had on the family life in the mining districts was incalculable; the women were rescued from servitude in the mines and restored to their natural place at home.

There was still much to do. In 1844 the factory question was again brought to the front by the demands of the working classes, and again Ashley was ready to champion their cause, and to propose that the working day should now be limited to eight hours for children, and to ten hours for grown men. In Parliament there was long and weary fighting over the details. The Tory Government did not wish to oppose the bill directly. Neither party had really faced the question or made up its mind. Expediency rather than justice was in the minds of the official politicians.

Such a straightforward champion as Lord Ashley was a source of embarrassment to these gentlemen, to be met by evasion rather than direct opposition. The radical John Bright, a strong opponent of State interference and equally straightforward in his methods, made a personal attack on Lord Ashley. He referred to the Dorset labourers, as if Ashley was indifferent to abuses nearer home, and left no one in doubt of his opinions. At the same time, Sir James Graham, the Home Secretary, did all in his power to defeat Ashley's bill by bringing forward alternative proposals, which he knew would be unacceptable to the workers. In face of such opposition most men would have given way. Ashley, who had been a consistent Tory all his life, was bitterly aggrieved at the treatment which his bill met with from his official leaders. He persevered in his efforts, relying on support from outside; but in Parliament the Government triumphed to the extent of defeating the Ten Hours Bill in March 1844 and again in April 1846. Still, the small majority (ten) by which this last division was decided showed in which direction the current was flowing, and when a few months later the Tories were ousted from office, the Whigs took up the bill officially, and in June 1847 Lord Ashley, though himself out of Parliament for the moment, had the satisfaction of seeing the bill become the law of the land.

There was great rejoicing in the manufacturing districts, and Lord Ashley was the hero of the day. The working classes had no direct representative in Parliament in those days: without his constant efforts neither party would have given a fair hearing to their cause. He had argued with politicians without giving away principles; he had stirred the industrial districts without rousing class hatred; he had been defeated time after time without giving up the struggle. Much has been added since then to the laws restricting the conditions of labour till, in the often quoted words of Lord Morley, the biographer of Cobden, we have 'a complete, minute, and voluminous code for the protection of labour... an immense host of inspectors, certifying surgeons and other authorities whose business it is to "speed and post o'er land and ocean" in restless guardianship of every kind of labour'. But these were the heroic days of the struggle for factory legislation, and also of the struggle for cheap food for the people. Reviewing these great events many years later the Duke of Argyll said, 'During that period two great discoveries have been made in the science of Government: the one is the immense advantage of abolishing restrictions on trade, the other is the absolute necessity of imposing restrictions on labour'. While Sir Robert Peel might with some justice contest with Cobden the honour of establishing the first principle, few will challenge Lord Ashley's right to the honour of securing the second.

Of the many religious and political causes which he undertook during and after this time, of the Zionist movement to repatriate the Jews, of the establishing of a Protestant bishopric at Jerusalem, of his attacks on the war with Sind and the opium trade with China, of his championship of the Nestorian Christians against the Turk, of his leadership of the great Bible Society, there is not space to speak. The mere list gives an idea of the width of his interests and the warmth of his sympathy.

Some of these questions were highly contentious; and Lord Ashley, who was a fervent Evangelical, was less than fair to churchmen of other schools. To Dr. Pusey himself he could write a kindly and courteous letter; but on the platform, or in correspondence with friends, he could denounce 'Puseyites' in the roundest terms. One cannot expect that a man of his character will avoid all mistakes. It was a time when feeling ran high on religious questions, and he was a declared partisan; but at least we may say that the public good, judged from the highest point, was his objective; there was no room for self-seeking in his heart. Nor did this wide extension of his activity mean neglect of his earlier crusades. On the contrary, he continued to work for the good of the classes to whom his Factory Bills had been so beneficial. Not content with prohibiting what was harmful, he went on to positive measures of good; restriction of hours was followed by sanitation, and this again by education, and by this he was led to what was perhaps the second most famous work of his life.

In 1843 his attention had already been drawn to the question of educating the neglected children, and he was making acquaintance at first hand with the work of the Ragged Schools, at that time few in number and poorly supported. He visited repeatedly the Field Lane School, in a district near Holborn notoriously frequented by the criminal classes, and soon the cause, at which he was to work unsparingly for forty years, began to move forward. He went among the poor with no thought of condescension. Simple as he was by nature, he possessed in perfection the art of speaking to children, and he was soon full of practical schemes for helping them. Sanitary reform was not neglected in his zeal for religion, and emigration was to be promoted as well as better housing at home; for, till the material conditions of life were improved, he knew that it was idle to hope for much moral reform. 'Plain living and high thinking' is an excellent ideal for those whose circumstances put them out of reach of anxiety over daily bread; it is a difficult gospel to preach to those who are living in destitution and misery.

The character of his work soon won confidence even in the most unlikely quarters. In June 1848 he received a round-robin signed by forty of the most notorious thieves in London, asking him to come and meet them in person at a place appointed; and on his going there he found a mob of nearly four hundred men, all living by dishonesty and crime, who listened readily and even eagerly to his brotherly words.

Several of them came forward in turn and made candid avowal of their respective difficulties and vices, and of the conditions of their lives. He found that they were tired of their own way of life, and were ready to make a fresh start; and in the course of the next few months he was able, thanks to the generosity of a rich friend, to arrange for the majority of them to emigrate to another country or to find new openings away from their old haunts.

But, apart from such special occasions, the work of the schools went steadily forward. In seven years, more than a hundred such schools were opened, and Lord Shaftesbury was unfailing in his attendance whenever he could help forward the cause. His advice to the managers to 'keep the schools in the mire and the gutter' sounds curious; but he was afraid that, as they throve, boys of more prosperous classes would come in and drive out those for whom they were specially founded. 'So long', he said, 'as the mire and gutter exist, so long as this class exists, you must keep the school adapted to their wants, their feelings, their tastes and their level.' And any of us familiar with the novels of Charles Dickens and Walter Besant will know that such boys still existed unprovided for in large numbers in 1850 and for many years after.

Thus the years went by. He succeeded to the earldom on his father's death in 1851. His heart was wrung by the early deaths of two of his children and by the loss of his wife in 1872. In his home he had his full share of the joys and sorrows of life, but his interest in his work never failed. If new tasks were taken up, it was not at the expense of the old; the fresh demand on his unwearied energies was met with the same spirit. At an advanced age he opened a new and attractive chapter in his life by his friendly meetings with the London costermongers. He gave prizes for the best-kept donkey, he attended the judging in person, he received in return a present of a donkey which was long cherished at Wimborne St. Giles. It is impossible to deal fully with his life in each decade; one page from his journal for 1882 shows what he could still do at the age of eighty-one, and will be the best proof of his persistence in well-doing. He began the day with a visit to Greenhithe to inspect the training ships for poor boys, at midday he came back to Grosvenor Square to attend a committee meeting of the Bible Society at his home, he then went to a public banquet in honour of his godson, and he finished with a concert at Buckingham Palace, thus keeping up his friendly relations with all classes in the realm. To the very last, in his eighty-fifth year, he continued to attend a few meetings and to visit the scenes of his former labours; and on October 1, 1885, full of years and full of honours, he died quietly at Folkestone, where he had gone for the sake of his health.

In this sketch attention has been drawn to his labours rather than to his honours. He might have had plenty of the latter if he had wished. He received the Freedom of the City of London and of other great towns. Twice he was offered the Garter, and he only accepted the second offer on Lord Palmerston's urgent request that he should treat it as a tribute to the importance of social work. Three times he was offered a seat in the Cabinet, but he refused each time, because official position would fetter his special work. He kept aloof from party politics, and was only roused when great principles were at stake. Few of the leading politicians satisfied him. Peel seemed too cautious, Gladstone too subtle, Disraeli too insincere. It was the simplicity and kindliness of his relative Palmerston that won his heart, rather than confidence in his policy at home or abroad. The House of Commons suited him better than the colder atmosphere of the House of Lords; but in neither did he rise to speak without diffidence and fear. It is a great testimony to the force of his conviction that he won as many successes in Parliament as he did. But the means through which he effected his chief work were committees, platform meetings, and above all personal visits to scenes of distress.

The nation would gladly have given him the last tribute of burial in Westminster Abbey, but he had expressed a clear wish to be laid among his own people at Wimborne St. Giles, and the funeral was as simple as he had wished it to be. His name in London is rather incongruously associated with a fountain in Piccadilly Circus, and with a street full of theatres, made by the clearing of the slums where he had worked: the intention was good, the result is unfortunate. More truly than in any sculpture or buildings his memorial is to be found in the altered lives of thousands of his fellow citizens, in the happy looks of the children, and in the pleasant homes and healthy workshops which have transformed the face of industrial England.

JOHN LAWRENCE

1811-79

1811. Born at Richmond, Yorkshire, March 4.

1823. School at Londonderry.

1827. Haileybury I.C.S. College.

1829. Goes out to India as a member of Civil Service.

1831. Delhi.

1834. Pānīpat.

1836. Etāwa.

1840-2. Furlough and marriage to Harriette Hamilton.

1844. Collector and Magistrate of Delhi and Pānīpat.

1845. First Sikh War.

1846. Governor of Jālandhar Doāb.

1848. Second Sikh War.

1849. Lord Dalhousie annexes Punjab. Henry and John Lawrence members of Punjab Board.

1852-3. New Constitution. John Lawrence, Chief Commissioner of Punjab.

1856. Oudh annexed. Henry Lawrence first Governor.

1857. Indian Mutiny. Death of Henry Lawrence at Lucknow (July). Punjab secured. Delhi retaken (September).

1858-9. Baronetcy; G.C.B. Return to England.

1864. Governor-General of India. Irrigation. Famine relief.

1869. Return to England. Peerage.

1870. Chairman of London School Board.

1876. Failure of eyesight.

1879. Death in London, June 27.

JOHN LAWRENCE
INDIAN ADMINISTRATOR

The north of Ireland and its Scoto-Irish stock has given birth to some of the toughest human material that our British Isles have produced. Of this stock was John Wesley, who at the age of eighty-five attributed his good health to rising every day at four and preaching every day at five. Of this was Arthur Wellesley, who never knew defeat and 'never lost a British gun'. Of this was Alexander Lawrence, sole survivor among the officers of the storming party at Seringapatam, who lived to rear seven stout sons, five of whom went out to service in India, two at least to win imperishable fame. His wife, a Miss Knox, came also from across the sea; and, if the evidence fails to prove Mr. Bosworth Smith's statement that she was akin to the great Reformer, she herself was a woman of strong character and great administrative talent. When we remember John Lawrence's parentage, we need not be surprised at the character which he bore, nor at the evidence of it to be seen in the grand rugged features portrayed by Watts in the picture in the National Portrait Gallery.

LORD LAWRENCE
From the painting by G. F. Watts in the National Portrait Gallery]

Of these parents John Laird Mair Lawrence was the fourth surviving son, one boy, the eldest, having died in infancy. He owed the accident of his birth in an English town to his father's regiment being quartered at the time in Yorkshire, his first schooling at Bristol to his father's residence at Clifton; but when he was twelve years old, he followed his elder brothers to Londonderry, where his maternal uncle, the Rev. James Knox, was Headmaster of the Free Grammar School, situated within the walls of that famous Protestant fortress. It was a rough school, of which the Lawrence brothers cherished few kindly recollections. It is difficult to ascertain what they learnt there: perhaps the grim survivals of the past, town-walls, bastions, and guns, made the deepest impression upon them. John's chief friend at school was Robert Montgomery, whom, many years later, he welcomed as a sympathetic fellow-worker in India; and the two boys continued their education together at Wraxall in Wiltshire, to which they were transferred in 1825. Here John spent two years, working at his books by fits and starts, and finding an outlet for his energy in climbing, kite-flying, and other unconventional amusements, and then his turn came to profit by the goodwill of a family friend, who was an influential man and a director of the East India Company. To this man, John Huddlestone by name, his brothers Alexander and George owed their commissions in the Indian cavalry, while Henry had elected for the artillery. John hoped for a similar favour, but was offered, in its place, a post in the Indian Civil Service. This was a cruel disappointment to him as he had set his heart on the army. In fact he was only reconciled to the prospect by the influence of his eldest sister Letitia, who held a unique place as the family counsellor now and throughout her life.

When he sailed first for India at the age of eighteen, John Lawrence had done little to give promise of future distinction. He had strong attachments to his mother and sister; outside the family circle he was not eager to make new friends. In his work and in his escapades he showed an independent spirit, and seemed to care little what others thought of him; even at Haileybury, at that time a training-school for the service of the East India Company, he was most irregular in his studies, though he carried off several prizes; and he seems to have impressed his fellows rather as an uncouth person who preferred mooning about the college, or rambling alone through the countryside, to spending his days in the pursuits which they esteemed.

When the time came for John Lawrence to take up his work, his brother Henry, his senior by five years, was also going out to India to rejoin his company of artillery, and the brothers sailed together. John had to spend ten weary months in Calcutta learning languages, and was very unhappy there. Ill-health was one cause; another was his distaste for strangers' society and his longing for home; it was only the definite prospect of work which rescued him from despondency. He applied for a post at Delhi; and, as soon as this was granted, he was all eagerness to leave Calcutta. But he had used the time well in one respect: he had acquired the power of speaking Persian with ease and fluency, and this stood him in good stead in his dealings with the princes and the peasants of the northern races, whose history he was to influence in the coming years.

Delhi has been to many Englishmen besides John Lawrence a city of absorbing interest. It had even then a long history behind it, and its history, as we in the twentieth century know, is by no means finished yet. It stands on the Jumna, the greatest tributary of the Ganges, at a point where the roads from the north-west reach the vast fertile basin of these rivers, full in the path of an invader. Many races had swept down on it from the mountain passes before the English soldiery appeared from the south-east; its mosques, its palaces, its gates, recall the memory of many princes and conquerors. At the time of Lawrence's arrival it was still the home of the heir of Akbar and Aurangzeb, the last of the great Mughals. The dynasty had been left in 1804, after the wars of Lord Wellesley, shorn of its power, but not robbed of its dignity or riches. As a result it had degenerated into an abuse of the first order, since all the scoundrels of the district infested the palace and preyed upon its owner, who had no work to occupy him, no call of duty to rouse him from sloth and sensuality. The town was filled with a turbulent population of many different tribes, and the work of the European officials was exacting and difficult. But at the same time it gave unique opportunities for an able man to learn the complexity of the Indian problem; and the knowledge which John Lawrence acquired there proved of incalculable value to him when he was called to higher posts.

At Delhi he was working as an assistant to the Resident, one of a staff of four or five, with no independent authority. But in 1834 he was given temporary charge of the district of Pānīpat, fifty miles to the north, and it is here that we begin to get some measure of the man and his abilities. The place was the scene of more than one famous battle in the past; armies of Mughals and Persians and Marāthīs had swept across its plains. Its present inhabitants were Jāts, a race widely extended through the eastern Punjab and the western part of the province of Agra. Originally invaders from the north, they espoused the religions of those around them, some Brahman, some Muhammadan, some Sikh, and settled down as thrifty industrious peasants; though inclined to peaceful pursuits, they still preserved some strength of character and were the kind of people among whom Lawrence might hope to enjoy his work. The duties of the magistrate are generally divided into judicial and financial. But, as an old Indian official more exhaustively stated it: 'Everything which is done by the executive government is done by the Collector in one or another of his capacities—publican, auctioneer, sheriff, road-maker, timber-dealer, recruiting sergeant, slayer of wild beasts, bookseller, cattle-breeder, postmaster, vaccinator, discounter of bills, and registrar.' It is difficult to see how one can bring all these departments under two headings; it is still more difficult to see how such diverse demands can possibly be met by a single official, especially by one little over twenty years of age coming from a distant country. No stay-at-home fitting himself snugly into a niche in the well-manned offices of Whitehall can expect to see his powers develop so rapidly or so rapidly collapse (whichever be his fate) as these solitary outposts of our empire, bearing, Atlas-like, a whole world on their shoulders.

With John Lawrence, fortunately, there was no question of collapse till many years of overwork broke down his physical strength. He grappled with the task like a giant, passing long days in his office or in the saddle, looking into everything for himself, laying up stores of knowledge about land tenure and agriculture, training his judgement to deal with the still more difficult problem of the workings of the Oriental mind. He had no friends or colleagues of his own at hand; and when the day's work was done he would spend his evenings holding an informal durbar outside his tent, chatting with all and sundry of the natives who happened to be there. The peoples of India are familiar with pomp and outward show such as we do not see in the more prosaic west; but they also know a man when they see one. And this young man with the strongly-marked features, curt speech, and masterful manner, sitting there alone in shirt-sleeves and old trousers as he listened to their tales, was an embodiment of the British rule which they learnt to respect—if not to love—for the solid benefits which it conferred upon them. He had an element of hardness in him; by many he was thought to be unduly harsh at different periods of his life; but he spared no trouble to learn the truth, he was inflexibly just in his decisions, and his reputation spread rapidly throughout the district. In cases of genuine need he could be extremely kind and generous; but he did not lavish these qualities on the first comer, nor did he wear his heart upon his sleeve. His informal ways and unconventional dress were a bugbear to some critics; his old waywardness and love of adventure was still alive in him, and he thoroughly enjoyed the more irregular sides of his work. Mr. Bosworth Smith has preserved some capital stories of the crimes with which he had to deal, and how the young collector took an active part in arresting the criminals—stories which some years later the future Viceroy dictated to his wife.

But, after two years thus spent in constant activity and ever-growing mastery of his work, he had to come down in rank; the post was filled by a permanent official, and John Lawrence returned to the Delhi staff as an assistant.

He soon received other 'acting appointments' in the neighbourhood of Delhi, one of which at Etāwa gave him valuable experience in dealing with the difficult revenue question. The Government was in the habit of collecting the land tax from the 'ryot' or peasant through a class of middle-men called 'talukdārs',[17] who had existed under the native princes for a long time. Borrowing perhaps from western ideas, the English had regarded the latter as landowners and the peasants as mere tenants; this had often caused grave injustice to the latter, and the officials now desired to revise the settlement in order to put all classes on a fair footing. In this department Robert Bird was supreme, and under his direction John Lawrence and others set themselves to measure out areas, to record the nature of the various soils, and to assess rents at a moderate rate. Still this was dull work compared to the planning of practical improvements and the conviction of dangerous criminals; and as, towards the end of 1839, Lawrence was struck down by a bad attack of fever, he was not sorry to be ordered home on long leave and to revisit his native land. He had been strenuously at work for ten years on end and he had well earned a holiday.

His father was now dead, and his favourite sister married, but of his mother he was for many years the chief support, contributing liberally of his own funds and giving his time and judgement to managing what the brothers put together for that purpose. In 1840 he was travelling both in Scotland and Ireland; and it was near Londonderry that he met his future wife, daughter of the Rev. Richard Hamilton, who, besides being rector of his parish, was an active justice of the peace. He met her again in the following summer, and they were married on August 26, 1841. Their life together was a tale of unbroken happiness, which was only ended by his death. A long tour on the Continent was followed by a severe illness, which threatened to forbid all prospect of work in India. However, by the end of that summer he had recovered his health enough to contemplate returning, and in October, 1842, he set sail to spend another sixteen years in labouring in India.

In 1843 he resumed work at Delhi, holding temporary posts till the end of 1844, when he became in his own right Collector and Magistrate of Delhi and Pānīpat. This time his position, besides involving much familiar work, threw him in the way of events of wider interest. Lord Hardinge, the Governor-General, on his way to the first Sikh war, came to Delhi, and was much impressed with Lawrence's ability; and when he annexed the Doāb[18] of Jālandhar and wanted a governor for it, he could find no one more suitable than the young magistrate, who had so swiftly collected 4,000 carts and sent them up laden with supplies on the eve of the battle of Sobraon.

This was a great step in advance and carried John Lawrence ahead of many of his seniors; but it was promotion that was fully justified by events. He was not wanting in self-confidence, and the tone of some of his letters to the Secretary at head-quarters might seem boastful, had not his whole career shown that he could more than make good his promise. 'So far as I am concerned as supervisor,' he says, 'I could easily manage double the extent of country'; and then, comparing his district with another, he continues: 'I only ask you to wait six months, and then contrast the civil management of the two charges.' As a fact, during the three years that he held this post, he was often acting as deputy for his brother Henry at Lahore, during his illness or absence, and this alone clears him of the charge of idle boasting. Jālandhar was comparatively a simple job for him, whatever it might be for others; he was able to apply his knowledge of assessment and taxation gained at Etāwa, and need only satisfy himself. At Lahore, on the other hand, he had to consider the very strong views held by his brother about the respect due to the vested rights of the chiefs; and he studiously set himself to deal with matters in the way in which his brother would have done. The Sirdars or Sikh chieftains had inherited traditions of corrupt and oppressive rule; but the chivalrous Henry Lawrence always looked at the noble side of native character; and, as by his personal gifts he was able to inspire devotion, so he could draw out what was good in those who came under his influence. The cooler and more practical John looked at both sides, at the traditions, good and evil, which came to them from their forefathers, and he considered carefully how these chiefs would act when not under his immediate influence. Above all, he looked to the prosperity and happiness of the millions of peasants out of sight, who toiled laboriously to get a living from the land.

The second Sikh war, which broke out in 1848, can only be treated here so far as it affected the fortunes of the Lawrences. Lord Gough's strategical blunders, redeemed by splendid courage, give it great military interest; but it was the new Viceroy, Lord Dalhousie, who decided the fate of the Punjab. He was a very able, hard-working Scotch nobleman, who devoted himself to his work in India for eight years with such self-sacrifice that he returned home in 1856 already doomed to an early death. But he was masterful and self-confident to a degree; and against his imperious will the impulsive forces of Charles Napier and Henry Lawrence broke like waves on a granite coast. He was not blind to their exceptional gifts, but to him the wide knowledge, coolness, and judgement of John Lawrence made a greater appeal; and when, after the victory of Chiliānwāla and the submission of the Sikh army in 1849, he annexed the Punjab, he decided to rule it by a Board and not by a single governor, and to direct the diverse talents of the brothers to a common end. He could not dispense with Henry's influence among the Sikh chieftains, and John's knowledge of civil government was of equal value.

Each would to a certain extent have his department, but a vast number of questions would have to be decided jointly by the Board, of which the third member, from 1850, was their old schoolfellow and friend Robert Montgomery. The friction which resulted was often intolerable. Without the least personal animosity, the brothers were forced into frequent conflicts of opinion; each was convinced of the justice of his attitude and most unwilling to sacrifice the interests of those in whom he was especially interested. After three years of the strain, Lord Dalhousie decided that it was time to put the country under a single ruler. For the honour of being first Chief Commissioner of the Punjab he chose the younger brother; and Sir Henry was given the post of Agent in Rājputāna, from which he was promoted in 1857 to be the first Governor of Oudh.

It was a tragic parting. The ablest men in the Punjab, like John Nicholson and Herbert Edwardes, regarded Sir Henry as a father, and many felt that it would be impossible to continue their work without him. No Englishman in India made such an impression by personal influence on both Europeans and Asiatics. As a well-known English statesman said: 'His character was far above his career, distinguished as that career was.' But there is little doubt, now, that for the development of the new province Lord Dalhousie made the right choice. And there is no higher proof of the magnanimity of John Lawrence than the way in which he won the respect, and retained the services, of the most ardent supporters of his brother. His dealings with Nicholson alone would fill a chapter; few lessons are more instructive than the way in which he controlled the waywardness of this heroic but self-willed officer, while giving full scope to his singular abilities.

The tale of John Lawrence's government of the Punjab is in some measure a repetition of his work at Pānīpat and Delhi. It had the same variety, it was carried out with the same thoroughness; but on this vast field it was impossible for him to see everything for himself. While directing the policy, he had to work largely through others and to leave many important decisions to his subordinates. The quality of the Punjab officials—of men who owed their inspiration to Henry Lawrence, or to John, or to both of them—was proved in many fields of government during the next thirty years. Soldiers on the frontier passes, judges and revenue officers on the plains, all worked with a will and contributed of their best. The Punjab is from many points of view the most interesting province in India. Its motley population, chiefly Musalmāns, but including Sikhs and other Hindus; its extremes of heat and cold, of rich alluvial soil and barren deserts; its vast water-supplies, largely running to waste; its great frontier ramparts with the historic passes—each of these gave rise to its own special problems. It is impossible to deal with so complex a subject here; all that we can do is to indicate a few sides of the work by which John Lawrence had so developed the provinces within the short period of eight years that it was able to bear the strain of the Mutiny, and to prove a source of strength and not of weakness. He put the right men in the right places and supported them with all his power. He broke up the old Sikh army, and reorganized the forces in such a way as to weaken tribal feeling and make it less easy for them to combine against us. He so administered justice that the natives came to know that an English official's word was as good as his bond. And, with the aid of Robert Napier and others, he so helped forward irrigation as to redeem the waste places and develop the latent wealth of the country. In all these years he had little recognition or reward. His chief, Lord Dalhousie, valued his work and induced the Government to make him K.C.B. in 1856; but to the general public at home he was still unknown.

In 1857 the crisis came. The greased cartridges were an immediate cause; there were others in the background. The sepoy regiments were too largely recruited from one race, the Poorbeas of the North-west Province, and they were too numerous in proportion to the Europeans; vanity, greed, superstition, fear, all influenced their minds. Fortunately, they produced no leader of ability; and, where the British officials were prompt and firm, the sparks of rebellion were swiftly stamped out; Montgomery at Lahore, Edwardes at Peshāwar, and many others, did their part nobly and disarmed whole regiments without bloodshed. But at Meerut and Cawnpore there was hesitation; rebellion raised its head, encouragement was given to a hundred local discontents, little rills flowed together from all directions, and finally two great streams of rebellion surged round Delhi and Lucknow. The latter, where Henry Lawrence met a hero's death in July, does not here concern us; but the reduction of Delhi was chiefly the work of John Lawrence, and its effect on the history of the Mutiny was profound.

He might well have been afraid for the Punjab, won by conquest from the most military race in India only eight years before, lying on the borders of our old enemy Afghānistān, garrisoned by 11,000 Europeans and about 50,000 native troops. It might seem a sufficient achievement to preserve his province to British rule, with rebellion raging all around and making inroads far within its borders. But as soon as he had secured the vital points in his own province (Multān, Peshāwar, Lahore), John Lawrence devoted himself to a single task, to recover Delhi, directing against it every man and gun, and all the stores that the Punjab could spare. Many of his subordinates, brave men though they were, were alarmed to see the Punjab so denuded and exposed to risks; but we now see the strength of character and determination of the man who swayed the fortunes of the north. He knew the importance of Delhi, of its geographical position and its imperial traditions; and he felt sure that no more vital blow could be struck at the Mutiny than to win back the city. The effort might seem hopeless; the military commanders might hesitate; the small force encamped on the historic ridge to the west of the town might seem to be besieged rather than besiegers. But continuous waves of energy from the Punjab reinforced them. One day it was 'the Guides', marching 580 miles in twenty-two days, or some other European regiment hastening from some hotbed of fanaticism where it could ill be spared;

another day it was a train of siege artillery, skilfully piloted across rivers and past ambushes; lastly, it was the famous moving column led by John Nicholson in person which restored the fortunes of the day. Through June, July, August, and half of September, the operations dragged wearily on; but thanks to the exertions of Baird Smith and Alexander Taylor, the chief engineers, an assault was at last judged to be feasible. After days of street fighting, the British secured control of the whole city on September 20th, and Nicholson, who was fatally wounded in the assault, lived long enough to hear the tale of victory. Without aid from England this great triumph had been won by the resources of the Punjab; and great was the moral effect of the news, as it spread through the bazaars.

This success did not exhaust Lawrence's energy. For months after, he continued to help Sir Colin Campbell in his operations against Lucknow, and to correspond with the Viceroy, Lord Canning, and others about the needs of the time. More perhaps than any one else, he laboured to check savage reprisals and needless brutality, and thereby incurred much odium with the more reckless and ignorant officers, who, coming out after the most critical hour, talked loudly about punishment and revenge. He was as cool in victory as he had been firm in the hour of disaster, and never ceased to look ahead to rebuilding the shaken edifice on sounder foundations when the danger should be past. It was only in the autumn of 1858, when the ship of State was again in smooth water, that he began to think of a holiday for himself. He had worked continuously for sixteen years; his health was not so strong as of old, and he could not safely continue at his post. He received a Baronetcy and the Grand Cross of the Bath from the Crown, while the Company recognized his great services by conferring on him a pension of £2,000 a year.

From these heroic scenes it is difficult to pass to the humdrum life in England, the receptions at Windsor, the parties in London, and the discussions on the Indian Council. He himself (though not indifferent to honourable recognition of his work) found far more pleasure in the quiet days passed in the home circle, the games of croquet on his lawn, and the occasional travels in Scotland and Ireland. Four years of repose were none too long, for other demands were soon to be made upon him. When Lord Elgin died suddenly in 1863, John Lawrence received the offer of the highest post under the Crown, and, before the end of the year, he was sailing for Calcutta as Governor-General of India.

In some ways he was able to fill the place without great effort. He had never been a respecter of persons; he had been quite indifferent whether his decisions were approved by those about him, and had always learnt to walk alone with a single eye to the public good. Also, he had such vast store of knowledge of the land and its inhabitants as no Viceroy before him for many decades. But the ceremonial fatigued him; and the tradition of working 'in Council', as the Viceroy must, was embarrassing to one who could always form a decision alone and had learnt to trust his own judgement.

Many of Lawrence's best friends and most trusted colleagues had left India, and he had, seated at his Council board, others who did not share his views, and who opposed the measures that he advocated. Especially was this true of the distinguished soldier Sir Hugh Rose; and Lawrence had to endure the same strain as in 1850, in the days of the Punjab board. But he was able to do great service to the country in many ways, and especially to the agricultural classes by pushing forward large schemes of irrigation. Finance was one of his strong points, and any expenditure which would be reproductive was sure of his support owing to his care for the peasants and his love of a sound budget. The period of his Viceroyalty was what is generally called uneventful—that is, it was chiefly given up to such schemes as promoted peace and prosperity, and did not witness any extension of our dominions. Even when Robert Napier's[19] expedition went to Abyssinia, few people in England realized that it was organized in India and paid for by India; and the credit for its success was given elsewhere.

But it is necessary to refer to one great subject of controversy, which was prominent all through Lawrence's career and with which his name is associated. This is the 'Frontier Policy' and the treatment of Afghānistān, on which two distinct schools of thought emerged. One school, ever jealous of the Russian advance, maintained that our Indian Government should establish agencies in Afghānistān with or without the consent of the Amīr; that it should interfere, if need be, to secure the throne for a prince who was attached to us; that British troops should be stationed beyond the Indus, where they could make their influence felt beyond our borders. The other maintained that our best policy was to keep within our natural boundaries, and in this respect the Indus with its fringe of desert was second only to the high mountain chains; that we should recognize the wild love of independence which the Afghāns felt, that we should undertake no obligations towards the Amīr except to observe the boundaries between him and us. If the Russians threatened our territories through Afghānistān, the natives would help us from hatred of the invaders; but if we began to establish agents and troops in their towns, we should ourselves become to them the hated enemy.

One school said that the Afghāns respected strength and would support us, if we seemed capable of a vigorous policy. The other replied that they resented foreign intrusion and would oppose Great Britain or Russia, if either attempted it. One said that we ought to have a resident in Kābul and Kandahār, the other said that it was a pity that we had ever occupied

Peshāwar, in its exposed valley at the foot of the Khyber Pass, and that Attock, where the Indus was bridged, was the ideal frontier post.

No one doubted that Lawrence would be found on the side of the less showy and less costly policy; and he kept unswervingly true to his ideal. The verdict of history must not be claimed too confidently in a land which has seen so many races come and go. At least it may be said that the men who advocated advance were unable to make it good. Few chapters in our history are more tragic than the Afghān Wars of 1838-42 and 1878-80, though the last was redeemed by General Roberts's great achievements. Our present policy is in accord with this verdict. There is to-day no British agency at Kābul or Kandahār; and the loyalty of the Amīrs, during some forty years of faithful adherence on our part to this policy, have been sufficiently firm to justify Lawrence's opposition to the Forward Policy. To-day it seems easy to vindicate his wisdom; but in 1878, when the Conservative Government kindled the war fever and allowed Lord Lytton to initiate a new adventure, it was not easy to stem the tide, and Lawrence came in for much abuse and unpopularity in maintaining the other view.

But long before this happened he had returned to England. His term of office was over early in 1869, and his work in India was finished. His last years at home were quiet, but not inactive. In 1870 he was invited to become the first chairman of the new School Board for London, and he held this office three years. Board work was always uncongenial to him, and the subject was, of course, unfamiliar; but he gave his best efforts to the cause and did other voluntary work in London. This came to an end in 1876, when his eyesight failed, and for nearly two years he had much suffering and was in danger of total blindness for a time. A second operation saved him from this, and in 1878 he put forth his strength in writing and speaking vigorously, but without success, against Lord Lytton's Afghān War. In June, 1879, he was stricken with sudden illness, and died a week later in his seventieth year. It was hardly to be expected that one who had spent himself so freely, amid such stirring events, should live beyond the Psalmist's span of life.

He had started at the bottom of the official ladder; by his own efforts he had won his way to the top; and his career will always be a notable example to those young Englishmen who cross the sea to serve the Empire in our great Dependency with its 300 million inhabitants. How the relations between India and Great Britain will develop—how long the connexion will last may be debated by politicians and authors; it is in careers like that of John Lawrence (and there were many such in the nineteenth century) that the noblest fruit of the connexion may be seen.

JOHN BRIGHT

1811-89

1811.	Born at Greenbank, Rochdale, November 16.
1827.	Leaves school. Enters his father's mill.
1839.	Marries Elizabeth Priestman (died 1841).
1841.	Joins Cobden in constitutional agitation for Repeal of Corn Laws.
1843.	Enters Parliament as Member for Durham.
1846.	Corn Laws repealed.
1847.	Marries Margaret Leatham (died 1878).
1847.	Member for Manchester.
1854-5.	Opposes Crimean War.
1856-7.	Long illness.
1857.	Unseated for Manchester. Member for Birmingham.
1861.	Supports the North in American Civil War.
1868.	President of Board of Trade in Gladstone's first Government.
1870.	Second long illness.
1880.	Chancellor of Duchy of Lancaster in Gladstone's second Government.
1882.	Resigns office over bombardment of Alexandria.
1886.	Opposes Gladstone's first Home Rule Bill.
1889.	Dies at Rochdale, March 29.

JOHN BRIGHT

TRIBUNE

The word 'tribune' comes to us from the early days of the Roman Republic; and even in Rome the tribunate was unlike all other magistracies. The holder had no outward signs of office, no satellites to execute his commands, no definite department to administer like the consul or the praetor. It was his first function to protest on behalf of the poorer citizens against the violent exercise of authority, and, on certain occasions, to thwart the action of other magistrates. He was to be the champion of the weak and helpless against the privileged orders; and his power depended on his courage, his eloquence, and the prestige of his office. England has no office of the sort in her constitutional armoury; but the word 'tribune' expresses, better than any other title, the position occupied in our political life by many of the men who have been the conspicuous champions of liberty, and few would contest the claim of John Bright to a foremost place among them. He, too, stood forth to vindicate the rights of the *plebs*; he, too, resisted the will of governments; and in no common measure did he give evidence, through forty years of public life, of the possession of the highest eloquence and the highest courage.

JOHN BRIGHT
From the painting by W. W. Ouless in the National Portrait Gallery

His early life gave little promise of a great career. He was born in 1811, the son of Jacob Bright, of Rochdale, who had risen by his own efforts to the ownership of a small cotton-mill in Lancashire, a man of simple benevolence and genuine piety, and a member of the Society of Friends—a society more familiar to us under the name of Quakers, though this name is not employed by them in speaking of themselves.

The boy left home early, and between the ages of eight and fifteen he was successively a pupil at five Quaker schools in the north of England. Here he enjoyed little comfort, and none of the aristocratic seclusion in which most statesmen have been reared at Eton and Harrow. He rubbed shoulders with boys of various degrees of rank and wealth, and learnt to be simple, true, and serious-minded; but he was in no way remarkable at this age. We hear little of his recreations, and still less of his reading; the school which pleased him most and did him most good was the one which he attended last, lying among the moors on the borders of Lancashire and Yorkshire. In the river Hodder he learnt to swim; still more he learnt to fish, and it was fishing which remained his favourite outdoor pastime throughout his life.

When school-days were over—at the age of fifteen—there was no question of the University: a rigorous life awaited him and he began at once to work in his father's business. The mill stood close beside his father's house at Greenbank near Rochdale, some ten miles northward from Manchester, and had been built in 1809 by Jacob Bright, out of a capital lent to him by two members of the Society of Friends. Here he received bales of new cotton by canal or from carriers, span it in his mill, and gave out the warp and weft thus manufactured to handloom weavers, whom he paid by the piece to weave it in the weaving chamber at the top of their own houses. He then sold the fully manufactured article in Manchester or elsewhere. In such surroundings, many a clever boy has developed into a hard-headed prosperous business man; material interests have cased in his soul, and he has been content to limit his thoughts to buying and selling, to the affairs of his factory and his town, and he has heard no call to other fields of work. But John Bright's education in books and in life was only just beginning, and though it may be regrettable that he missed the leisured freedom of university life, we must own that he really made good the loss by his own effort (and that without neglecting the work of the mill), and thereby did much to strengthen the independence of his character.

In the mill he was the earliest riser, and often spent hours before breakfast at his books. History and poetry were his favourite reading, and periodicals dealing with social and political questions; his taste was severe and had the happiest effect in chastening his oratorical style. To him, as to the earnest Puritans of the seventeenth century, the Bible and Milton were a peculiar joy; no other stories were so moving, no other music so thrilling to the ear. In his family there was no want of good talk. His mother, who died in 1830, was a woman of great gifts, who helped largely in developing the minds of her children. After her death John continued to live with his sisters, who were clever and original in mind, becoming the leader in the home circle, where views were freely exchanged on the questions of the day.

The Society of Friends was adverse to political discussion, as interfering with the religious life. But the Brights could not be kept from such a field of interest; and during these years theirs, like many other quiet homes, was stirred by the excitement roused by the fortunes of the Reform Bill.

The mill, too, did much to educate him. In the Rochdale factory there was no marked separation as at Manchester between rich and poor. Master and men lived side by side, knew one another's family history and fortunes, and fraternized over their joys and sorrows. Even in those days of backward education 'Old Jacob' made himself responsible for the schooling of his workmen's children; his son, too, made personal friends among those working under him and kept them throughout his life. Outside the mill Rochdale offered opportunities which he readily took. In 1833 he became one of the founders and first president of a debating society, and he began early to address Bible meetings and to lecture on temperance in his native town, moved by no conscious idea of learning to speak in public, but by the simple desire to be useful in good work. In such holidays as he took he was eager to travel abroad and to learn more of the outside world, and before he started at the age of twenty-four on his longest travels (a nine months' journey to Palestine and the eastern Mediterranean) he had, by individual effort, fitted himself to hold his own with the best students of the universities in width of outlook and capacity for mastering a subject. Like them, he had his limitations and his prejudices; but however we may admire wide toleration in itself, depth and intensity of feeling are often of more value to a man in enabling him to influence his fellows.

The year of Queen Victoria's accession may be counted a landmark in the life of this great Victorian. Then for the first time he met Richard Cobden, who was destined to extend his labours and to share his glory; and in the following year he began to co-operate actively in the Free Trade cause, attending meetings in the Rochdale district and gradually developing his power of speaking. It was about this time that he came to know his first wife, Elizabeth Priestman, of the Society of Friends, in Newcastle-on-Tyne, a woman of refined nature and rare gifts, whom he was to marry in 1839 and to lose in 1841. Then it was that he built the house 'One Ash', facing the same common as the house in which he was born. Here he lived many years, and here he died in the fullness of time, a Lancashire man, content to dwell among his own people, in his native town, and to forgo the grandeur of a country house. It was from here that he was called in the decisive hour of his life to take part in a national work with which his name will ever be associated. At the moment when Bright was prostrated with grief at his wife's death Cobden appeared on the scene and made his historic appeal. He urged his friend to put aside his private grief, to remember the miseries of so many other homes, miseries due directly to the Corn Laws, to put his shoulder to the wheel, and never to rest till they were repealed.

Cobden had been less happy than Bright in his schooling. His father's misfortune led to his spending five years at a Yorkshire school of the worst type, and seven more as clerk in the warehouse of an unsympathetic uncle. Like Bright, he had early to take the lead in his own family; also, like Bright, he had to educate himself; but he had a far harder struggle, and the enterprise which he showed in commerce in early manhood would have left him the possessor of a vast fortune, had he not preferred to devote his energies to public causes. The two men were by nature well suited to complement one another. If Cobden was the more ingenious in explaining an argument, Bright was more forcible in asserting a principle. If Cobden could, above all other men, convince the intellects of his hearers, Bright could, as few other speakers, kindle their spirits for a fray. His figure on a platform was striking. His manly expressive face, with broad brow, straight nose, and square chin, was essentially English in type. Though in the course of his political career he discarded the distinctive Quaker dress, he never discarded the Quaker simplicity. His costume was plain, his style of speaking severe, his bearing dignified and restrained. Only when his indignation was kindled at injustice was he swept far away from the calmness of Quaker tradition.

The Corn Laws were a sequel to the Napoleonic wars and to the insecurity of foreign trade which these caused. While war lasted it had inflated prices, and brought to English growers of corn a period of extraordinary prosperity. When peace came, to escape from a sudden fall in prices, the landed proprietors, who formed a majority of the House of Commons, had fixed by Act of Parliament the conditions under which corn might be imported from abroad. This measure was to perpetuate by law, in time of peace, the artificial conditions from which the people had unavoidably suffered by the accident of war. The legislators paid no heed to the growth of population, which was enormous, or to the distress of the working classes, who needed time to adjust themselves to the rapid changes in industry. Even the middle classes suffered, and the poor could only meet such trouble by 'clemming' or self-starvation. A noble duke, speaking in all good faith, advised them to 'try a pinch of curry powder in hot water', as making the pangs of hunger less intolerable. He met with little thanks for his advice from the sufferers, who demanded a radical cure. Parliament as a whole showed few signs of wishing to probe the question more deeply, and shut its eyes to the evidence of distress, whether shown in peaceful petitions or in disorderly riots. Many of the members were personally humane men and good landlords; but there were no powerful newspapers to enlighten them, and they knew little of the state of the manufacturing districts.

The cause had now found its appropriate champions. We in this day are familiar with appeals to the great mass of the people: we know the story of Midlothian campaigns and Belfast reviews; we hear the distant thunder from Liverpool, Manchester, or Birmingham, when the great men of Parliament go down from London to thrill vast audiences in the provincial towns. But the agitation of the Anti-Corn-Law League was a new thing. It was initiated by men unknown outside the Manchester district; few of the thousands to whom it was directed possessed the vote; and yet it wrought one of the greatest changes of the nineteenth century, a change of which the influence is perhaps not yet spent. In this campaign, Cobden and Bright were, without doubt, the leading spirits.

The movement filled five years of Bright's life. His hopes and fears might alternate—at one moment he was stirred to exultation over success, at another to regrets at the break-up of his home life, at another to bitter complaints and hatred of the landed interest—but his exertions never relaxed. As he was so often absent, the business at Rochdale had to be entrusted to his brother. Whenever he could be there, Bright was at his home with his little motherless daughter; but his efforts on the platform were more and more appreciated each year, and the campaign made heavy demands upon him.

At the opening of the Free Trade Hall in Manchester, on the site of the 'Peterloo' riots, he won a signal triumph. The vast audience was enthusiastic: several of them also were discriminating in their praise. One lady said that the chief charm of Mr. Bright was in the simplicity of his manner, the total absence of anything like showing off; another that she should never attend another meeting if he were announced to speak, as she could not bear the excitement. Simplicity and profound emotion were the secrets of his influence. The London Opera House saw similar scenes once a month, from 1843 till the end of the struggle. Villages and towns, and all classes of society, were instructed in the principles of the League and induced to help forward the cause. Not only did the wealthy factory owner, conscious as he was of the loss which the high price of food inflicted on the manufacturing interest, contribute his thousands; the factory hand too contributed his mite to further the welfare of his class. Even farmers were led to take a new view of the needs of agriculture, and the country labourer was made to see that his advantage lay in the success of the League. It was a farm-hand who put the matter in a nutshell at one of the meetings: 'I be protected,' he said, 'and I be starving.'

In 1843 Bright joined his leader in Parliament as member for Durham city, though his Quaker relatives disapproved of the idea that one of their society should so far enter the world and take part in its conflicts. In the House of Commons he met with scant popularity but with general respect. He was no mob orator of the conventional type. The simplicity and good taste of his speeches satisfied the best judges. He expressed sentiments hateful to his hearers in such a way that they might dislike the speech, but could not despise the speaker. Even when he boldly attacked the Game Laws in an assembly of landowners, the House listened to him respectfully, and the spokesman of the Government thanked him for the tone and temper of his speech, admitting that he had made out a strong case. But it was in the country and on the platform that the chief efforts of Cobden and Bright were made, and their chief successes won.

In 1845 they had an unexpected but most influential ally. Nature herself took a hand in the game. From 1842 to 1844 the bad effects of the Corn Laws were mitigated by good harvests and by the wise measures of Peel in freeing trade from various restrictions. But in 1845 first the corn, and then the potato crop, failed calamitously. Peel's conscience had been uneasy for years: he had been studying economics, and his conclusions did not square with the orthodox Tory creed. So when the Whig leader, Lord John Russell, ventured to express himself openly for Free Trade in his famous Edinburgh letter of November 28, Peel at last saw some chance of converting his party. It has already been told in this book how at length he succeeded in his aims, how he broke up his party but saved the country, and how in the hour of mingled triumph and defeat he generously gave to Cobden the chief credit for success. Whigs and Tories might taunt one another with desertion of principles, or might claim that their respective leaders collaborated at the end; certainly the question would never have been put before the Cabinet or the House of Commons as a Government measure but for the untiring efforts of the two Tribunes. History can show few greater triumphs of Government by moral suasion and the art of speech. Throughout, violence had been eschewed, even though men were starving, and appeals had been made solely to the justice and expediency of their case. Nothing illustrates better the sincerity and disinterestedness of John Bright than his conduct in these last decisive months. The tide was flowing with him; the opposition was reduced to a shadow. He might have enjoyed the luxury of applause from Radicals, Whigs, and the more advanced Tories, and won easy victories over a hostile minority. But the cause was now in the safe hands of Peel, whose honesty they respected and whose generalship they trusted; so Cobden and Bright were content to stand aside and watch. Instead of carping at his tardy conversion, Bright wrote in generous praise of Peel's speech: 'I never listened', he said, 'to any human being speaking in public with so much delight.' His heart was in the cause and not in his own advancement. When he did rise to speak, it was to vindicate Peel's honour and his statesmanship.

A few months later this honourable alliance came to an abrupt end. Bright was forced, by the same incorruptible sense of right and by the absence of all respect of persons, to oppose Peel in the crisis of his fate. The Government brought in an Irish Coercion Bill, which was naturally opposed by the Whigs. The Protectionist Tories saw their chance of taking revenge on Peel for repealing the Corn Laws and made common cause with their enemies; and from very different motives, Bright went into the same lobby. His conscience forbade him to support any coercive measure. No Prime Minister could please him as much as Peel; but no surrender, no mere evasion of responsibilities was possible in the case of a measure of which he disapproved. So firm was the bed-rock of principle on which Bright's political conduct was based; and it was to this uncompromising sincerity above all that he owed the triumphs of his oratory.

His method as an orator is full of interest.[20] In his youth he had begun by writing out and learning his speeches in full; but, before he quitted Rochdale for a wider theatre, he had discarded this rather mechanical method, and trusted more freely to his growing powers. He still made careful preparation for his speeches. He tells us how he often composed them in bed, as Carlyle's 'rugged Brindley' wrestled in bed with the difficulties of his canal-schemes, the silence and the dim light favouring the birth of ideas. He prepared words as well as ideas; but he only committed to memory enough to be a guide to him in marking the order and development of his thoughts, and filled up the original outline according to the inspiration of the moment. A few sentences, where the balance of words was carefully studied; a few figures of speech, where his imagination had taken flight into the realm of poetry; a few notable illustrations from history or contemporary politics, with details of names and figures,—these would be found among the notes which he wrote on detached slips of paper and dropped successively into his hat as each milestone was attained. As compared with his illustrious rival Gladstone, he was very sparing of gesture, depending partly on facial expression, still more on the modulations of his voice, to give life to the words which he uttered. His reading had formed his diction, his constant speaking had taught him readiness, and his study of great questions at close quarters and his meditation on them supplied him with the facts and the conclusions which he wished to put forward; but the fire which kindled this material to white heat was the passion for great principles which glowed in his heart. He himself in 1868, in returning thanks for the gift of the Freedom of the City of Edinburgh, quoted with obvious sincerity a sentence from his favourite Milton: 'True eloquence I find to be none but the serious and hearty love of Truth.'

Bright's public life was in the main a tale of devotion to two great causes, the Repeal of the Corn Laws, consummated in 1846, and the extension of the Franchise, which was not realized till twenty years later. But he found time to examine other questions and to utter shrewd opinions on the government of India and of Ireland, and to influence English sentiment on the Crimean War and the War of Secession in the United States. In advance of his time, he wished to develop cotton-growing in India and so to prevent the great industry of his own district being dependent on America alone. He attacked the existing board of directors and preferred immediate control by the Crown; and, while wishing to preserve the Viceroy's supremacy over the whole, he spoke in favour of admitting Indians to a larger share in the government of the various provinces. Many of the best judges of to-day are now working towards the same end, but at the time he met with little support. It is interesting to find that both on India and on Ireland similar views were put forward by men so different as John Bright and Benjamin Disraeli. Mr. Trevelyan has preserved the memory of several episodes in which they were connected with one another and of attempts which Disraeli made to win Bright's support and co-operation. Bright could cultivate friendships with politicians of very different schools without being induced to deviate by a hair's breadth from the cause which his principles dictated, and he could treat his friends, at times, with refreshing frankness. When Disraeli warmly admired one of his greatest speeches and expressed the wish that he himself could emulate it, the outspoken Quaker replied: 'Well, you might have made it, if you had been honest.'

It was the young Disraeli who, as early as 1846, had attributed the Irish troubles to 'a starving population, an absentee aristocracy, and an alien church'. It was Bright who never hesitated, when opportunity arose, to work for the Disestablishment of the Church in Ireland and for the security of Irish tenants in their holdings. A succession of measures, carried by Liberals and Conservatives from Gladstone to George Wyndham, have made us familiar with the idea of land purchase in Ireland; but Bright had been there as early as 1849 and had learnt for himself. Though at the end of his life he was a stubborn opponent of Gladstone's Home Rule Bill, he had long ago won the gratitude of Ireland as no other Englishman of his day, and his name has been preserved there in affectionate remembrance.

In 1854, the year of the Crimean War, Bright reached the zenith of his oratorical power, and at the same time touched the nadir of his popularity. Public opinion was setting strongly against Russia. In stemming the tide of war the so-called 'Manchester school' had a difficult task, and was severely criticized. The idea of the 'balance of power' made little appeal to Bright; and as a Quaker he was reluctant to see England interfering in a quarrel which did not seem to concern her. The satirists indeed scoffed unfairly at the doctrine of 'Peace at any price'; for Bright was content to put aside the principle and to argue the case on pure political expediency. But his attacks on the wars of the last century were too often couched in an offensive tone with personal references to the peerages won in them, and he spoke at times too bitterly of the diplomatic profession and especially of our ambassador at Constantinople. Nothing shows so clearly the danger of the imperfect education which was forced on Bright by necessity, and which he had done so much to remedy, as his attitude to foreign and imperial politics. In his home he had too readily imbibed the crude notion that our Empire existed to provide careers for the needy cadets of aristocratic families, and that our foreign policy was inspired by self-seeking officials who cared little for moral principles or for the lives of their fellow countrymen. A few months spent with Lord Canning at Calcutta, or with the Lawrences at Lahore, frequent intercourse with men of the calibre of Lord Lyons or Lord Cromer, would have enlightened him on the subject and prevented him from uttering the unwarranted imputations which he did. Yet in his great parliamentary speeches of 1854 he rose high above all pettiness and made a deep impression on a hostile house. Damaging though his speech of December 22 was to the Government, no minister attempted to reply. Palmerston, Russell, and Gladstone, with all their power, were unequal to the task. Disraeli told Bright that a few more such speeches 'would break up the Government'; and Delane, the famous editor of *The Times*, wrote that 'Cobden and Bright would be our ministers but for their principle of peace at any price'.

But Bright was not thinking of office or of breaking up Governments: he was thinking of the practical end in view. His next great speech was on February 23, 1855, when a faint hope of peace appeared. It was most conciliatory in tone, and was a solemn appeal to Palmerston to use his influence in ending the war. This was known as 'the Angel of Death' speech, from a famous passage which occurs in it. At the end he was 'overloaded with compliments', but the minister, who was hampered by Russian intrigues with Napoleon, seemed deaf to all appeals, and Bright again returned to the attack. Till the last days of the war, he continued to raise his voice on behalf of peace; but his exertions had told on his strength, and for the greater part of two years he had to abandon public life and devote himself to recovering his health.

Six years later he was to prove that 'peace at any price' was no fair description of his attitude. The Southern States of America seceded on the question of State rights and the institution of slavery, and the Federal Government declared war on them as rebels. This time it was not a war for the balance of power, but one fought to vindicate a moral principle, and Bright was strongly in favour of fighting it to a finish. For different reasons most of our countrymen favoured the South, but he appealed for British sympathy for the other side, on the ground that no true Briton could abet slavery. He was the most prominent supporter of the North, for long the only prominent one, but he gradually made converts and did much to wipe away the reproach which attached to the name of Englishmen in America, when the North triumphed in the end. The war ended in 1865 with the surrender of General Lee at Appomattox, and Bright wrote in his journal, 'This great triumph of the Republic is the event of our age'.

But long before 1865 the question of Reform and of the extension of the franchise had been revived. Gladstone might speak in favour of the principle in 1864; Russell might introduce a Reform Bill in 1866; a year later Disraeli might 'dish the Whigs'; and Whig and Tory might wrangle over the question who were the friends of the 'working man', but Bright had made his position clear to his friends in 1846. He began a popular movement in 1849 and for the next fifteen years of his life it was the object dearest to his heart. He was not afraid to walk alone. When his old fellow worker, Cobden, refused his aid, on the ground that he was not convinced of the need for extending the franchise, Bright himself assumed the lead and bore the brunt of the battle. Till 1865 his main obstacle was Palmerston, who since he took the helm in the worst days of the Crimean War and conducted the ship of State into harbour, occupied an impregnable position. Palmerston was dear to 'the man in the street', shared his prejudices and understood his humours; and nothing could make him into a serious Democrat or reformer. Even after Palmerston's death, Bright's chief opponent was to be found in the Whig ranks, in Robert Lowe, who was a master of parliamentary eloquence and who managed, in 1866, to wreck Lord John Russell's Reform Bill in the House. But Bright had his revenge in the country. Such meetings as ensued in the great provincial towns had not been seen for twenty years: the middle class and the artisans were fused as in the great Repeal struggle of 1846. At Glasgow as many as 150,000 men paraded outside the town, and no hall could contain the thousands who wished to hear the great Tribune. He claimed that eighty-four per cent. of his countrymen were still excluded from the vote, and he bluntly asserted that the existing House of Commons did not represent 'the intelligence and the justice of the nation, but the prejudices, the privileges, and the selfishness, of a class'.

But however blind many of this class might still be to the signs of the times, they found an astute leader in Disraeli, who had few principles and could trim his sails to any wind. The Tory Reform Bill, which he put forward in February 1867, came out a very different Bill in July, after discussion in the Cabinet, which led to the resignation of three ministers, and after debates in the House of Commons, where it was roughly handled. The principle of household suffrage was conceded, and another million voters were added to the electorate. Disraeli had made a greater change of front than any which he could attribute to Peel, and that without conviction, for reasons of party expediency. The real triumph belonged to Bright. 'The Bill adopted', he writes, 'is the precise franchise I recommended in 1858.' He had not only roused the country by his platform speeches, he had carefully watched the Bill in all its stages through the House, and gradually transformed it till it satisfied the aspirations of the people. He had been content to work with Disraeli so long as he could further the cause of Reform; and he only quarrelled with that statesman finally when, in 1878, he revived the anti-Russian policy of Palmerston.

During this strenuous time his domestic life was happy and tranquil. After the death of his first wife he had remained a widower for six years, and in 1847 he had married Margaret Leatham, who bore him seven children and shared his joys and sorrows in no ordinary measure for thirty years. Whenever politics took him away from his Rochdale home, he wrote constantly to her, and his letters throw most valuable light on his inmost feelings. She died in 1878, and after this his life was pitched in a different key. The outer world might suppose that high political office was crowning his career, but his enthusiasm and his power were ebbing and his physical health failed him more than once. He was as affectionate to his children, as friendly to his neighbours, as true to his principles; but the old fire was gone.

The outward events of his life from 1867 to 1889 must be passed over lightly. Against his own wishes he was persuaded by Gladstone to join the Cabinet in 1868 and again in 1880. His name was a tower of strength to the Government with the newly-enfranchised electors, but he himself had little taste for the routine of office. At Birmingham, for which he had sat since 1857, he compared himself to the Shunammite woman who refused the offer of advancement at court, and replied to the prophet, 'I dwell among mine own people'. But events were too strong for him: he was drawn first to Westminster to share in the government of the country, and then to Osborne to visit the Queen. Both the Queen and he were nervous at the prospect, but the interview passed off happily.[21] Family affections and sorrows were a bond between them, and he talked to her with his usual frankness and simplicity. Even the difficult question of costume was settled by a compromise, and the usual gold-braided livery was replaced by a sober suit of black. Ministerial work in London might have proved irksome to him; but his colleagues in the Cabinet were indulgent, and no excessive demands were made upon his strength. It was recognized that Bright was no longer in the fighting line. In 1870 he was incapacitated by a second long illness, and he had little share in the measures carried through Parliament for Irish land purchase and national education.

His official career was finally closed in 1882, when the bombardment of Alexandria seemed to open a new and aggressive chapter in our Eastern policy. Bright was true to his old principles and resigned office.

He severed himself still more from the official Liberals in 1886, when he refused to follow Gladstone into the Home Rule camp. He disliked the methods of Parnell, the obstruction in Parliament, and the campaign of lawlessness in Ireland. His own victories had not been won so, and he had a great respect for the traditions of the House. He also believed that the Home Rule Bill would vitally weaken the unity of the realm. But no personal bitterness entered into his relations with his old colleagues: he did not attack Gladstone, as he had attacked Palmerston in 1855. From his death-bed he sent a cordial message to his old chief, and received an answer full of high courtesy and affection.

His illness lasted several months. From the autumn of 1888 he lay at One Ash, weak but not suffering acutely; and on March 27, 1889, he quietly passed away. His old friend Cobden had preceded him more than twenty years, having died in 1865, and had been buried at his birthplace in Sussex, where he had made himself a peaceful home in later life. Bright proved himself equally faithful to the home of his earliest years. He was laid to rest in the small burying-ground in front of the Friends' meeting-house where he had worshipped as a child. In his long career he had served noble causes, and scaled the heights of fame, and the crowds at his funeral testified to the love which his neighbours bore him. He had never willingly been absent for long from his native town. His life, compared with that of Disraeli or Gladstone, seems almost bleak in its simplicity, varied as it was by so few excursions into other fields. But two strong passions enriched it with warmth and glow, his family affections and his zeal for the common good. These filled his heart, and he was content that it should be so.

Type of the wise who soar but never roam,
True to the kindred points of Heaven and Home.

CHARLES DICKENS
From the painting by Daniel Maclise in the National Portrait Gallery

CHARLES DICKENS

1812-1870

1812.   Born at Landport, Portsmouth, February 7.

1816.   Parents move to Chatham; 1821, to London.

1822.   Father bankrupt and in prison. Charles in blacking warehouse.

1827.   Charles enters lawyer's office.

1831.   Reporters' Gallery in Parliament.

1836.   Marries Catherine Hogarth. Publishes *Sketches by Boz*.

1837.   *Pickwick Papers*. 1838. *Nicholas Nickleby*.

1842.   First American journey. 1843. *Martin Chuzzlewit*.

1844-5. Eleven months' residence in Italy, chiefly at Genoa.

1846.   Editor of *Daily News* for a few weeks.

1846-7. Six months at Lausanne; three months at Paris. *Dombey and Son*.

1849-50. *David Copperfield*.

1850.   Editor of weekly periodical, *Household Words*.

1851-2. Manager of theatrical performances. 1852. *Bleak House*.

1853.   Italian tour: Rome, Naples, and Venice.

1856.   Purchase of Gadshill House, near Rochester.

1858.   Beginning of public readings.

1859.   *Tale of Two Cities* appears in *All the Year Round*.

1860.   Gadshill becomes his home instead of London.

1867.   Second American journey. Public readings in America.

1869.   April, collapse at Chester. Readings stopped.

1870.   Dies at Gadshill, June 9.

CHARLES DICKENS
NOVELIST AND SOCIAL REFORMER

In these days when critics so often repeat the cry of 'art for art's sake' and denounce Ruskin for bringing moral canons into his judgements of pictures or buildings, it is dangerous to couple these two titles together, and to label Dickens as anything but a novelist pure and simple. And indeed, all would admit that the creator of Sam Weller and Sarah Gamp will live when the crusade against 'Bumbledom' and its abuses is forgotten and the need for such a crusade seems incredible. But when so many recent critics have done justice to his gifts as a creative artist, this aspect of his work runs no danger of being forgotten. Moreover, when we are considering Dickens as a Victorian worthy and as a representative man of his age, it is desirable to bring out those qualities which he shared with so many of his great contemporaries. Above all, we must remember that Dickens himself would be the last man to be ashamed of having written 'with a purpose', or to think that the fact should be concealed as a blemish in his art. There was nothing in which he felt more genuine pride than in the thought that his talents thus employed had brought public opinion to realize the need for many practical reforms in our social condition. If these old abuses have mostly passed away, we may be thankful indeed; but we cannot feel sure that in the future fresh abuses will not arise with which the example of Dickens may inspire others to wage war. His was a strenuous life; he never spared himself nor stinted his efforts in any cause for which he was fighting; and if he did not win complete victory in his lifetime, he created the spirit in which victory was to be won.

Charles Dickens was born in 1812, the second child of a large family, his father being at the time a Navy clerk employed at Portsmouth. Of his birthplace in Commercial Road Portsmouth is justifiably proud; but we must think of him rather as a Kentishman and a Londoner, since he never lived in Hampshire after his fourth year. The earliest years which left a distinct impress on his mind were those passed at Chatham, to which his father moved in 1816. This town and its neighbouring cathedral city of Rochester, with their narrow old streets, their riverside and dockyard, took firm hold of his memory and imagination. To-day no places speak more intimately of him to the readers of his books. Here he passed five years of happy childhood till his father's work took the family to London and his father's improvidence plunged them into misfortune.

For those who know Wilkins Micawber it is needless to describe the failings of Mr. Dickens; for others we may be content to say that he was kindhearted, sanguine and improvident, quite incapable of the steady industry needed to support a growing family. When his debts overwhelmed him and he was carried off to the Marshalsea prison, Charles was only ten years old, but already he took the lead in the house. On him fell the duty of pacifying creditors at the door, and of making visits to the pawn-broker to meet the daily needs of the household. His initiation into life was a hard one and it began cruelly soon. If he was active and enterprising beyond his years, with his nervous high-strung temperament he was capable of suffering acutely; and this capacity was now to be sorely tried. For a year or more of his life this proud sensitive child had to spend long hours in the cellars of a warehouse, with rough uneducated companions, occupied in pasting labels on pots of boot-blacking. This situation was all that the influence of his family could procure for him; and into this he was thrust at the age of ten with no ray of hope, no expectation of release. His shiftless parents seemed to acquiesce in this drudgery as an opening for their cleverest son; and instead of their helping and comforting him in his sorrow, it was he who gave his Sundays to visiting them in prison and to offering them such consolation as he could. The iron burnt deep into his soul. Long after, in fact till the day when the district was rebuilt and changed out of knowledge, he owned that he could not bear to revisit the scene; so painful were his recollections, so vivid his sense of degradation. Twenty-five years later he narrated the facts to his friend and biographer John Forster in a private conversation; and he only recurred to the subject once more when under the disguise of a novel he told the story of the childhood of David Copperfield. By shifting the horror from the realm of fact to that of fiction, perhaps he lifted the weight of it from the secret recesses of his heart.

When his father's debts were relieved, the child regained his freedom from servitude, but even then his schooling was desultory and ineffective. Well might the elder Dickens, in a burst of candour, say to a stranger who asked him about his son's education, 'Why indeed, sir, ha! ha! he may be said to have educated himself.'

At the age of fifteen Charles embarked again on his career as a wage-earner. At first he was taken into a lawyer's office, where he filled a position somewhat between that of office-boy and clerk, and two years later he was qualifying himself by the study of shorthand for the profession of a parliamentary reporter, which his father was then following. He entered 'the Gallery' in 1831, first representing the *True Sun* and later the well-known *Morning Chronicle*; and at intervals he enlarged his experiences by journeys into the provinces to report political meetings. Thus it was that he familiarized himself with the mail coaches, the wayside hostelries, and the rich variety of types that were to be found there; with London in most of its phases he was already at home. So, when in 1834 he made his first attempts at writing in periodical literature, although he was only twenty-two years old, he had a wealth of first-hand experiences quite outside the range of the man who is just finishing his leisurely passage through a public school and university: of schools and offices, of parliaments and prisons, of the street and of the high road, he had been a diligent and observant critic; for many years he had practised the maxim of Pope: 'The proper study of mankind is Man.'

Friends sprang up wherever he went. His open face, his sparkling eye, his humorous tongue, his ready sympathy, were a passport to the goodwill of those whom he met; few could resist the appeal. Many readers will be familiar with the early portrait by Maclise; but his friends tell us how little that did justice to the lively play of feature, 'the spirited air and carriage' which were indescribable. On the top of a mail coach, on a fresh morning, they must have won the favour of his fellow travellers more easily than Alfred Jingle won the hearts of the Pickwickians. And beneath the radiant cheerfulness of his manner, the quick flash of observation and of speech, there was in him an element of hard persistence and determination which would carry him far. If the years of poverty and neglect had failed to chill his hopes and break his spirit, there was no fear that he would tire in the pursuit of his ambition when fortune began to smile upon him. He had touched life on many sides. He had kept his warmth of sympathy, his buoyancy, his capacity for rising superior to ill-fortune; and the years of adversity had only deepened his feeling for all that were oppressed. He had much to learn about the craft of letters; but he already had the first essential of an author—he had something to say.

The year 1836 is a definite landmark in the life of Dickens. In this year he married; in this year he gave up the practice of parliamentary reporting, published the *Sketches by Boz*, and began the writing of *The Pickwick Papers*. This immortal work achieved wide popularity at once. Criticism cannot hope to do justice to the greatness of Sam Weller, to the humours of Dingley Dell and Eatanswill, to the adventures of the hero in back gardens or in prison, on coaches or in wheelbarrows. Every one must read them in the original for himself. In this book Dickens reached at once the height of his success in making his fellow countrymen laugh with him at their own foibles. If in the art of constructing a story, in the depiction of character, in deepening the interest by the alternation of happiness and misfortune, he was to go far beyond his initial triumph,—still with many Dickensians, who love him chiefly for his liveliness of observation and broad humour, Pickwick remains the prime favourite.

The effect of this success on the fortunes of the author was immediate and lasting. Henceforth he could live in a comfortable house and look forward to a family life in which his children should be free from all risk of repeating his own experience. He could afford himself the pleasures and the society which he needed, and he became the centre of a circle of friends who appreciated his talents and encouraged him in his career. His relations with his publishers, though not without incident, were generally of the most cordial kind. If Dickens had the self-confidence to estimate his own powers highly, and the shrewd instinct to know when he was getting less than his fair share in a bargain, yet in a difference of opinion he was capable of seeing the other side, and he was loyal in the observance of all agreements.

The five years which followed were so crowded with various activities that it is difficult to date the events exactly, especially when he was producing novels in monthly or weekly numbers. Generally he had more than one story on the stocks. Thus in 1837, before *Pickwick* was finished, *Oliver Twist* was begun, and it was not itself complete before the earlier numbers of *Nicholas Nickleby* were appearing. In the same way *The Old Curiosity Shop* and *Barnaby Rudge*, which may be dated 1840 and 1841, overlapped one another in the planning of the stories, if not in the execution of the weekly parts. There is no period of Dickens's life which enables us better to observe his intense mental activity, and at the same time the variety of his creations. Here we have the luxuriant humour of Mrs. Nickleby and the Crummles family side by side with the tragedy of Bill Sikes and the pathos of Little Nell. Here also we can see the gradual development of constructive power in the handling of the story. But for our purpose it is more significant to notice that we here find Dickens's pen enlisted in the service of the noblest cause for which he fought, the redemption from misery and slavery of the children of his native land. Lord Shaftesbury's life has told us what their sufferings were and how the machinery of Government was slowly forced to do its part; and Dickens would be the last to detract from the fame of that great philanthropist, whose efforts on many occasions he supported and praised. But there were wide circles which no philanthropist could reach, hearts which no arguments or statistics could rouse; men and women who attended no meetings and read no pamphlets but who eagerly devoured anything that was written by the author of *The Pickwick Papers*. To them Smike and Little Nell made a personal and irresistible appeal; they could not remain insensible to the cruelty of Dotheboys Hall and to the depravity of Fagin's school; and if these books did not themselves recruit active workers to improve the conditions of child life, at least society became permeated with a temper which was favourable to the efforts of the reformers.

As far back as the days of his childhood at Rochester Dickens had been indignant at what he had casually heard of the Yorkshire schools; and his year of drudgery in London had made him realize, in other cases beside his own, the degradation that followed from the neglect of children. On undertaking to handle this subject in *Nicholas Nickleby*, he journeyed to Yorkshire to gather evidence at first hand for his picture of Dotheboys Hall. And for many years afterwards he continued to correspond with active workers on the subject of Ragged Schools and on the means of uplifting children out of the conditions which were so fruitful a source of crime. He discovered for himself how easily miscreants like Fagin could find recruits in the slums of London, and how impossible it was to bring up aright boys who were bred in these neglected homes. Even where efforts had been begun, the machinery was quite inadequate, the teachers few, the schoolrooms cheerless and ill-equipped. Mr. Crotch[22] has preserved a letter of 1843 in which Dickens makes the practical offer of providing funds for a washing-place in one school where the children seemed to be suffering from inattention to the elementary needs. His heart warmed towards individual cases and he faced them in practical fashion; he was not one of those reformers who utter benevolent sentiments on the platform and go no further.

Critics have had much to say about Dickens's treatment of child characters in his novels; the words 'sentimental' and 'mawkish' have been hurled at scenes like the death of Paul Dombey and Little Nell and at the more lurid episodes in *Oliver Twist*. But Dickens was a pioneer in his treatment of children in fiction; and if he did smite resounding blows which jar upon critical ears, at least he opened a rich vein of literature where many have followed him. He wrote not for the critics but for the great popular audience whom he had created, comprising all ages and classes, and world-wide in extent. The best answer to such criticism is to be found in the poem which Bret Harte dedicated to his memory in 1870, which beautifully describes how the pathos of his child-heroine could move the hearts of rough working men far away in the Sierras of the West. Nor did this same character of Little Nell fail to win special praise from literary critics so fastidious as Landor and Francis Jeffrey.

In 1842 he embarked on his first voyage to America. Till then he had travelled little outside his native land, and this expedition was definitely intended to bear fruit. Before starting he made a bargain with his publishers to produce a book on his return. The *American Notes* thus published, dealing largely with institutions and with the notable 'sights' of the country, have not retained a prominent place among his works; with *Martin Chuzzlewit* and its picture of American manners it is different. This stands alone among his writings in having left a permanent heritage of ill-will. Reasons in abundance can be found for the bitterness caused. He portrayed the conceit, the self-interest, the disregard for the feelings of others which the less-educated American showed to foreigners in a visible and often offensive guise; and the portraits were so life-like that no arrow fails to hit the mark. The American people were young; they had made great strides in material prosperity, they had not been taught to submit to the lash by satirists like Swift or more kindly mentors like Addison. Their own Oliver Wendell Holmes had not yet begun to chastise them with gentle irony. So they were aghast at Dickens's audacity, and indignant at what seemed an outrage on their hospitality, and few stopped to ask what elements of truth were to be found in the offending book. No doubt it was one-sided and unfair; Dickens, like most tourists, had been confronted by the louder and more aggressive members of the community and had not time to judge the whole. In large measure he recanted in subsequent writings; and on his second visit the more generous Americans showed how little rancour they bore. But the portraits of Jefferson Brick and Elijah Pogram will live; with Pecksniff, 'Sairey' Gamp, and other immortals they bear the hall-mark of Dickens's creative genius.

To America he did not go again for twenty-five years; but, as he grew older, he seemed to feel increasing need for change and variety in his mode of life. In 1844 he went for nearly twelve months to Italy, making his head-quarters at Genoa; and in 1846 he repeated the experiment at Lausanne on the lake of Geneva. Later, between 1853 and 1856, he spent a large part of three summers in a villa near Boulogne. Though he desired the change for reasons connected with his work, and though in each case he formed friendly connexions with his neighbours, it cannot be said that his books show the influence of either country. His genius was British to the core and he remained an Englishman wherever he went. He complained when abroad that he missed the stimulus of London, where the lighted streets, through which he walked at night, caused his imagination to work with intensified force. But even in Genoa he proved capable of writing *The Chimes*, which is as markedly English in temper as anything which he wrote.

The same spirit of restlessness comes out in his ventures into other fields of activity at home. At one time he assumed the editorship of a London newspaper; but a few weeks showed that he was incapable of editorial drudgery and he resigned. His taste for acting played a larger part in his life; and in 1851 and other years he put an enormous amount of energy into organizing public theatrical performances with his friends in London. He always loved the theatre. Macready was one of his innermost circle, and he had other friends on the stage. Indeed there were moments in his life when it seemed that the genius of the novelist might be lost to the world, which would have found but a sorry equivalent in one more actor of talent on the stage, however brilliant that talent was. But the main current of his life went on in London with diligent application to the book or books in hand; or at Broadstairs, where Dickens made holiday in true English fashion with his children by the sea.

In the years following the American voyage the chief landmarks were the production of *Dombey and Son* (begun in 1846) and *David Copperfield* (begun in 1849). From many points of view they may be regarded as his masterpieces, where his art is best seen in depicting character and constructing a story, though the infectious gaiety of the earlier novels may at times be missed. Dickens's insight into human nature had ripened, and he had learnt to group his lesser figures and episodes more skilfully round the central plot. And *David Copperfield* has the peculiar interest which attaches to those works where we seem to read the story of the author's own life. Evidently we have memories here of his childhood, of his school-days and his apprenticeship to work, and of the first gleams of success which met him in life. It is generally assumed that the book throws light on his own family relations; but it would be rash to argue confidently about this, as the inventive impulse was so strong in him. At least we may say that it is the book most necessary for a student who wishes to understand Dickens himself and his outlook on the world.

Also *David Copperfield* may be regarded as the central point and the culmination of Dickens's career as a novelist. Before it, and again after it, he had a spell of about fifteen years' steady work at novel writing, and no one would question that the first spell was productive of the better work. *Bleak House*, *Hard Times*, *Little Dorrit*, *Our Mutual Friend* all show evidence of greater effort and are less happy in their effect. No man could live the life that Dickens had lived for fifteen years and not show some signs of exhaustion; the wonder is that his creative power continued at all. He was capable of brilliant successes yet. *The Tale of Two Cities* is among the most thrilling of his stories, while *Edwin Drood* and parts of *Great Expectations* show as fine imagination and character drawing as anything which he wrote before 1850; but there is no injustice in drawing a broad distinction between the two parts of his career.

His home during the most fertile period of his activity was in Devonshire Terrace, near Regent's Park, a house with a garden of considerable size. Here he was within reach of his best friends, who were drawn from all the liberal professions represented in London. First among them stands John Forster, lawyer, journalist, and author, his adviser and subsequently his biographer, the friend of Robert Browning, a man with a genius for friendship, unselfish, loyal, discreet and wise in counsel. Next came the artists Maclise and Clarkson Stanfield, the actor Macready, Talfourd, lawyer and poet, Douglas Jerrold and Mark Lemon, the two famous contributors to *Punch*, and some fellow novelists, of whom Harrison Ainsworth was conspicuous in the earlier group and Wilkie Collins in later years. Less frequent visitors were Carlyle, Thackeray, and Bulwer Lytton, but they too were proud to welcome Dickens among their friends. With some of these he would walk, ride, or dine, go to the theatre or travel in the provinces and in foreign countries. His biographer loves to recall the Dickens Dinners, organized to celebrate the issue of a new book, when songs and speeches were added to good cheer and when 'we all in the greatest good-humour glorified each other'. Dickens always retained the English taste for a good dinner and was frankly fond of applause, and there was no element of exclusive priggishness about the cordial admiration which these friends felt for one another and their peculiar enthusiasm for Dickens and his books. Around him the enthusiasm gathered, and few men have better deserved it.

When he was writing he needed quiet and worked with complete concentration; and when he had earned some leisure he loved to spend it in violent physical exercise. He would suddenly call on Forster to come out for a long ride on horseback to occupy the middle of the day; and his diligent friend, unable to resist the lure of such company, would throw his own work to the winds and come. Till near the end of his life Dickens clung to these habits, thinking nothing of a walk of from twenty to thirty miles; and there seems reason to believe that by constant over-exertion he sapped his strength and shortened his life. But lameness in one foot, the result of an illness early in 1865, handicapped him severely at times; and in the same year he sustained a rude shock in a railway accident where his nerves were upset by what he witnessed in helping the injured. He ought to have acquired the wisdom of the middle-aged man, and to have taken things more easily, but with him it was impossible to be doing nothing; physical and mental activity succeeded one another and often went together with a high state of nervous tension.

This love of excitement sometimes took forms which modern taste would call excessive and unwholesome. His attendance at the public execution of the Mannings in 1849, his going so often to the Morgue in Paris, his visit to America to 'the exact site where Professor Webster did that amazing murder', may seem legitimate for one who had to study crime among the other departments of life; but at times he revels in gruesome details in a way which jars on our feeling, and betrays too theatrical a love of sensation. However, no one could say that Dickens is generally morbid, in view of the sound and hearty appreciation which he had for all that is wholesome and genial in life.

In many ways the latter part of his life shows a less even tenor, a less steady development. Though he was so domestic in his tastes and devoted to his children, his relations with his wife became more and more difficult owing to incompatibility of temperament; and from 1858 they found it desirable to live apart. This no doubt added to his restlessness and the craving for excitement, which showed itself in the ardour with which he took up the idea of public readings. These readings are only less famous than his writings, so prodigious was their success. His great dramatic gifts, enlisted in the service of his own creations, made an irresistible appeal to the public, and till the day of his collapse, ten years later, their popularity showed no sign of waning. The amount of money which he earned thereby was amazing; the American tour alone gave him a net profit of £20,000; and he expected to make as much more in two seasons in England. But he paid dearly for these triumphs, being often in trouble with his voice, suffering from fits of sleeplessness, aggravating the pain in his foot, and affecting his heart. In spite, then, of the success of the readings, his faithful friends like Forster would gladly have seen him abandon a practice which could add little to his future fame, while it threatened to shorten his life. But, however arduous the task which he set himself, when the moment came Dickens could brace himself to meet the demands and satisfy the high expectations of his audience. His nerves seemed to harden, his voice to gain strength; his spirit flashed out undimmed, and he won triumph after triumph, in quiet cathedral cities, in great industrial towns, in the more fatiguing climate of America and before the huge audiences of Philadelphia and New York. He began his programme with a few chosen pieces from *Pickwick* and the Christmas Books, and with selected characters like Paul Dombey and Mrs. Gamp; he added Dotheboys Hall and the story of David Copperfield in brief; in his last series, against the advice of Forster, he worked up the more sensational passages from *Oliver Twist*. His object, he says, was 'to leave behind me the recollection of something very passionate and dramatic, done with simple means, if the act would justify the theme'. It was because the art of reading was unduly strained that Forster protested, and his judgement is confirmed by Dickens's boast (perhaps humorously exaggerated) that 'at Clifton we had a contagion of fainting, and yet the place was not hot—a dozen to twenty ladies taken out stiff and rigid at various times'. The physical effects of this fresh strain soon appeared. After a month his doctor ordered him to cease reading; and, though he resumed it after a few days' rest, in April 1869 he had a worse attack of giddiness and was obliged to abandon it permanently. The history of these readings illustrates the character of Dickens perhaps better than any other episode in his later life.

But the same restless energy is visible even in his life at Gadshill, which was his home from 1860 to 1870. The house lies on the London road a few miles west of Rochester, and can easily be seen to-day, almost unaltered, by the passer-by. It had caught his fancy in his childhood before the age of ten when he was walking with his father, and his father had promised that, if he would only work hard enough, he might one day live in it. The associations of the place with the Falstaff scenes in *Henry IV* had also endeared it to him; and so, when in 1855 he heard that it was for sale, he jumped at the opportunity. For some years after purchasing it he let it to tenants, but from 1860 he made it his permanent abode. It has no architectural features to charm the eye; with its many changes and additions made for comfort, its bow-windows and the plantations in the garden, it is a typical Victorian home. Here Dickens could live at ease, surrounded by his children, his dogs, his books, his souvenirs of his friends, and the Kentish scenery which he loved. To the north lay the flat marshlands of the lower Thames, to the south and west lay rolling hills crowned with woodlands, with hop gardens on the lower slopes; to the east lay the valley of the Medway with the quaint old streets of Rochester and the bustling dockyard of Chatham. All that makes the familiar beauty and richness of English landscape was here, above all the charm of associations. So many names preserved memories of his books. To Rochester the Pickwickians had driven on their first search for knowledge; to Cobham Mr.

Winkle had fled, and at the 'Leather Bottle' his friends had found him; in the marshlands Joe Gargery and Pip had watched for the escaped convict; in the old gateway by the cathedral Jasper had entertained Edwin Drood on the eve of his disappearance; along that very high-road over which Dickens's windows looked the child David Copperfield had tramped in his journey from London to Dover.

Meanwhile, though his creative vein may have been less fertile than of old, his efforts for the good of his fellow men were no less continuous and sincere. His first books had aimed at killing by ridicule certain social institutions which had sunk into abuses. The pictures of parliamentary elections, of schools, of workhouses, had not only created a hearty laugh, but they had disposed the public to listen to the reformers and to realize the need for reform. As he grew older he went deeper into the evil, and he also blended his reforming purpose better with his story. The characters of Mr. Dombey and the Chuzzlewits are not mere incidents in the tale, nor are they monstrosities which call forth immediate astonishment and horror. But in each case the ingrained selfishness which spreads misery through a family is the very mainspring of the story; and the dramatic power by which Dickens makes it reveal itself in action has something Shakespearian in it. Here there is still a balance between the different elements, the human interest and the moral lesson, and as works of art they are on a higher plane than *Hard Times*, where the purpose is too clearly shown. Still if we wish to understand this side of Dickens's work, it is just such a book as *Hard Times* that we must study.

It deals with the relation of classes to one another in an industrial district, and especially with the faults of the class that rose to power with the development of manufacturing. Mr. Gradgrind and Mr. Bounderby, the well-meaning pedant and the offensive parvenu, preach the same gospel. Political economy, as they understand it, is to rule life, and this dismal science is not concerned with human well-being and happiness, but only with the profit and loss on commercial undertakings. Hard facts then are to be the staple of education; memory and accurate calculation are to be cultivated; the imagination is to be driven out. In depicting the manner of this education Dickens rather overshoots the mark. The visit of Mr. Gradgrind to Mr. M'Choakumchild's school (when the sharp-witted Bitzer defines the horse according to the scientific handbook, while poor Cissy, who has only an affection for horses, indulges in fancies and collapses in disgrace) is too evident a caricature. But the effects of this kind of teaching are painted with a powerful hand, and we see the faculty for joy blighted almost in the cradle. And the lesson is enforced not only by the working man and his family but by Gradgrind's own daughter, who pitilessly convicts her father of having stifled every generous impulse in her and of having sacrificed her on the altar of fancied self-interest.

Side by side with the dismal Mr. Gradgrind is the poor master of the strolling circus, Mr. Sleary, with his truer philosophy of life. He can see the real need that men have for amusement and for brightness in their lives; and, though he lives under the shadow of bankruptcy, he can hold his head up and preach the gospel of happiness. This was a cause which never failed to win the enthusiastic advocacy of Dickens. He fought, as men still have to fight today, against those Pharisees who prescribe for the working classes how they should spend their weekly day of freedom; he supported the opening on Sunday of parks, museums, and galleries; whole-heartedly he loved the theatre and the circus, and he wished as many as possible to share those delights. In defiance of 'Mrs. Grundy' he ventured to maintain that the words 'music-hall' and 'public-house', rightly understood, should be held in honour. It is one thing to hate drunkenness and indecency; it is quite another to assume that these must be found in the poor man's place of recreation, and this roused him to anger. To him 'public-house' meant a place of fellowship, and 'music-hall' a place of song and mirth; and if some critics complain of an excess of material good-cheer in his picture of life, Dickens is certainly here in sympathy with the bulk of his fellow-countrymen.

Another cause in which Dickens was always ready to lead a crusade was the amendment of the Poor Law. This will remind us of the early days of Oliver Twist, of such a friendless outcast as Jo in *Bleak House*, of the struggle of Betty Higden in *Our Mutual Friend* and her determination never to be given up to 'the Parish'. But, even more than the famous novels, the casual writings of Dickens in his own magazines and elsewhere throw light on his activities in this cause and on the researches which he made into the working of the system. Mr. Crotch describes visits which he paid to the workhouses in Wapping and Whitechapel, quoting his comments on the 'Foul Ward' in one, on the old men's ward in the other, and on the torpor of despair which settled down on these poor wrecks of humanity. Could such a system, he asked himself, be wise which robbed men not of liberty alone but of all hope for the future, which left them no single point of interest except the statistics of their fellows who had gone before them and who had been finally liberated by death? A still more striking passage, just because Dickens here shows unusual restraint and moderation in his language, tells us of the five women whom he saw sleeping all night outside the workhouse through no fault of any official, but simply because there was no room for them inside and because society had nothing to offer, no form of 'relief' which could touch these unfortunates. Many will be familiar with passages in Ruskin, where he denounces similar tragedies due to our inhuman disregard of what is happening at our doors.

Though the most valuable part of his work was the effective appeal to the hearts of his brother men, Dickens had the practical wisdom to suggest definite remedies in some cases. He saw that the districts in the East End of London, even with a heavy poor rate, failed to supply adequate relief for their waifs and strays, while the wealthy inhabitants of the West End, having few paupers, paid on their riches a rate that was negligible, and he boldly suggested the equalization of rates. All London should jointly share the burden of maintaining those for whose welfare they were responsible and should pay shares proportioned to their wealth. This wise reform was not carried into effect till some thirty or forty years later; but the principle is now generally accepted. Though in this case, as in his famous attack on the Court of Chancery in *Bleak House*, Dickens failed in obtaining any immediate effect, it is unquestionable that he influenced the minds of thousands and changed the temper in which they looked at the problem of the poor. In this nothing that he wrote was more powerful than the series of Christmas Books, in which his imagination, with the power of a Rembrandt, threw on to a smaller canvas the lights and shades of London life, the grim background of mean streets, and the cheerful virtues which throw a glamour over their humble homes. His advocacy of these social causes came to be known far and wide and contributed a second element to the popularity won by his novels; long before his death Dickens stood on a pinnacle alone, loved by the vast reading public among those who toil in our towns and villages, and wherever English is read and understood. He was not only their entertainer, but their friend and brother; he had been through his days of sorrow and suffering and he had kept that vast fund of cheerfulness which overflowed into his books and gladdened the lives of so many thousands. When he died in 1870 after a year of intermittent illness, following on his breakdown over the public readings, there was naturally a widespread desire that he should be buried in Westminster Abbey, as a great Englishman and a true representative of his age. During life he had expressed his desire for a private funeral, unheralded in the press, and he had thought of two or three quiet churches in the neighbourhood of Rochester and Gadshill. These particular graveyards were found to be already closed, and the family consented to a compromise by which their father should be buried in the Abbey at an early hour when no strangers would be aware of it. After his body was laid to rest, the people were admitted to pay their homage; the universality and the sincerity of their feelings was shown in a wonderful way. Among men of letters he had reigned in the hearts of the people, as Queen Victoria reigned among our sovereigns. In the annals of her reign his name will outlive those of soldiers, of prelates, and of politicians.

The causes for which he fought have not all been won yet. Officialdom still dawdles over the work of the State, hearts are still broken by the law's delays, the path of crime still lies too easily open to the young. Vast progress has been made; a humane spirit is to be found in the working of our Government, and a truer knowledge of social problems is spreading among all classes. But the world cannot afford to relegate Charles Dickens to oblivion, and shows no desire to do so; his books are and will be a wellspring of cheerfulness, of faith in human nature, and of true Christian charity from which all will do well to drink.

ALFRED TENNYSON

1809-92

1809.	Born at Somersby, Lincolnshire, August 6.
1816-20.	At school at Louth.
1820-7.	Educated at home.
1827.	*Poems by Two Brothers*, Charles and Alfred.
1828-31.	Trinity College, Cambridge.
1830-2.	Early volumes of poetry published.
1833.	Death of Arthur Hallam at Vienna.
1837.	High Beech, Essex.
1840.	Tunbridge Wells.
1842.	Collected poems, including 'Morte d'Arthur' and 'English Idyls'.
1846.	Cheltenham.
1847.	*The Princess*.
1850.	*In Memoriam*, printed and given to friends before March; published June. Marriage, June. Poet Laureate, November.
1852.	'Ode on the Death of the Duke of Wellington.'
1853.	Becomes tenant—1856, owner—of Farringford, Isle of Wight.
1855.	*Maud*.
1859.	First four 'Idylls of the King' published.
1864.	*Enoch Arden*.
1869.	Second home at Aldworth, near Haslemere.
1875-84.	*Plays* (1875 'Queen Mary', 1876 'Harold', 1884 'Becket').
1880.	*Ballads and other Poems* ('The Revenge', &c.).

1884. Created a Peer of the realm.

1892. October 6, death at Aldworth. October 12, funeral at Westminster Abbey.

TENNYSON
Poet

The Victorians, as a whole, were a generation of fighters. They battled against Nature's forces, subduing floods and mountain barriers, pestilence and the worst extremes of heat and cold; they also went forth into the market-place and battled with their fellow men for laws, for tariffs, for empire. Their triumphs, like those of the Romans, are mostly to be seen in the practical sphere. But there were others of that day who chose the contemplative life of the recluse, and who yet, by high imaginings, contributed in no less degree to enrich the fame of their age; and among these the first name is that of Alfred Tennyson, the most representative of Victorian poets.

ALFRED, LORD TENNYSON
From the painting by G. F. Watts in the National Portrait Gallery

His early environment may be said to have marked him out for such a life. He was born in one of the remotest districts of a rural county. The village of Somersby lies in a hollow among the Lincolnshire wolds, twenty miles east of Lincoln, midway between the small towns of Spilsby, Horncastle, and

Louth. There are no railways to disturb its peace; no high roads or broad rivers to bring trade to its doors. The 'cold rivulet' that rises just above the village flows down some twenty miles to lose itself in the sea near Skegness; in the valley the alders sigh and the aspens quiver, while around are rolling hills covered by long fields of corn broken by occasional spinneys. It is not a country to draw tourists for its own sake; but Tennyson knew, as few other poets know, the charm that human association lends to the simplest English landscape, and he cherished the memory of these scenes long after he had gone to live among the richer beauties of the south. From the garners of memory he drew the familiar features of this homely land showing that he had forgotten

No grey old grange, or lonely fold,
Or low morass and whispering reed,
Or simple stile from mead to mead,
Or sheepwalk up the winding wold.[23]

There are days when the wolds seem dreary and monotonous; but if change is wanted, a long walk or an easy drive will take us from Somersby, as it often took the Tennyson brothers, to the coast at Mablethorpe, where the long rollers of the North Sea beat upon the sandhills that guard the flat stretches of the marshland. Here the poet as a child used to lie upon the beach, his imagination conjuring up Homeric pictures of the Grecian fleet besieging Troy; and if, on his last visit before leaving Lincolnshire, he found the spell broken, he could still describe vividly what he saw with the less fanciful vision of manhood.

Grey sandbanks, and pale sunsets, dreary wind,
Dim shores, dense rains, and heavy-clouded sea![24]

These wide expanses of sea, sand, and sky figure many times in his poetry and furnish a background for the more tragic scenes in the *Idylls of the King*.

Nor does the vicarage spoil the harmony of the scene, an old-fashioned low rambling house, to which a loftier hall adjoining, with its Gothic windows, lends a touch of distinction. The garden with one towering sycamore and the wych-elms, that threw long shadows on the lawn, opened on to the parson's field, where on summer mornings could be heard the sweep of the scythe in the dewy grass. Here Tennyson's father had been rector for some years when his fourth child Alfred was born in August 1809, the year which also saw the birth of Darwin and Gladstone. The family was a large one; there were eight sons and four daughters, the last of whom was still alive in 1916. Alfred's education was as irregular as a poet's could need to be, consisting of a few years' attendance at Louth Grammar School, where he suffered from the rod and other abuses of the past, and of a larger number spent in studying literature at home under his father's guidance. These left him a liberal amount of leisure which he devoted to reading at large and roaming the country-side. His father was a man of mental cultivation far beyond the average, well fitted to expand the mind of a boy of literary tastes and to lead him on at a pace suited to his abilities. He had suffered from disappointments which had thrown a shadow over his life, having been disinherited capriciously by his father, who was a wealthy man and a member of Parliament. The inheritance passed to the second brother, who took the name of Tennyson d'Eyncourt; and though the Rector resented the injustice of the act, he did not allow it to embitter the relations between his own children and their cousins. His character was of the stern, dominating order, and both his parishioners and his children stood in awe of him; but the gentle nature of their mother made amends. She is described by Edward FitzGerald, the poet's friend, as 'one of the most innocent and tender-hearted ladies I ever met, devoted to husband and children'. In her youth she had been a noted beauty, and in her old age was not too unworldly to remember that she had received twenty-five proposals of marriage. It was from her that the family derived their beauty of feature, while in their strength of intellect they resembled rather their father. One of Alfred's earliest literary passions was a love of Byron, and he remembered in after life how as a child he had carved on a rock the woful tidings that his hero was dead. In this period he was already writing poetry himself, though he did not publish his first volume till after he had gone up to Cambridge.

From this home life, filled with leisurely reading, rambling, and dreaming, he was sent in 1828 to join his brother Frederick at Trinity College, Cambridge, and he came into residence in February of that year. Cambridge has been called the poets' University. Here in early days came Spenser and Milton, Dryden and Gray; and—in the generation preceding Tennyson—Wordsworth, Coleridge, and Byron had followed in their steps. However little we can trace directly the development of the poetic gift to local influence, at least we can say that Tennyson gained greatly by the time he spent within its walls. He came up an unknown man without family connexions to help him, and without the hall-mark of any famous school upon him. Shy and retiring by nature as he was, he might easily have failed to win his way to notice. But there was something in his appearance, in his manner, and in the personality that lay behind, which never failed to impress observers, and gradually he attached to himself the most brilliant undergraduates of his time and became a leader among them. Thackeray and FitzGerald were in residence; but it was not till later that he came to know them well, and we hear more of Spedding (the editor of Bacon), of Alford and Merivale (deans of Canterbury and Ely), of Trench (Archbishop of Dublin), of Lushington, who married one of his sisters, and of Arthur

Hallam, who was engaged to another sister at the time of his early death. Hallam came from Eton, where his greatest friend had been W. E. Gladstone, and he had not been long at Cambridge before he was led by kindred tastes and kindred nature into close friendship with Tennyson. In the judgement of all who knew him, a career of the highest usefulness and distinction was assured to him. His intellectual force and his high aspirations would have shone in the public service; and at least they won him thus early the affection of the noblest among his compeers, and a fame that is almost unique in English literature.

Much has been written about the society which these young men formed and which they called 'the Apostles'. The name has been thought to suggest a certain complacency and mutual admiration. But enough letters and personal recollections of their talk have been preserved to show how simple and unaffected the members were in their intercourse with one another. They had their enthusiasms, but they had also their jests. Their humour was not perhaps the boisterous fun of William Morris and Rossetti, but it was lively and buoyant enough to banish all suspicion of priggishness. Just because their enthusiasm was for the best in literature and art, Tennyson was quickly at home among them. Already he had learnt at home to love Shakespeare and Milton, Coleridge and Keats, and no effort was required, in this circle of friends, to keep his reading upon this high level. *Lycidas* was always a special favourite of Tennyson's, and appreciation of it seemed to him a sure 'touchstone of poetic taste'. In conversation he did not tend to declaim or monopolize the talk. He was noted rather for short sayings and for criticisms tersely expressed. He had his moods, contemplative, genial or gay; but all his utterances were marked by independence of thought, and his silence could be richer than the speech of other men. But for display he had no liking. In fact, so reluctant was he to face an audience of strangers, that when in 1829 it was his duty to recite his prize poem in the senate-house, he obtained leave for Merivale to read it on his behalf. On the other hand, he was ready enough to impart to his real friends the poems that he wrote from time to time, and he would pass pleasant hours with them reciting old ballads and reading aloud the plays of Shakespeare. His sonorous voice, his imagination, and his feeling for all the niceties of rhythm made his reading unusually impressive, as we know from the testimony of many who heard him.

The course of his education is, in fact, more truly to be found in this free companionship than in the lecture room or the examination hall. His opinion of the teaching which he received from the Dons was formed and expressed in a sonnet of 1830, though he refrained from publishing it for half a century. He addresses them as 'you that do profess to teach and teach us nothing, feeding not the heart'—and complains of their indifference to the movements of their own age and to the needs of their pupils. For, despite the ferment which was spreading in the realms of theology, of politics, and of natural science, the Dons still taught their classics in the dry pedantic manner of the past, and refused to face the problems of the nineteenth century. For Tennyson, whose mind was already capacious and deep, these problems had a constant attraction, and he had to fall back upon solitary musings and on talks with Hallam and other friends. Partly perhaps because he missed the more rigorous training of the schools, we have to wait another ten years before we see marks of his deeper thinking in his work. He was but groping and feeling his way. In the 'Poems, chiefly Lyrical' which he produced in 1830, rich images abound, play of fancy and beauty of expression; but there are few signs of the power of thought which he was to show in later volumes.

After three years thus spent, by no means unfruitfully, though it was only by his prize poem of 'Timbuctoo' that he won public honours, he was called away from Cambridge by family troubles and returned to Somersby in February 1831. His father had broken down in health, and a month later he died, suddenly and peacefully, in his arm-chair. After the rector's death an arrangement was made that the family should continue to inhabit the Rectory; and Tennyson, who was now his mother's chief help and stay, settled down to a studious life at home, varied by occasional visits to London. The habit of seclusion was already forming. He was much given to solitary walking and to spending his evening in an attic reading by himself. But this was not due to moroseness or selfishness, as we can see from his intercourse with family and friends. He would willingly give hours to reading aloud to his mother, or sit listening happily while his sisters played music. From this time indeed he seems to have taken his father's place in the home; and with Hallam and other friends he continued on the same affectionate terms. He had not Dickens's buoyant temper and love of company, nor did he indulge in the splenetic outbursts of Carlyle. He could, when it was needed, find time to fulfil the humblest duties and then return with contentment to his solitude. But his thoughts seemed naturally to lift him above the level of others, and he was most truly himself when he was alone. Apart from his eyesight, which began to trouble him at this time, he was enjoying good health, which he maintained by a steady regime of physical exercise. His strength and his good looks were alike remarkable.[25] As his friend Brookfield laughingly said, 'It was not fair that he should be Hercules as well as Apollo'.

Another volume of verse appeared in 1832; and its appearance seems to have been due rather to the urgent persuasion of his friends than to his own eagerness to appear in print. Though J. S. Mill and a few other critics wrote with good judgement and praised the book, it met with a cold reception in most places, and the *Quarterly Review*, regardless of its blunder over Keats, spoke of it in most contemptuous terms. All can recognize to-day how unfair this was to the merits of a volume which contained the 'Lotos-Eaters', 'Oenone', and the 'Lady of Shalott'; but the effect of the harsh verdict on the poet, always sensitive about the reception of his work, was unfortunate to a degree. For a time it seemed likely to chill his ardour and stifle his poetic gifts at the very age when they ought to be bearing fruit. He writes of himself at this time as 'moping like an owl in an ivy bush, or as that one sparrow which the Hebrew mentioneth as sitting on the house-top'; and, despite his friendship with Hallam, which was closer than ever since the latter's engagement to his sister Emily, he had thoughts of settling abroad in France or Italy, since he found, or fancied that he found, in England too unsympathetic an atmosphere.

Such a decision would have been disastrous. Residence abroad might suit the robust, many-sided genius of Robert Browning with his gift for interpreting the thoughts of other nations and other times; it would have been fatal to Tennyson, whose affections were rooted in his native soil, and who had a special call to speak to Englishmen of English scenes and English life.

The following year brought him a still severer shock in the loss of his beloved friend, Arthur Hallam, who was taken ill at Vienna and died there a few days later, to the deep sorrow of all who knew him. Many besides Tennyson have borne witness to his character and gifts; thanks to their tribute, and above all to the verses of *In Memoriam*, though his life was all too short to realize the promise of his youth, his name will be preserved. The gradual growth of Tennyson's elegy can be discerned from the letters of his friends, to whom from time to time he read some of the stanzas which he had completed. Even in the first winter after Hallam's death, he wrote a few lines in the manuscript book which he kept by him for the purpose during the next fifteen years, and which he was within an ace of losing in 1850, just when the poem was completed and ready for publication. As a statesman turns from his private sorrow to devote himself to a public cause, so the poet's instinct was to find comfort in the practice of his art. Under the stress of feelings aroused by this event and under the influence of a wider reading, his mind was maturing. We hear of a steady discipline of mental work, of hours given methodically to Italian and German, to theology and history, to chemistry, botany, and other branches of science. Above all, he pondered now, as he did later so constantly, on the mystery of death and life after death. Outwardly this seems the most uneventful period of his career; but, in their effect on his mind and work, these years were very far from being wasted. When next, in 1842, he emerges from seclusion to offer his verses to the public, he had enlarged the range of his subjects and deepened his powers of thought. We see less richness in the images, less freedom in the play of fancy, but there is a firmer grip of character, a surer handling of the problems affecting the life of man.

Underground was flowing the hidden stream of *In Memoriam*, unknown save to the few; only in part were the fruits of this period to be seen in the two volumes containing 'English Idyls' and other new poems, along with a selection of earlier lyrics now revised and reprinted.

The distinctive quality of the book is given by the word Idyl, which was to be so closely connected with Tennyson's fame. Here he is working in a small compass, but he breaks fresh ground in describing scenes of English village life, and shows that he has used his gifts of observation to good purpose. Better than the slight sketches of character, of girls and their lovers, of farmers and their children, are the landscapes in which they are set; and many will remember the charming passages in which he describes the morning songs of birds in a garden, or the twinkling of evening lights in the still waters of a harbour. More original and more full of lyrical fervour was 'Locksley Hall', where he expresses many thoughts that were stirring the younger spirits of his day. Perhaps the most perfect workmanship, in a volume where much calls for admiration, is to be found in 'Ulysses', which the poet's friend Monckton Milnes gave to Sir Robert Peel to read, in order to convince him that Tennyson's work merited official recognition. His treatment of the hero is as far from the classical spirit as anything which William Morris wrote. He preserves little of the directness or fierce temper of the early epic. Rather does his Ulysses think and speak like some bold adventurer of the Renaissance, with the combination of ardent curiosity and reflective thought which was the mark of that age. Even so Tennyson himself, as he passed from youth to middle life, and from that to old age, was ever trying to achieve one more 'work of noble note', and yearning

To follow knowledge like a sinking star
Beyond the utmost bound of human thought.

But between this and the production of his next volume comes the most unhappy period in the poet's career, when his friends for a time despaired of his future and even of his life. At the marriage of his brother Charles in 1836, Tennyson had fallen in love with the bride's sister, Emily Sellwood; and in the course of the next three or four years they became informally engaged to one another. But his prospects of earning enough money to support a wife seemed so remote that in 1840 her family insisted on breaking off the engagement, and the lovers ceased to write to one another. Even the volumes of 1842, while winning high favour with cultivated readers, and stirring enthusiasm at the Universities, failed to attract the larger public and to make a success in the market. So when he sustained a further blow in the loss of his small fortune owing to an unwise investment, his health gave way and he fell into a dark mood of hypochondria. His star seemed to be sinking, just as he was winning his way to fame. Thanks to medical attention, aided by his own natural strength and the affections of his friends, he was already rallying in 1845, when Peel conferred on him the timely honour of a pension; and he was able not only to continue working at *In Memoriam*, but also to produce in 1847 *The Princess*, which gives clear evidence of renewed cheerfulness and vigour. Dealing as it does, half humorously, with the question of woman's education and her claim to a higher place in the scheme of life, it illustrates the interest which Tennyson, despite his seclusion, felt in social questions of the day. From this point of view it may be linked with *Locksley Hall* and *Maud*; but in *The Princess* the treatment is half humorous and the setting is more artificial. Tennyson's lyrical power is seen at its best in the magical songs which occur in the course of the story or interposed between the different scenes. They have deservedly won a place in all anthologies. His facility in the handling of blank verse is also remarkable. Lovers of Milton may regret the massive grandeur of an earlier style; but, as in every art, so in poetry, we pay for advance in technical accomplishment, in suppleness and melodious phrasing, by the loss of other qualities which are difficult to recapture.

Meanwhile *In Memoriam* was approaching completion; and this the most central and characteristic of his poems illustrates, more truly than a narrative of outward events, the phases through which Tennyson had been passing. Desultory though the method of its production be, and loose 'the texture of its fabric', there is a certain sequence of thought running through the cantos. We see how from the first poignancy of grief, when he can only brood passively over his friend's death, he was led to questioning the basis of his faith, shaken as it was by the claims of physical science—how from those doubts of his own, he was led to think of the universal trouble of the world—how at length by throwing himself into the hopes and aspiration of humanity he attained to victory and was able to put away his personal grief, believing that his friend's soul was still working with him in the universe for the good of all. At intervals, during the three years mirrored in the poem, we get definite notes of time. We see how the poet is affected each year as the winter and the spring come round, and how the succeeding anniversaries of Hallam's death stir the old pain in varying degree. But we must not suppose that each section was composed at the time represented in this scheme. Seventeen years went to the perfecting of the work; it is impossible to tell when each canto was first outlined and how often it was re-written; and we must be content with general notions of its development. The poet's memory was fully charged. As he could recall so vividly the Lincolnshire landscape when he was living in the south, so he could portray the emotions of the past though he had entered on a new period of life fraught with a different spirit.

Thus many elements go to make up the whole, and readers of *In Memoriam* can choose what suits their mood. To some, who wish to compare the problems of different ages, chief interest will attach to that section where the active mind wakes up to the conflict between science and faith. It was a difficult age for poets and believers. The preceding generation had for a time been swept far from their bearings by the tornado of the French Revolution. Some of them found an early grave while still upholding the flag; others had won back to harbour when their youth was past and ended their days in calm—if not stagnant—waters. But the advance of scientific discoveries and the scientific spirit sapped the defences of faith in more methodical fashion, and Tennyson's mind was only too open to all the evidence of natural law and the stern lessons of the struggle for life. To understand the influence of Tennyson on his age it is necessary to inquire how he reconciled religion with science; but this is too large a subject for a biographical sketch, and valuable studies have been written which deal with it more or less fully, by Stopford Brooke[26] and many others.

To Queen Victoria, and to others who had been stricken in their home affections, the human interest outweighed all others; the sorrow of those who gave little thought to systems of philosophy or religion was instinctively comforted by the note of faith in a future life and by the haunting melodies in which it found expression.

Many were content to return again and again to those passages where the beauty of nature is depicted in stanzas of wonderful felicity. No such gift of observation had yet ministered to their delight. Readers of Mrs. Gaskell will be reminded of the old farmer in *Cranford* revelling in the new knowledge which he has gained of the colour of ash-buds in March. So too we are taught to look afresh at larch woods in spring and beech woods in autumn, at the cedar in the garden and the yew tree in the churchyard. We are vividly conscious of the summer's breeze which tumbles the pears in the orchard, and the winter's storm when the leafless ribs of the wood clang and gride. As the perfect stanza lingers in our memory, our eyes are opened and we are taught to observe the marvels of nature for ourselves. Here, more than anywhere else, is he the true successor of Wordsworth, the Wordsworth of the daisy, the daffodil, and the lesser celandine, though following a method of his own—at once a disciple and a master.

But other influences than those of nature were coming into his life. In 1837 the Tennyson family had been compelled to leave Somersby; and the poet, recluse though he was, showed that he could rouse himself to meet a practical emergency with good sense. He took charge of all arrangements and transplanted his mother successively to new homes in Essex and Kent. This brought him nearer to London and enlarged considerably his circle of friends. The list of men of letters who welcomed him there is a long one, from Samuel Rogers to the Rossettis, and includes poets, novelists, historians, scholars, and scientists. The most interesting, to him and to us, was Carlyle, then living at Chelsea, who had published his *French Revolution* in

1837, and had thereby become notable among literary men. Carlyle's judgements on the poet and his poems have often been quoted. At first he was more than contemptuous over the latter, and exhorted Tennyson to leave verse and rhyme and apply himself to prose. But familiar converse, in which both men spoke their opinions without reserve, soon enlightened 'the sage', and he delighted in his new friend. Long after, in 1879, he confessed that 'Alfred always from the beginning took a grip at the right side of every question'. He could not fail to appreciate the man when he saw him in the flesh, and it is he who has left us the most striking picture of Tennyson's appearance in middle life. In 1842 he wrote to Emerson: 'Alfred is one of the few... figures who are and remain beautiful to me;—a true human soul... one of the finest-looking men in the world. A great shock of rough dusty-dark hair, bright-laughing hazel eyes, massive aquiline face, most massive yet most delicate, of sallow-brown complexion, almost Indian-looking; clothes cynically loose, free-and-easy;—smokes infinite tobacco. His voice is musical metallic,—fit for loud laughter and piercing wail, and all that may lie between; speech and speculation free and plenteous: I do not meet, in these late decades, such company over a pipe!' Not only were pipes smoked at home, but walks were taken in the London streets at night, with much free converse, in which art both were masters, but of which Carlyle, no doubt, had the larger share. Tennyson was a master of the art of silence, which Carlyle could praise but never practice; but when he spoke his remarks rarely failed to strike the bell.

Another comrade worthy of special notice was FitzGerald, famous to-day as the translator of Omar Khayyam, and also as the man whom two great authors, Tennyson and Thackeray, named as their most cherished friend. He was living a hermit's life in Suffolk, dividing his day between his yacht, his garden, and his books; and writing, when he was in the humour, those gossipy letters which have placed him as a classic with Cowper and Lamb. From time to time he would come to London for a visit to a picture gallery or an evening with his friends; and for many years he never failed to write once a year for news of the poet, whose books he might criticize capriciously, but whose image was always fresh in his affectionate heart. Of his old Cambridge circle Tennyson honoured, above all others, 'his domeship' James Spedding, of the massive rounded head, of the rare judgement in literature, of the unselfish and faithful discharge of all the duties which he could take upon himself. Great as was his edition of Bacon, he was by the common consent of his friends far greater than anything which he achieved, and his memory is most worthily preserved in the letters of Tennyson, and of others who knew him. In London he was present at gatherings where Landor and Leigh Hunt represented the elder generation of poets; but he was more familiar with his contemporaries Henry Taylor and Aubrey de Vere. It is the latter who gives us an interesting account of two meetings between

Wordsworth and his successor in the Laureateship.[27] The occasions when Tennyson and Browning met one another and read their poetry aloud were also cherished in the memory of those friends who were fortunate enough to be present.[28] Differing as they did in temperament and in tastes, they were rivals in generosity to one another and indeed to all their brethren who wielded the pen of the writer. To meet such choice spirits Tennyson would leave for a while his precious solitude and his books. London could not be his home, but it became a place of pleasant meetings and of friendships in which he found inspiration and help.

Thus it was that Tennyson spent the quiet years of meditation and study before he achieved his full renown. This was no such sensational event as Byron's meteoric appearance in 1812; but one year, 1850, is a clear landmark in his career. This was the date of the publication of *In Memoriam* and of his appointment, on the death of Wordsworth, to the office of Poet Laureate. This year saw the end of his struggle with ill-fortune and the end of his long courtship. In June he was married, at Shiplake on the Thames, to Emily Sellwood. Henceforth his happiness was assured and he knew no more the restlessness and melancholy which had clouded his enjoyment of life. His course was clear, and for forty years his position was hardly questioned in all lands where the English tongue was spoken. Noble companies of worshippers might worthily swear allegiance to Thackeray and Browning; but by the voice of the people Dickens and Tennyson were enthroned supreme.

To deal with all the volumes of poetry that Tennyson published between 1850 and his death would be impossible within the limits of these pages. In some cases he reverted to themes which he had treated before and he preserved for many years the same skill in craftsmanship. But in *Maud*, in *The Idylls of the King*, and in the historical dramas, unquestionably, he broke new ground.

Partly on account of the scheme of the poem, partly for the views expressed on questions of the day, *Maud* provoked more hostile criticism than anything which he wrote; yet it seems to have been the poet's favourite work. The story of its composition is curious. It was suggested by a short lyric which Tennyson had printed privately in 1837 beginning with the words 'Oh, that 'twere possible after long grief'. His friend, Sir John Simeon, urged him to write a poem which would lead up to and explain it; and the poet, adopting the idea, used *Maud* as a vehicle for much which he was feeling in the disillusionment of middle life. The form of a monodrama was unfamiliar to the public and has difficulties of its own. Tennyson has combined action, proceeding somewhat spasmodically, with a skilful study of character, showing us the exaggerated sensibility of a nature which under the successive influence of misanthropy, hope, love, and tragic disappointment, may easily pass beyond the border-land of insanity. In the scene where love is triumphant, Tennyson touches the highest point of lyrical passion; but there are jarring notes introduced in the satirical descriptions of Maud's brother and of the rival who aspires to her hand. And in the later cantos where, after the fatal quarrel, the hero is driven to moody thoughts and dark presages of woe, there are passages which seem to be charged with the doctrine that England was being corrupted by long peace and needed the purifying discipline of war. For this the poet was taken to task by his critics; and, though it is unfair in dramatic work to attribute to an author the words of his characters, Tennyson found it difficult to clear himself of suspicion, the more so that the Crimean War inspired at this time some of his most popular martial ballads and songs.

The Idylls of the King had a different fate and achieved instant popularity. The first four were published in 1859 and within a few months 10,000 copies were sold. Tennyson's original design, formed early in life, had been to build a single epic on the Arthurian theme, which seemed to him to give scope, like Virgil's *Aeneid*, for patriotic treatment. 'The greatest of all poetical subjects' he called it, and it haunted his mind perpetually. But if Virgil found such a task difficult nineteen hundred years before, it was doubly difficult for Tennyson to satisfy his generation, with scientific historians raking the ash heaps of the past, and pedants demanding local colour. In shaping his poem to meet the requirements of history he was in danger of losing that breadth of treatment which is essential for epic poetry. He fell back on the device of selecting episodes, each a complete picture in itself, and grouping them round a single hero. The story is placed in the twilight between the Roman withdrawal and the conquests of the Saxons, when the lamp of history was glimmering most faintly. In these troublous times a king is miraculously sent to be a bulwark to the people against the inroads of their foes. He founds an order of Knighthood bound by vows to fight for all just and noble causes, and upholds for a time victoriously the standard of chivalry within his realm, till through the entrance of sin and treachery the spell is broken and the heathen overrun the land. After his last battle, in the far west of our island, the king passes away to the supernatural world from which he came. This last episode had been handled many years before, and the 'Morte d'Arthur', which had appeared in the volume of 1842, was incorporated into the 'Passing of Arthur' to close the series of Idylls.

With what admixture of allegory this story was set out it is hard to say—Tennyson himself could not in later years be induced to define his purpose—but it seems certain that many of the characters are intended to symbolize higher and lower qualities. According to some interpretations King Arthur stands for the power of conscience and Queen Guinevere for the heart.

Galahad represents purity, Bors rough honesty, Percivale humility, and Merlin the power of the intellect, which is too easily beguiled by treachery. So the whole story is moralized by the entrance, through Guinevere and Lancelot, of sin; by the gradual fading, through the lightness of one or the treachery of another, of the brightness of chivalry; and by the final ruin which shatters the fair ideal.

But there is no need to darken counsel by questions about history or allegory, if we wish, first and last, to enjoy poetry, for its own sake. Here, as in Spenser's *Faerie Queene*, forth go noble knights with gentle maidens through the enchanted scenes of fairyland; for their order and its vows they are ready to dare all. Lawlessness is tamed and cruelty is punished, and no perilous quest presents itself but there is a champion ready to follow it to the end. And if severe critics tell us that they find no true gift of story-telling here, let us go for a verdict to the young. They may not be good judges of style, or safe interpreters of shades of thought, but they know when a story carries them away; and the *Idylls of the King*, like the Waverley Novels, have captured the heart of many a lover of literature who has not yet learnt to question his instinct or to weigh his treasures in the scales of criticism. And older readers may find themselves kindled to enthusiasm by reflective passages rich in high aspiration, or charmed by descriptions of nature as beautiful as anything which Tennyson wrote.

In the historical plays, which occupied a large part of his attention between 1874 and 1879, Tennyson undertook a yet harder task. He chose periods when national issues of high importance were at stake, such as the conflict between the Church and the Crown, between the domination of the priest and the claim of the individual to freedom of belief. He put aside all exuberance of fancy and diction as unsuited to tragedy; he handled his theme with dignity and at times with force, and attained a literary success to which Browning and other good judges bore testimony. Of Becket in particular he made a sympathetic figure, which, in the skilful hands of Henry Irving, won considerable favour upon the stage. But the times were out of joint for the poetic drama, and he had not the rich imagination of Shakespeare, nor the power to create living men and women who compel our hearts to pity, to horror, or to delight. For the absence of this no studious reading of history, no fine sentiment, no noble cadences, can make amends, and it seems doubtful whether future ages will regard the plays as anything but a literary curiosity.

On the other hand, nothing which he wrote has touched the human heart more genuinely than the poems of peasant life, some of them written in the broadest Lincolnshire dialect, which Tennyson produced during the years in which he was engaged on the Idylls and the plays. 'The Grandmother', 'The Northern Cobbler', and the two poems on the Lincolnshire farmers of following generations, were as popular as anything which the Victorian Age produced, and seem likely to keep their pre-eminence. The two latter illustrate, by their origin, Tennyson's power of seizing on a single impression, and building on it a work of creative genius. It was enough for him to hear the anecdote of the dying farmer's words, 'God A'mighty little knows what he's about in taking me! And Squire will be mad'; and he conceived the character of the man, and his absorption in the farm where he had lived and worked and around which he grouped his conceptions of religion and duty. The later type of farmer was evoked similarly by a quotation in the dialect of his county: 'When I canters my herse along the ramper, I 'ears "proputty, proputty, proputty"'; and again Tennyson achieved a triumph of characterization. It is here perhaps that he comes nearest to the achievements of his great rival Browning in the field of dramatic lyrics.

Apart from the writing and publication of his poems, we cannot divide Tennyson's later life into definite sections. By 1850 his habits had been formed, his friendships established, his fame assured; such landmarks as are furnished by the birth of his children, by his journeyings abroad, by the homes in which he settled, point to no essential change in the current of his life. Of the perfect happiness which marriage brought to him, of the charm and dignity which enabled Mrs. Tennyson to hold her place worthily at his side, many witnesses have spoken. Two sons were born to him, one of whom died in 1886, while the other, named after his lost friend, lived to write the Memoir which will always be the chief authority for our knowledge of the man. His homes soon became household words—so great was the spell which Tennyson cast over the hearts of his readers. Farringford, at the western end of the Isle of Wight, was first tenanted by him in 1853, and was bought in 1856. Here the poet enjoyed perfect quiet, a genial climate and the proximity of the sea, for which his love never failed. It was a very different coast to the bleak sandhills and wide flats of Mablethorpe. Above Freshwater the noble line of the Downs rises and falls as it runs westward to the Needles, where it plunges abruptly into the sea; and here on the springy turf, a tall romantic figure in wide-brimmed hat and flowing cloak, the poet would often walk. But Farringford, lying low in the shelter of the hills, proved too hot in summer; Freshwater was discovered by tourists too often inquisitive about the great; and so, after ten or twelve years, he was searching for another home, some remoter fastness set on higher ground. This he discovered on the borders of Surrey and Sussex near Haslemere, where Black Down rises to a height of 900 feet above the sea and commands a wide prospect over the blue expanse of the weald. Here he found copses and commons haunted by the song of birds, here he raised plantations close at hand to shelter him from the rude northern winds, and here he built the stately house of Aldworth where, some thirty years later, he was to die.

To both houses came frequent guests. For, shy as he was of paying visits, he loved to see in his own house men and women who could talk to him as equals—nor was he always averse to those of reverent temper, so they were careful not to jar on his fastidious tastes. In some ways it was a pity that he did not come to closer quarters with the rougher forces that were fermenting in the industrial districts. It might have helped him to a better understanding of the classes that were pushing to the front, who were to influence so profoundly the England of the morrow. But the strain of kindly sympathy in Tennyson's nature can be seen at its best in his intercourse with cottagers, sailors, and other humble folk who lived near his doors. The stories which his son tells us show how the poet was able to obtain an insight into their minds and to write poems like 'The Grandmother' with artistic truth. And no visitor received a heartier welcome at Farringford than Garibaldi, who was at once peasant and sailor, and who remained so none the less when he had become a hero of European fame. To Englishmen of nearly every cultured profession Tennyson's hospitality was freely extended—we need only instance Professor Tyndall, Dean Bradley, James Anthony Froude, Aubrey de Vere, G. F. Watts, Henry Irving, Hubert Parry, Lord Dufferin, and that most constant of friends, Benjamin Jowett, pre-eminent among the Oxford celebrities of the day. Among his immediate neighbours he conceived a peculiar affection for Sir John Simeon, whose death in 1870 called forth the stanzas 'In the Garden at Swainston'; and no one was more at home at Farringford than Julia Cameron, famous among early photographers, who has left us some of the best likenesses of the poet in middle and later life.

Tennyson was not familiar with foreign countries to the same degree as Browning, nor was he ever a great traveller. When he went abroad he needed the help of some loyal friend, like Francis Palgrave or Frederick Locker, to safeguard him against pitfalls, and to shield him from annoyance. When he was too old to stand the fatigue of railway journeys, he was willing to be taken for a cruise on a friend's yacht; and thus he visited many parts of Scotland and the harbours of Scandinavia. Amid new surroundings he was not always easy to please; bad food or smelly streets would call forth loud protests and upset him for a day; but his friends found it worth their while to risk some anxiety in order to enjoy his keen observation and the originality of his talk. Wherever he went he took with him his stored wisdom on Homer, Dante, and the 'Di maiores' of literature; and when Gladstone, too, happened to be one of the party on board ship, the talk must have been well worth hearing. As in his youth, so now, Tennyson's mind moved most naturally on a lofty plane and he was most at home with the great poets of the past; and with the exception of a few poems like 'All along the valley', where the torrents at Cauteretz reminded him of an early visit with Hallam to the Pyrenees, we can trace little evidence in his poetry of the journeys which he made. But we can see from his letters that he was kindled by the beauty of Italian cities and their treasures. In every picture-gallery which he visited he showed his preference for Titian and the rich colour of the Venetian painters. He refused to be bound by the conventional English taste for Alpine scenery, and broke out into abuse of the discoloured water in the Grindelwald glacier—'a filthy thing, and looking as if a thousand London seasons had passed over it'. In all places, among all people, he said what he thought and felt, with independence and conviction.

One incident connecting him with Italy is worthy of mention as showing that the poet, who 'from out the northern island' came at times to visit them, was known and esteemed by the people of Italy. When the Mantuans celebrated in 1885 the nineteenth centenary of the death of Virgil, the classic poet to whom Tennyson owed most, they asked him to write an ode, and nobly he rose to the occasion, attaining a felicity of phrase which is hardly excelled in the choicest lines of Virgil himself. But it is as the laureate of his own country that he is of primary interest, and it is time to inquire how he fulfilled the functions of his office, and how he rendered that office of value to the State.

When he was first appointed, Queen Victoria had let him know that he was to be excused from the obligation of writing complimentary verse to celebrate the doings of the court. Of his own accord he composed occasional odes for the marriages of her sons, and showed some of his practised skill in dignifying such themes; but it is not here that he found his work as laureate. He achieved greater success in the poems which he wrote to honour the exploits of our army and navy, in the past or the present. In his ballad of 'The Revenge', in his Balaclava poems, in the 'Siege of Lucknow', he struck a heroic note which found a ready echo in the hearts of soldiers and sailors and those who love the services. Above all, in the great ode on the death of the Duke of Wellington he has stirred all the chords of national feeling as no other laureate before him, and has enriched our literature with a jewel which is beyond price.

The Arthurian epic failed to achieve its national aim, and the historical dramas, though inspired by great principles which have helped to shape our history, never touched those large circles to which as laureate he should appeal. Some might judge that his function was best fulfilled in the lyrics to be found scattered throughout his work which praise the slow, ordered progress of English liberties. Passages from *Maud* or *In Memoriam* will occur to many readers, still more the three lyrics generally printed together at the end of the 1842 poems, beginning with the well-known tines, 'Of old sat Freedom on the heights', 'Love thou thy land', and 'You ask me why though ill at ease'. Here we listen to the voice of English Liberalism uttered in very different tones from those of Byron and Shelley, expressing the mind of one who recoiled from French Revolutions and had little sympathy with their aims of universal equality. In this he represented very truly that Victorian movement which was guided by Cobden and Mill, by Peel and Gladstone, which conferred such practical benefits upon the England of their day; but it is hardly the temper that we expect of an ardent poet, at any rate in the days of his youth. The burning passion of Carlyle, Ruskin, or William Morris, however tempered by other feelings, called forth a heartier response in the breast of the toiling multitudes.

It may be that the claim of Tennyson to popular sovereignty will, in the end, rest chiefly on the pleasure which he gave to many thousands of his fellow-countrymen, a pleasure to be renewed and found again in English scenes, and in thoughts which coloured grey lives and warmed cold hearts, which shed the ray of faith on those who could accept no creeds and who yet yearned for some hope of an after-life to cheer their declining days. That he gave this pleasure is certain—to men and women of all classes from Samuel Bamford,[29] the Durham weaver, who saved his pence to buy the precious volumes of the 'thirties, to Queen Victoria on her throne, who in the reading of *In Memoriam* found one of her chief consolations in the hour of widowhood.

It was given to Tennyson to live a long life, and to know more joy than sorrow—to be gladdened by the homage of two hemispheres, to lament the loss of his old friends who went before him (Spedding in 1881, FitzGerald in 1883, Robert Browning in 1889), to write his most famous lyric 'Crossing the Bar' at the age of 80, and to be soothed and strengthened to the end by the presence of his wife. For some weeks in the autumn of 1892 he lay in growing weakness at Aldworth taking farewell of the sights and sounds that he had loved so long. To him now it had come to hear with dying ears 'the earliest pipe of half-awakened birds' and to see with dying eyes 'the casement slowly grow a glimmering square'. Early on October 5 he had an access of energy, and called to have the blinds drawn up—'I want', he said, 'to see the sky and the light'. The next day he died, and a week later a country wagon bore the coffin to Haslemere. Thence it passed to Westminster, where his dust was to be laid beside that of Browning, among the great men who had gone before. In what mood he faced death we can learn from his own words:

Spirit, nearing yon dark portal at the limit of thy human state,
Fear not thou the hidden purpose of that Power which alone is great,
Nor the myriad world, His shadow, nor the silent Opener of the Gate![30]

CHARLES KINGSLEY
From a drawing by W. S. Hunt in the National Portrait Gallery

CHARLES KINGSLEY

1819-75

1819. Born at Holne on Dartmoor, June 12.

1830-6. Father rector of Clovelly.

1832. Grammar School at Helston, Cornwall.

1836. Father rector of St. Luke's, Chelsea. C. K. to King's College, London.

1838-42. Magdalene College, Cambridge.

1842. Ordained at Farnham. Curate of Eversley.

1844. Marriage to Fanny Grenfell. Friendship with F. D. Maurice.

1844. Rector of Eversley.

1848. Chartist riots. 'Parson Lot' pamphlets.

1850. *Alton Locke* published.

1855. *Westward Ho!* published.

1857. *Two Years Ago* published.

1859. Chaplain to the Queen.

1860. Professor of Modern History at Cambridge.

1864. Tour in the south of France.

1869. Canon of Chester.

1870. Tour to the West Indies.

1873. Canon of Westminster.

1874. Tour to California.

1875. Death at Eversley, January 23.

CHARLES KINGSLEY
PARISH PRIEST

If Charles Kingsley had been born in Scandinavia a thousand years earlier, one more valiant Viking would have sailed westward from the deep fiords of his native home to risk his fortunes in a new world, one who by his courage, his foresight, and his leadership of men was well fitted to be captain of his bark. The lover of the open-air life, the searcher after knowledge, the fighter that he was, he would have been in his element, foremost in the fray, most eager in the quest. But it was given to him to live in quieter times, to graft on the old Norse stock the graces of modern culture and the virtues of a Christian; and in a peaceful parish of rural England he found full scope for his gifts. There he taught his own and succeeding generations how full and beneficent the life of a parish priest can be. Our villages and towns produced many notable types of rector in the nineteenth century, Keble, Hawker, Hook, Robertson, Dolling, and scores of others; but none touched life at more points, none became so truly national a figure as Charles Kingsley in his Eversley home.

His father was of an old squire family; like his son he was a clergyman, a naturalist, and a sportsman. His mother, a Miss Lucas, came from Barbados; and while she wrote poetry with feeling and skill, she had also a practical gift of management. His father's calling involved several changes of residence. Those which had most influence on his son were his removal in 1824 to Barnack, on the edge of the fens, still untamed and full of wild life, and in 1830 to Clovelly in North Devon. More than thirty years later, when asked to fill up the usual questions in a lady's album, he wrote that his favourite scenery was 'wide flats and open sea'. He was precocious as a child and perpetrated poems and sermons at the age of four; but very early he developed a habit of observation and a healthy interest in things outside himself. Such a nature could not be indifferent to the beauty of Clovelly, to the coming and going of its fishermen, and to the romance and danger of their lives. The steep village-street nestling among the woods, the little harbour sheltered by the sandstone cliffs, the wide view over the blue water, won his lifelong affection.

His parents talked of sending him to Eton or Rugby, but in the end they decided to put him with Derwent Coleridge, the poet's son, at the Grammar School of Helston. Here he had the scenery which he loved, and masters who developed his strong bent towards natural science; and here he laid the foundations of his knowledge of botany, which remained all his life his favourite recreation. He was an eager reader, but not a close student of books; fond of outdoor life, but not skilled in athletic games; capable of much effort and much endurance, but rather irregular in his spurts of energy. A more methodical training might have saved him some mistakes, but it might also have taken the edge off that fresh enthusiasm which made intercourse with him at all times seem like a breath of moorland air. Here he developed an independence of mind and a fearlessness of opinion which is rarely to be found in the atmosphere of a big public school.

At the age of seventeen, when his father was appointed to St. Luke's, Chelsea, he left Helston and spent two years attending lectures at King's College, London, and preparing for Cambridge. These were by no means among his happier years. He disliked London and he rebelled against the dullness of life in a vicarage overrun with district visitors and mothers' meetings. His father, a strong evangelical, objected to various forms of public amusement, and Charles, though loyal and affectionate to his parents, fretted to find no outlet for his energies. He made a few friends and devoured many books, but his chief delight was to get away from town to old west-country haunts. Nor was his life at Cambridge entirely happy. His excitability was great: his self-control was not yet developed. Rowing did not exhaust his physical energy, which broke out from time to time in midnight fishing raids and walks from Cambridge to London. He wasted so much of his time that he nearly imperilled his chance of taking a good degree, and might perhaps count himself lucky when, thanks to a heroic effort at the eleventh hour, his excellent abilities won him a first class in classics. At this time he was terribly shaken by religious doubts. But in one of his vacations in 1839 he met Fanny Grenfell, his future wife, and soon he was on such a footing that he could open to her his inmost thoughts. It was she who helped him in his wavering decision to take Holy Orders; and, when he went down in 1842, he set himself to read seriously and thoroughly for Ordination. Early in 1844 he was admitted to deacon's orders at Farnham.

His first office marked out his path through life. With a short interval between his holding the curacy and the rectory of Eversley,[31] he had his home for thirty-three years at this Hampshire village so intimately connected with his name. Eversley lies on the borders of Berkshire and Hampshire, in the diocese of Winchester, near the famous house of Bramshill, on the edge of the sandy fir-covered waste which stretches across Surrey. To understand the charm of its rough commons and self-sown woods one must read Kingsley's *Prose Idylls*, especially the sketch called 'My Winter Garden'. There he served for a year as curate, living in bachelor quarters on the green, learning to love the place and its people: there, when Sir John Cope offered him the living in 1844, he returned a married man to live in the Rectory House beside the church, which may still be seen little altered to-day. A breakdown from overwork, an illness of his wife's, a higher appointment in the Church, might be the cause of his passing a few weeks or even months away; but year in, year out, he gave of his very best to Eversley for thirty-three years, and to it he returned from his journeys with all the more ardour to resume his work among his own people. The church was dilapidated, the Rectory was badly drained, the parish had been neglected by an absentee rector. For long periods together Kingsley was too poor to afford a curate: when he had one, the luxury was paid for by extra labour in taking private pupils. He had disappointments and anxieties, but his courage never faltered. He concentrated his energies on steady progress in things material and moral, and whatever his hand found to do, he did it with his might.

The church and its services called for instant attention. The Holy Communion had been celebrated only three times a year; the other services were few and irregular; on Sundays the church was empty and the alehouse was full. The building was badly kept, the churchyard let out for grazing, the whole place destitute of reverence. What the service came to be under the new Rector we can read on the testimony of many visitors. The intensity of his devotion at all times, the inspiration which the great festivals of the Church particularly roused in him, changed all this rapidly. He did all he could to draw his parishioners to church; but he had no rigid Puritanical views about the Sabbath. A Staff-College officer, who frequently visited him on Sundays, tells us of 'the genial, happy, unreserved intercourse of those Sunday afternoons spent at the Rectory, and how the villagers were free to play their cricket—"Paason he do'ant objec'—not 'e—as loik as not, 'e'll come and look on".' All his life he supported the movement for opening museums to the public on Sundays, and this at a time when few of the clergy were bold enough to speak on his side. The Church was not his only organ for teaching. He started schools and informal classes. In winter he would sometimes give up his leisure to such work every evening of the week. The Rectory, for all its books and bottles, its fishing-rods and curious specimens, was not a mere refuge for his own work and his own hobbies, but a centre of light and warmth where all his parishioners might come and find a welcome. He was one of the first to start 'Penny Readings' in his parish, to lighten the monotony of winter evenings with music, poetry, stories, and lectures; and though his parish was so wide and scattered, he tried to rally support for a village reading-room, and kept it alive for some years.

His afternoons were regularly given to parish visiting, except when there were other definite calls upon his time. He soon came to know every man, woman, and child in his parish. His sympathies were so wide that he could make himself at home with every one, with none more so than the gipsies and poachers, who shared his intimate knowledge of the neighbouring heaths and of the practices, lawful and unlawful, by which they could be made to supply food. He would listen to their stories, sympathize with their troubles and speak frankly in return. There was no condescension. One of his pupils speaks of 'the simple, delicate, deep respect for the poor', which could be seen in his manner and his talk among the cottagers. He could be severe enough when severity was needed, as when he compelled a cruel farmer to kill 'a miserable horse which was rotting alive in front of his house'; and he could deal no less drastically with hypocrisy. When a professional beggar fell on his knees at the Rectory gate and pretended to pray, he was at once ejected by the Rector with every mark of indignation and contumely. But the weak and suffering always made a special appeal to him. Though it was easy to vex and exasperate him, he could always put away his own troubles in presence of his own children or of any who needed his help. He had that intense power of sympathy which enabled him to understand and reach the heart.

From a letter to his greatest friend, Tom Hughes, written in 1851, we get a glimpse of a day in his life—'a sorter kinder sample day'. He was up at five to see a dying man and stayed with him till eight. He then went out for air and exercise, fished all the morning and killed eight fish. He went back to his invalid at three. Later he spent three hours attending a meeting convoked by his Archdeacon about Sunday schools, and at 10.30 he was back in his study writing to his friends.

But though he himself calls this a 'sample day', it does no justice to one form of his activities. Most days in the year he would put away all thought of fishing, shut himself up in his study morning and evening, and devote himself to reading and writing. Great care was taken over his weekly sermons. Monday was, if possible, given to rest; but from Tuesday till Friday evening they took up the chief share of his thoughts. And then there were the books that he wrote, novels, pamphlets, history lectures, scientific essays, on which he largely depended to support his wife and family. Besides this he kept up an extensive correspondence with friends and acquaintances. Many wrote to consult him about political and religious questions; from many he was himself trying to draw information on the phenomena of the science which he was trying to study at the time. Among the latter were Geikie, Lyell, Wallace, and Darwin himself, giants among scientific men, to whom he wrote with genuine humility, even when his name was a household word throughout England. His books can sometimes be associated with visits to definite places which supplied him with material. It is not difficult to connect *Westward Ho!* with his winter at Bideford in 1854, and *Two Years Ago* with his Pen-y-gwryd fishing in 1856. Memories of *Hereward the Wake* go back to his early childhood in the Fens, of *Alton Locke* to his undergraduate days at Cambridge. But he had not the time for the laborious search after 'local colour' with which we are familiar to-day. The bulk of the work was done in his study at Eversley, executed rapidly, some of it too rapidly; but the subjects were those of which his mind was full, and the thoughts must have been pursued in many a quiet hour on the heathery commons or beside the streams of his own neighbourhood.

About his books, his own judgement agreed with that of his friends. 'What you say about my "Ergon" being poetry is quite true. I could not write *Uncle Tom's Cabin* and I can write poetry:... there is no denying it: I do feel a different being when I get into metre: I feel like an otter in the water instead of an otter ashore.' The value of his novels is in their spirit rather than in their artistic form or truth; but it is foolish to disparage their worth, since they have exercised so marked an influence on the characters and lives of so many Englishmen, especially our soldiers and sailors, inspiring them to higher courage and more unselfish virtue. Perhaps the best example of his prose is the *Prose Idylls*, sketches of fen-land, trout streams, and moors, which combine his gifts so happily, his observation of natural objects, and the poetic imagination with which he transfuses these objects and brings them near to the heart of man. There were very few men who could draw such joy from familiar English landscapes, and could communicate it to others. The cult of sport, of science, and of beauty has here become one and has found its true high priest. In poetry his more ambitious efforts were *The Saint's Tragedy*, a drama in blank verse on the story of St. Elizabeth of Hungary, and *Andromeda*, a revival of the old Greek legend in the old hexameter measure. But what are most sure to live are his lyrics, 'Airlie Beacon', 'The Three Fishers', 'The Sands of Dee', with their simplicity and true note of song.

The combination of this poetic gift with a strong interest in science and a wide knowledge of it is most unusual; but there can be no mistaking the genuine feeling which Charles Kingsley had for the latter. It took one very practical form in his zeal for sanitation. In 1854 when the public, so irrational in its moments of excitement, was calling for a national fast-day on account of the spread of cholera, he heartily supported Lord Palmerston, who refused to grant it. He held it impious and wrong to attribute to a special visitation from God what was due to the blindness, laziness, and selfishness of our governing classes. His article in *Fraser's Magazine* entitled 'Who causes pestilence?' roused much criticism: it said things that comfortable people did not like to hear, and said them frankly; it was far in advance of the public opinion of that time, but its truth no one would dispute to-day. And what his pen did for the nation, his example did for the parish. He drained unwholesome pools in his own garden, and he persuaded his neighbours to do the same. He taught them daily lessons about the value of fresh air and clean water: no details were too dull and wearisome in the cause. To many people his novels, like those of Dickens and Charles Reade, are spoilt by the advocacy of social reforms. The novel with a purpose was characteristic of the early Victorian Age, and both in *Alton Locke* and in *Two Years Ago* he makes little disguise of the zeal with which he preaches sanitary reform. Of the more attractive sciences, which he pursued with equal intensity, there is little room to speak. Botany was his first love and it remained first to the end. Zoology at times ran it close, and his letters from seaside places are full of the names of marine creatures which he stored in tanks and examined with his microscope. A dull day on the coast was inconceivable to him. Geology, too, thrilled him with its wonders, and was the subject of many letters.

Side by side with his hobby of natural history went his love of sport: it was impossible for him to separate the one from the other. Fishing was his chief delight; he pursued it with equal keenness in the chalk streams of Hampshire, in the salmon rivers of Ireland, in the desolate tarns on the Welsh mountains. In the visitors' book of the inn at Pen-y-gwryd, Tom Hughes, Tom Taylor, and he left alternate quatrains of doggerel to celebrate their stay, written *currente calamo*, as the spirit prompted them. This is Charles Kingsley's first quatrain:

I came to Pen-y-gwryd in frantic hopes of slaying
Grilse, salmon, three-pound red-fleshed trout and what else there's no saying:
But bitter cold and lashing rain and black nor'-eastern skies, sir,
Drove me from fish to botany, a sadder man and wiser.

Each had his disappointment through the weather, which each expressed in verse; but it took more than bad weather to damp the spirits of three such ardent open-air enthusiasts. Hunting was another favourite sport, though he rarely indulged himself in this luxury, and only when he could do so without much expense. But whenever a friend gave him a mount, Kingsley was ready to follow the Berkshire hounds, and with his knowledge of the country he was able to hold his own with the best.

Let us try to imagine him then as he walked about the lanes and commons of Eversley in middle life, a spare upright figure, above the middle height, with alert step, informal but not slovenly in dress, with no white tie or special mark of his profession. His head was one to attract notice anywhere with the grand hawk-like nose, firm mouth, and flashing eye. The deep lines furrowed between the brows gave his face an almost stern expression which his cheery conversation soon belied. He might be carrying a fishing-rod or a bottle of medicine for a sick parishioner, or sometimes both: his faithful Dandie Dinmont would be in attendance and perhaps one of his children walking at his side. His walk would be swift and eager, with his eye wandering restlessly around to observe all that he passed: 'it seemed as if no bird or beast or insect, scarcely a cloud in the sky, passed by him unnoticed, unwelcomed.' So too with humanity—in breadth of sympathy he resembled 'the Shirra', who became known to every wayfarer between Teviot and Tweed. Gipsy boy, farm-hand, old grandmother, each would be sure of a greeting and a few words of talk when they met the Rector on his rounds. In society he might at times be too impetuous or insistent, when questions were stirred in which he was deeply interested. Tennyson tells us how he 'walked hard up and down the study for hours, smoking furiously and affirming that tobacco was the only thing that kept his nerves quiet'. Green compares him to a restless animal, and Stopford Brooke speaks of his quick-rushing walk, his keen face like a sword, and his body thinned out to a lath, and complains that he 'often screams when he ought to speak'. But this excitability was soothed by the country, and in his own parish he was at his best. He would never have been so beloved by his parishioners, if they had not found him willing to listen as well as to advise and to instruct.

His first venture into public life met with less general favour. The year 1848 saw many upheavals in Europe. On the Continent thrones tottered and fell, republics started up for a moment and faded away. In England it was the year of the Chartist riots, and political and social problems gave plenty of matter for thought. Monster meetings were held in London, which were not free from disorder. The wealthier classes and the Government were alarmed, troops were brought up to London and the Duke of Wellington put in command. Events seemed to point to outbreaks of violence and the starting of a class-war. Frederick Denison Maurice, whom above all men living Kingsley revered, was the leader of a group of men who were greatly stirred by the movement. They saw that more than political reform and political charters were needed; and, while full of sympathy for the working classes, they were not minded to say smooth things and prophesy Utopias in which they had no belief. Filled with the desire to help his fellow-men, indignant at abuses which he had seen with his own eyes, Kingsley came at once to their side. He went to London to see for himself, attended meetings, wrote pamphlets, and seemed to be promoting agitation. The tone in which he wrote can best be seen by a few words from the pamphlet addressed to the 'Workmen of England', which was posted up in London. 'The Charter is not bad, if the men who use it are not bad. But will the Charter make you free? Will it free you from slavery to ten-pound bribes? Slavery to gin and beer? Slavery to every spouter who flatters your self-conceit and stirs up bitterness and headlong rage in you? That I guess is real slavery, to be a slave to one's own stomach, one's pocket, one's own temper.' This is hardly the tone of the agitator as known to us to-day. With his friends Kingsley brought out a periodical, *Politics for the People*, in which he wrote in the same tone. 'My only quarrel with the Charter is that it does not go far enough in reform.... I think you have fallen into the same mistake as the rich of whom you complain, I mean the mistake of fancying that legislative reform is social reform, or that men's hearts can be changed by Act of Parliament.' He did not limit himself to denouncing such errors. He encouraged the working man to educate himself and to find rational pleasures in life, contributing papers on the National Gallery and bringing out the human interest of the pictures. 'Parson Lot', the *nom de guerre* which Kingsley adopted, became widely known for warm-hearted exhortations, for practical and sagacious counsels.

Two years later he published *Alton Locke*, describing the life of a young tailor whose mind and whose fortunes are profoundly influenced by the Chartist movement. From a literary point of view it is far from being his best work; and the critics agreed to belittle it at the time and to pass it over with apology at his death. But it received a warm welcome from others. While it roused the imagination of many young men and set them thinking, the veteran Carlyle could speak of 'the snatches of excellent poetical description, occasional sunbursts of noble insight, everywhere a certain wild intensity which holds the reader fast as by a spell'.

Should any one ask why a rector of a country parish mixed himself up in London agitation, many answers could be given. His help was sought by Maurice, who worked among the London poor. Many of the questions at issue affected also the agricultural labourer. Only one who was giving his life to serve the poor could effectively expose the mistakes of their champions. The upper classes, squires and merchants and politicians, had shut their eyes and missed their chances. So when the ship is on fire, no one blames the chaplain or the ship's doctor for lending a hand with the buckets.[32]

That his efforts in London met with success can be seen from many sources besides the popularity of *Alton Locke*. He wrote a pamphlet entitled 'Cheap Clothes and Nasty', denouncing the sweaters' shops and supporting the co-operative movement, which was beginning to arise out of the ashes of Chartism. Of this pamphlet a friend told him that he saw three copies on the table in the Guards' Club, and that he heard that captains in the Guards were going to the co-operative shop in Castle Street and buying coats there. A success of a different kind and one more valued by Kingsley himself was the conversion of Thomas Cooper, the popular writer in Socialist magazines, who preached atheistical doctrines weekly to many thousand working men. Kingsley found him to be sincerely honest, spent infinite time in writing him friendly letters, discussing their differences of opinion, and some years later had the joy of inducing him to become an active preacher of the Gospel. But most of the well-to-do people, including the clergy, were prejudiced against Kingsley by his Radical views. On one occasion he had to face a painful scene in a London church, when the vicar who had invited him to preach rose after the sermon and formally protested against the views to which his congregation had been listening. Bishop Blomfield at first sided with the vicar; but in the end he did full justice to the sincerity and charity of Kingsley's views and sanctioned his continuing to preach in the Diocese.

It was his literary successes which helped most to break down the prejudice existing against him in society. *Hypatia*, published in 1853, had a mixed reception; but *Westward Ho!* appearing two years later, was universally popular. His eloquence in the pulpit was becoming known to a wider circle, largely owing to officers who came over from Aldershot and Sandhurst to hear him; and early in 1859 he was asked to preach before the Queen and Prince Consort. His appointment as chaplain to the Queen followed before the year was out; and this made a great difference in his position and prospects. What he valued equally was the hearty friendship which he formed with the Prince Consort. They had the same tastes, the same interests, the same serious outlook on life. A year later came a still higher distinction when Kingsley was appointed Professor of Modern History at Cambridge. His history lectures, it is generally agreed, are not of permanent value as a contribution to the knowledge of the subject. With his parish work and other interests he had no time for profound study. But his eloquence and descriptive powers were such as to attract a large class of students, and many can still read with pleasure his lectures on *The Roman and the Teuton*, in which he was fired by the moral lessons involved in the decay of the Roman empire and the coming of the vigorous young northern races. Apart from his lectures he had made his mark in Cambridge by the friendly relations which he established with many of the undergraduates and the personal influence which he exercised. But he knew better than any one else his shortcomings as an historian, the preparation of his lectures gave him great anxiety and labour, and in 1869 he resigned the office.

The next honour which fell to him was a canonry at Chester, and in 1873, less than two years before his death, he exchanged it for a stall at Westminster. These historic cities with their old buildings and associations attracted him very strongly: preaching in the Abbey was even dangerously exciting to a man of his temperament. But while he gave his services generously during his months of office, as at Chester in founding a Natural History Society, he never deserted his old work and his old parish. Eversley continued to be his home, and during the greater part of each year to engross his thoughts.

Literature, science, and sport were, as we have seen, the three interests which absorbed his leisure hours. A fourth, partaking in some measure of all three, was travel, a hobby which the strenuous pursuit of duty rarely permitted him to indulge. Ill-health or a complete breakdown sometimes sent him away perforce, and it is to this that he chiefly owed his knowledge of other climes. He has left us some fascinating pictures of the south of France, the rocks of Biarritz, the terrace at Pau, the blue waters of the Mediterranean, and the golden arches of the Pont du Gard; but the voyages that thrilled him most were those that he took to America, when he sailed the Spanish main in the track of Drake and Raleigh and Richard Grenville. The first journey in 1870 was to the West Indies; the second and longer one took him to New York and Quebec, and across the continent to the Yosemite and San Francisco. This was in 1874, the last year of his life, and he was received everywhere with the utmost respect and goodwill. His name was now famous on both sides of the Atlantic, and the voice of opposition was stilled. The public had changed its attitude to him, but he himself was unchanged. He had the same readiness to gather up new knowledge, and to get into friendly touch with every kind of man, the same reluctance to talk about himself. Only the yearning towards the unseen was growing stronger. The poet Whittier, who met him at Boston, found him unwilling to talk about his own books or even about the new cities which he was visiting, but longing for counsel from his brother poet on the high themes of a future life and the final destiny of the human race.

While he was in California he was taken ill with pleurisy; and when he came back to England he had so serious a relapse in the autumn that he could hardly perform his duties at Westminster. He had never wished for long life, his strength was exhausted, the ardent soul had worn out its sheath. A dangerous illness of his wife's, threatening to leave him solitary, hastened the end. For her sake he fought a while against the pneumonia which set in, but the effort was in vain, and on January 23, in his own room at Eversley, he met his death contented and serene. Twenty years before he had said, 'God forgive me if I am wrong, but I look forward to it with an intense and reverent curiosity'.

These words of his sum up some of his most marked characteristics. Of his 'curiosity' there is no need to say more: all his life he was pursuing eager researches into rocks, flowers, animals, and his fellow-men. 'Intensity' has been picked out by many of his friends as the word which, more than any other, expresses the peculiar quality of his nature. This does not mean a weak excitability. His letters to J. S. Mill on the women-suffrage movement show that this hysterical element, which was often to be found in the women supporting it, was what most he feared. He himself defines it well—'my blessed habit of intensity. I go at what I am about as if there was nothing else in the world for the time being.' This quality, which many great men put into their work, Kingsley put both into his work and into his play-time. Critics will say that he paid for it: it is easy to quote the familiar line: 'Neque semper arcum tendit Apollo.' But Horace is not the poet to whom Charles Kingsley would go for counsel: he would only say that he got full value in both, and that he never regretted the bargain.

But it would be no less true to say that 'Reverence' is the key-note of his character. This fact was impressed on all who saw him take the services in his parish church, and it was an exaltation of reverence which uplifted his congregation and stamped itself on their memories. It is seen, too, in his political views. The Radical Parson, the upholder of Chartism, was in many ways a strong Tory. He had a great belief in the land-owning classes, and an admiration for what remained of the Feudal System. He believed that the old relation between squire and villagers, if each did his duty, worked far better than the modern pretence of Equality and Independence. Like Disraeli, like Ruskin, and like many other men of high imagination, he distrusted the

Manchester School and the policy that in the labour market each class should be left to fend for itself. Radical as he was, he defended the House of Lords and the hereditary system. So, too, in Church questions, though he was an anti-Tractarian, he had a great reverence for the Athanasian Creed and in general was a High Churchman. He had none of the fads which we associate with the Radical party. Total abstinence he condemned as a rigid rule, though there was no man more severe in his attitude to drunkenness. He believed that God's gifts were for man's enjoyment, and he set his face against asceticism. He trained his own body to vigorous manhood and he had remarkable self-control; and he wished to help each man to do this for himself and not to be driven to it by what he considered a false system. Logically it may be easy to find contradictions in the views which he expressed at different times; but his life shows an essential unity in aim and practice.

It has been the fashion to label Charles Kingsley and his teaching with the nickname of 'Muscular Christianity', a name which he detested and disclaimed. It implied that he and his school were of the full-blooded robust order of men, who had no sympathy for weakness, and no message for those who could not follow the same strenuous course as themselves. As a fact Kingsley had his full share of bodily illnesses and suffered at all times from a highly-wrought nervous organization; when pain to others was involved, he was as tender and sympathetic as a woman. He was a born fighter, too reckless in attack, as we see in his famous dispute with Cardinal Newman about the honesty of the Tractarians. But he was not bitter or resentful. He owned himself that in this case he had met a better logician than himself: later he expressed his admiration for Newman's poem, 'The Dream of Gerontius', and in his letters he praises the tone in which the Tractarians write—'a solemn and gentle earnestness which is most beautiful and which I wish I may ever attain'. The point which Matthew Arnold singles out in estimating his character is the width of his sympathies. 'I think', he says, 'he was the most generous man I have ever known, the most forward to praise what he thought good, the most willing to admire, the most incapable of being made ill-natured or even indifferent by having to support ill-natured attacks himself. Among men of letters I know nothing so rare as this.' To the gibe about 'Muscular Christianity' Kingsley had his own answer. He said that with his tastes and gifts he had a special power of appealing to the wild rough natures which were more at home in the country than the town, who were too self-forgetful, and too heedless of the need for culture and for making use of their opportunities. Jacob, the man of intellect, had many spiritual guides, and the poor outcast, Esau, was too often overlooked. As he said, 'The one idea of my life was to tell Esau that he has a birthright as well as Jacob'. When he was laid to his rest in Eversley churchyard, there were many mourners who represented the cultured classes of the day; but what gave its special character to the occasion was the presence of keepers and poachers, of gipsies, country rustics, and huntsmen, the Esaus of the Hampshire village, which was the fit resting-place for one who above all was the ideal of a parish priest.

GEORGE FREDERICK WATTS

1817-1904

1817. Born in London, February 23.

1827. Begins to frequent the studio of William Behnes.

1835. Enters Royal Academy Schools.

1837. Working in his own studio. 'Wounded Heron' and two portraits in Royal Academy exhibition.

1842. Success in Parliament House competition: 'Caractacus' cartoon.

1843-7. Living with Lord and Lady Holland at Florence.

1847. Success in second competition: 'Alfred' cartoon.

1848. Early allegorical pictures.

1850. Friendship with the Prinseps. Little Holland House.

1851. National series of portraits begun.

1852. Begins Lincoln's Inn Hall fresco: finished 1859.

1856. With Sir Charles Newton to Halicarnassus.

1865. Correspondence with Charles Rickards of Manchester.

1867. Elected A.R.A. and R.A. in same year. Portraits. Carlyle. W. Morris.

1872. New home at Freshwater, Isle of Wight. 'The Briary.' Little Holland House sold.

1877. Grosvenor Gallery opened. 1881. Watts exhibition there (200 pictures).

1882. D.C.L., Oxford; LL.D., Cambridge.

1886. November; marries Miss Fraser Tytler. Winter in Egypt.

1890. New home at Limnerslease, Compton.

1895. National Portrait Gallery opened.

1896. New Gallery exhibition (155 pictures).

1897. Gift of pictures to new Tate Gallery.

1902. Order of Merit.

1904. Death at Compton, July 1.

GEORGE FREDERICK WATTS
Artist

The great age of British art was past before Queen Victoria began her long and memorable reign. Reynolds and Gainsborough had died in the last years of the eighteenth century, Romney and Hoppner in the first decade of the nineteenth; Lawrence, the last of the Georgian portrait-painters, did not live beyond 1830. Of the landscapists Crome died in 1821 and Constable in 1837. Turner, the one survivor of the Giants, had done three-quarters of his work before 1837 and can hardly be reckoned as a Victorian worthy.

GEORGE FREDERICK WATTS
From a painting by himself in the National Portrait Gallery

In the reign of Queen Victoria many thousands of trivial anecdotic pictures were bought and sold, were reproduced in Art Annuals and Christmas Numbers and won the favour of rich amateurs and provincial aldermen—so much so that Victorian art has been a favourite target for the shafts of critics formed in the school of Whistler and the later Impressionists. But however just some of their strictures may be, it is foolish to condemn an age wholesale or to shut our eyes to the great achievements of those artists who, rising above the general level, dignified the calling of the painter just when the painters were most rare. These men formed no single movement progressing in a uniform direction. The study of pure landscape is best seen in the water-colour draughtsmen, Cotman, Cox, and de Wint; of landscape as a setting for the life of the people, in Fred Walker and George Mason. Among figure-painters the 'Pre-Raphaelites', Rossetti, Holman Hunt, and Millais, with their forerunner Madox Brown, are the first to win attention by their earnestness, their romantic imagination, and their intense feeling for beauty: in these qualities Burne-Jones carried on their work and retained the allegiance of a cultured few to the very end of the century. Two solitary figures are more difficult to class, Alfred Stevens and Watts. Each learnt fruitful lessons from prolonged study of the great art of the past; yet each preserves a marked originality in his work. More than any other artists of their age they realized the unity of art and the dependence of one branch upon another. Painting should go hand in hand with sculpture, and both minister to architecture. So the world might hope once more to see public buildings nobly planned and no less nobly decorated, as in the past it saw the completion of the Parthenon and the churches of mediaeval Italy. It was unfortunate that they received so little encouragement from the public, and that their example had so narrow an influence. St. Paul's can show its Wellington monument, Lincoln's Inn its fresco; but year after year subject-pictures continued to be painted on an ambitious scale, which after a few months' exhibition on the walls of Burlington House passed to their tomb in provincial museums, or reappeared as ghosts in the sale-room only to fetch a derisory price and to illustrate the fickle vagaries in the public taste.

In the early life of George Frederick Watts, who was born in a quiet street in West Marylebone, there are few incidents to narrate, there is little brightness to enliven the tale. His father, a maker of musical instruments, was poor; his mother died early; his home-life was overshadowed by his own ill-health and the uncertain moods of other members of the family. His education was casual and consisted mostly of reading books under the guidance of his father, who had little solid learning, but refined tastes and an inventive disposition. In his Sundays at home, where the Sabbatarian rule limited his reading, he became familiar with the stories of the Old Testament; he discovered for himself the Waverley Novels and Pope's translation of the *Iliad*; and he began from early years to use his pencil with the eager and persistent enthusiasm which marks the artist born.

For a rich artistic nature it was a starved life, but he made the most of such chances as came in his way. He was barely ten years old when he found his way to the studio of a sculptor named William Behnes, a man of Hanoverian extraction, an indifferent sculptor but possessed of a real talent for drawing; and from his more intellectual brother, Charles Behnes, he learnt to widen his interest in literature. In this halting and irregular process of education he received help, some years later, from another friend of foreign birth, Nicholas Wanostrocht, a Belgian, who under the assumed name of 'Felix' became a leading authority on the game of cricket. Wanostrocht was a cultivated man of very wide tastes, and it was largely through his encouragement that Watts gave to the study of the French and Italian languages, and to music, what little time he could spare from his professional work. London was to render him greater services than this. Thanks to his visits to the British Museum, he had, while still in his teens, come under a mightier spell. Though few Englishmen had yet learnt to value their treasures, the Elgin Marbles had been resting there for twenty years. But now, two years before Queen Victoria's accession, there might be seen, standing rapt in admiration before the works of Phidias, a boy of slender figure with high forehead, delicately moulded features, and disordered hair, one who, as we can see from the earliest portrait which Mrs. Watts has preserved in her biography, had something of the unearthly beauty of the young Shelley. He was physically frail, marked off from ordinary men by a grace that won its way quickly to the hearts of all who were susceptible to spiritual charm. Untaught though he was, he had the eye to see for himself the grandeur of these relics of Greece, and throughout his life they remained one of the guiding influences in his development, one of the standards which he set up before himself, though all too conscious that he could not hope to reach that height. We see their influence in his treatment of drapery, of horses, of the human figure, in his idealization of types, in the flowing lines of his compositions, and in the grouping of his masses. Compared to the hours which he spent in the British Museum, the lessons in the Royal Academy schools seem unimportant. He attended classes there for some months in 1835, but the teaching was poor and its results disappointing. William Hilton, R.A., who then occupied the post of Keeper, gave him some kind words of encouragement, but in general he came and went unnoticed, and he soon returned to his solitary self-training in his own studio. If we know little of his teaching in art, we know still less of his personal life during the time when he was laying the foundations of his success by study and self-discipline. Early rising was an art which he acquired early, and maintained throughout life; long after he felt the spur of necessity, even after the age of 80, he could rise at four when there was work to be done; and, living as he did on the simplest diet, he often achieved his best results at an hour when other men were still finishing their slumbers. His shyness and sensitiveness, combined with precarious health and weak physique, would seem to equip him but poorly in the struggle for life; but his steady persistence, his high conception of duty, his faith in his art, joined to that power which he had of winning friends among the noblest men and women of his day, were to carry him triumphantly through to the end.

The career of Watts as a public man began in 1843 when he had reached the age of 26. The British Government, not often guilty of fostering art or literature, may claim at least the credit for having drawn him out of his seclusion at the very moment when his genius was ripening to bear fruit. In 1834 the Palace of Westminster, so long the home of the Houses of Parliament, had been burnt to the ground. The present buildings were begun by Sir Charles Barry in 1840, and, with a view to decorating them with wall-paintings, the Board of Works wisely offered prizes for cartoons, hoping thereby to attract the best talent of the country. In June 1843 they had to judge between 140 designs by various competitors, and to award prizes varying in value from £300 to £100. Of the three first prizes one fell to Watts, hitherto unknown beyond the narrow circle of his friends, for a design displaying 'Caractacus led in triumph through the streets of Rome'. This cartoon, however, was not employed for its original purpose: it fell into the hands of an enterprising, if inartistic, dealer, who cut it up and sold such fragments as he judged to be of value in the state of the picture market at the time. What was far more important was the encouragement given to the artist by such a success at a critical time of his life, and the opportunity which the money furnished him to travel abroad and enrich his experiences before his style was formed. He had long wished to visit Italy; and, after spending a few weeks in France, he made his leisurely way (at a pace incredible to us to-day) to Florence and its picture galleries. On the steamer between Marseilles and Leghorn he was fortunate in making friends with a Colonel Ellice and his wife, and a few weeks later they introduced him to Lord Holland, the British Minister at Florence.

The story goes that Watts went to be the guest of Lord and Lady Holland for four days and remained there for four years—a story which is a tribute to the discernment of the latter and not a satire upon Watts, who was the last man in the world to take advantage of hospitality or to thrust himself into other people's houses. No doubt it is not to be taken too literally, but at least it is so far true that he very quickly became intimate with his host and hostess and found a home where he could pursue his art under ideal conditions. The value and the danger of patronage have been often discussed. Democracy may provide a discipline for artists and men of letters which is often salutary in testing the sincerity of their devotion to art and literature; but, in such a stern school, men of genius may easily founder and miss their way.

However that may be, Watts found just the haven which was needed for a nature like his. So far he had known but little appreciation, and had lived with few who were his peers. Now he was cheered by the favour of men and women who had known the best and whose favour was well worth the winning. But he kept his independence of spirit. He lived in a palace, but his diet was as sparing as that of a hermit. He feasted his eyes on the great works of the Renaissance, but he preserved his originality, and continued to work, with fervour and enhanced enthusiasm, on the lines which he had already marked out for himself. He did not copy with the hand, but he drank in new lessons with the eyes and dreamed new dreams with the spirit.

The Hollands had two houses, one in the centre of the city, the other, the Villa Medicea di Careggi, lying on the edge of the hills some two or three miles to the north. This latter had been a favourite residence of the first Cosimo; here Lorenzo had died, turning his face to the wall, unshriven by Savonarola; and here Watts decorated an open *loggia* in fresco, to bear witness to its latest connexion with the patronage of Art. Between the two houses he passed laborious but tranquil days, studying, planning, training his hand to mastery, but enjoying in his leisure all that such a home could give him of varied entertainment. Music and dancing, literature and good company, all had their charms for him, though none of them could beguile him into neglecting his work. Fortune had tried him with her frowns and with her smiles; under temptations of both sorts he remained but more faithful to his calling.

His health gave cause for anxiety from time to time, but he delighted in the sunshine and the genial climate of the South, and in general he was well enough to enjoy what Florence could give him of beautiful form and colour, and even to travel farther afield. One year he pushed as far as Naples, stopping on the way for a hurried glance at Rome. On this memorable day the Sistine chapel and its paintings were kept to the last; and Watts, high though his expectations were, was overwhelmed at what he saw. 'Michelangelo', he said, 'stands for Italy, as Shakespeare does for England.' So the four years went by till in 1847 this halcyon period came to an end. The Royal Commission of Fine Arts was offering prizes for fresco-painting, and Watts felt that he must put his growing powers to the test and utilize what he had learnt. This time he chose for his subject 'Alfred inciting the English to resist the Danes by sea'. He was busy at work in the early months of 1847 making many sketches in pencil for the figures, and by April he was on his way home, bringing with him the 'Alfred' almost finished and five other canvases in various stages of completion. The picture was placed in Westminster Hall for competition in June, and soon after he was announced to be the winner of one of the three £500 prizes. When the Commissioners decided to purchase his picture for the nation, he refused to take more than £200 for it, though he might easily have obtained a far higher price. This is one of the earliest instances in which he displayed that signal generosity which marked his whole career.

During the next three years his life was rather desultory. He was hoping to return to Italy and did not find it easy to settle down in London. He changed his studio two or three times. He planned various works, but felt chilled at the absence of any clear encouragement from new patrons or from the general public. His success in 1847 had not been followed by any commissions for the sort of work he loved: interest in the decoration of public buildings was still spasmodic and too rare.

He made the acquaintance of Mr. Ruskin; but, friendly though they were in their personal relations, they did not see eye to eye in artistic matters. Ruskin seemed to lay too much emphasis on points of secondary importance, and to fail in judging the work of Michelangelo and the greatest masters. So Watts thought, and many years later, in conversation with Jowett, declared, chary though he was of criticizing his friends. To-day there is little doubt whose judgement was the truer, even had Ruskin not weakened his position by so often contradicting himself. Besides Ruskin, Watts was beginning to make other friends, and was a member of the Cosmopolitan Club, which counted among its members Sir Robert Morier, Sir Henry Layard, FitzGerald, Palgrave, and Spedding. The large painting of the 'Story from Boccaccio', which now hangs in the Watts room of the Tate Gallery, hung for many years on the walls of this club and was presented to the nation in 1902. How frequently Watts attended the club or other social gatherings at this time we do not know. His name figures little in the biographies and memoirs of Londoners, and he himself would not have wished the record of his daily life to be preserved. His modesty in all personal matters is uncontested, and even if his subsequent offer of his pictures to the nation smacks somewhat of presumption, his motive was something other than conceit. His portraits were an historical record of the worthiest men of his own time: his allegories were of value, so he felt, not for their technical accomplishments, but for the high moral lessons which they tried to convey. The artist himself was at ease only in retirement and privacy. Yet complete isolation was not good for him. Ill-health still dogged his steps, and the dejection which came over him in the years 1849 and 1850 is to be seen in the gloomiest pictures which he ever painted. Their titles and subjects alike recall the more tragic poems of Thomas Hood. But the eclipse was not to last for long, and in 1850 Watts owed his recovery to a happy chance encounter with friends who were to give him a new haven of refuge and gladden his life for thirty years to come.

A high Indian official, James Pattle, had been the father of five daughters who were famous for their beauty, and from their tastes and character were particularly fitted to be the friends of artists and poets. If Lady Somers was the most beautiful of the sisters and Mrs. Cameron the most artistic, their elder sister Mrs. Prinsep proved to be Watts's surest friend. Her husband, Thoby Prinsep, was a member of the India Council in Whitehall, a large-hearted man, full of knowledge and full of kindliness. Mrs. Prinsep herself was mistress of the domestic arts in no common degree, from skilful cookery to the holding of a literary *salon*. She and her husband realized what friendship could do for a nature like that of Watts, and they provided him with an ideal home, where he was nursed back to health, relieved of care, and cheered by constant sympathy and affection. It was Watts who discovered this home for them in a quiet corner of London, that has not yet lost all its charm. Behind Holland House and adjoining its park was a smaller property with a rambling old-fashioned house, built in the days when London was still far away. At Little Holland House the Prinseps lived for a quarter of a century. Here the sisters came and went freely with their children who were growing up around them. Here were gatherings of their friends, among whom Tennyson, Thackeray, Rossetti, and Burne-Jones might be met from time to time; and here Watts remained a constant inmate, giving regular hours to his work, enjoying their society in his leisure, a special favourite with the children, who admitted him to their confidence and called him by pet names. There was no lionizing, no striving after brilliance; all work that was genuine and of high intention received due honour, and Watts could hope here to carry to fruition the noble visions which he had seen since the days of his youth.

These visions had little to do with the exhibitions of Burlington House, the winning of titles, or the acquisition of worldly wealth. Watts cherished the old Greek conception of willing service to the community. And he was alive to the special needs of an age when men were struggling for gain, and when 'progress' was measured by material riches. To him, if to few others, it seemed tragic that, in the wonderful development of industrial Britain, art, which had spoken so eloquently to citizens of Periclean Athens and to Florence in the Medicean age, should remain without expression or sign of life. For a moment our Government had seemed to hear the call, and the stimulus of the Westminster competitions had been of value; but the interest died away all too quickly, and the attention of the general public was never fully roused. If the latter could be won, Watts was only too willing to give the time and the knowledge which he had acquired. The building of the great railway stations in London seemed to offer a chance, and Watts approached the directors of the North Western Company with a humble petition. All that he asked for was wall space and the payment of his expenses in material. Had his request been granted, Euston might have enjoyed pre-eminence among railway stations, and passengers for the north might have passed through, or waited in, a National Gallery of their own. But the Railway Director's mind is slow to move; inventions leave him cold, and imagination is not to be weighed in the scale against dividends and quick returns. The Company declined the offer on the ground of expense, while their architect is said to have been seriously alarmed at the idea of any one tampering with his building.

Another proposal met with a heartier response. The men of law proved more generous than the men of commerce. The new Hall at Lincoln's Inn was being built by Mr. Philip Hardwick, in the Tudor style. Benchers and architect alike cordially welcomed Watts's offer to decorate a blank wall with fresco. The work could only be carried on during the legal vacations, and it proved a long business owing to the difficulties of the process and to the interruptions caused by the artist's ill-health. Watts planned it in 1852, began work in 1853, and did not put the finishing touch till 1859. The subject was a group of famous lawgivers, in which the chief figures were Moses, Mahomet, Justinian, Charlemagne, and Alfred, and it stands to-day as the chief witness to his powers as a designer on a grand scale.

Before this he had already dedicated to national service his gift of portrait-painting. The head of Lord John Russell, painted in 1851, is one of the earliest portraits known to have been painted with this intention, though it is impossible to fix with accuracy the date when such a scheme took shape. In 1899, with the same patriotic intention, he was at work on a painting of Cecil Rhodes. In this half-century of activity he might have made large sums of money, if he had responded to the urgent demands of those men and women who were willing to pay high prices for the privilege of sitting to him; but few of them attained their object. His earlier achievements were limited to a few families from whom he had received help and encouragement when he was unknown. First among these to be remembered are the various generations of that family whose name is still preserved at South Kensington in the Ionides collection of pictures. Next came the Hollands, of whom he painted many portraits at Florence; and a third circle, naturally enough, was that of the Prinseps. In general he was most unwilling to undertake, as a mere matter of business, commissions from individuals unknown to him. He found portrait-painting most exhausting in its demands upon him. He threw his whole soul into the work, straining to see and to reproduce all that was most noble in his sitters. His nervous temperament made him anxious at starting, while his high standard of excellence made him often dissatisfied with what he had accomplished. Even when he was painting Tennyson, a personal friend, he was miserable at the thought of the responsibility which he had undertaken; and in 1879 he gave up a commission to paint Gladstone, feeling that he was not realizing his aim. So far as mere money was concerned, he would have preferred to leave this branch of his profession, the most lucrative of all, perhaps the most suited to his gifts, severely on one side, and to confine himself to the allegorical subjects which he felt to be independent of external claims.

In the years after 1850, when he was first living at Little Holland House, Watts formed some of the friendships with brother artists which added so much pleasure to his life. Foremost among these friends was Frederic Leighton, the most famous President whom the Royal Academy has known since the days of Reynolds, a man of many accomplishments, linguist, orator, and organizer, as well as sculptor and painter, the very variety of whose gifts have perhaps prevented him from obtaining proper recognition for the things which he did really well. The worldly success which he won brought him under the fire of criticism as no other artist of the time; but, apart from his merits as a draughtsman and a sculptor he was a man of singularly generous temper, a staunch friend and a champion of good causes. These qualities, and his sincere admiration for all noble work, endeared him to Watts; and, at one time, Leighton paid daily visits to his studio to exchange views and to see his friend's work in progress.

For a while Rossetti frequented the circle, but this wayward spirit drifted into other paths, and the chief service which he did to Watts was to introduce to him Edward Burne-Jones, most refined of artists and most lovable of men. The latter's work commanded Watts's highest admiration, and his friendship was valued to the end. To many lovers of painting these two remain the embodiment of all that is purest and loftiest in Victorian art; and though their treatment of classic subjects and of allegory were so different their pictures were often hung side by side in exhibitions and their names were coupled together in the current talk of the time. Burne-Jones was markedly Celtic in his love of beautiful pattern, in the ghostly refinement of his figures, in the elaborate fancifulness of his imagery. Watts had more of the full-blooded Englishman in his nature, and his art was simpler, grander, more universal. If we may compare them with the great men of the Renaissance, Burne-Jones recalled the grace of Botticelli, Watts the richness and power of Veronese or of Titian.

Those who went to Little Holland House and saw the circle of the Prinseps adorned by these artists, and by such writers as Tennyson, Henry Taylor,[33] and Thackeray, had a singular impression of harmony between the men and their surroundings; and if they had been asked who best expressed the spirit of these gatherings, they would probably have pointed to the 'Signor', as Watts came to be called among his intimate friends—to the slight figure with the small delicately-shaped head, who seemed to recall the atmosphere of Florence in the Middle Ages, when art was at once a craft and a religion. But few who saw the grace and old-fashioned courtesy with which he moved among young and old would have guessed what fire and persistency were in him, that he would outlive all his generation, and be still wielding a vigorous brush in the early years of the century to come.

One interlude in this busy yet tranquil life came in 1856 when he was asked to accompany Sir Charles Newton's party to the coast of Asia Minor. Newton was to explore the ruins of Halicarnassus on behalf of the British Government, and a man-of-war was placed at his disposal. The opportunity of seeing Grecian lands in this leisurely fashion was too good to be missed, and Watts spent eight happy months on board. He showed his power of adapting himself to a new situation, made friends with the sailors, and sang 'Tom Bowling' at their Christmas concert. Incidentally he visited Constantinople, as it was necessary to get a 'firman' from the Porte, was commended to the famous ambassador Lord Stratford de Redcliffe and painted two portraits of him, one of which is in the National Portrait Gallery to-day. He also enjoyed a cruise through the Greek Islands, where the scenery with its rich colour and bold pure outlines was specially calculated to charm him. He painted few landscapes in his long career, but both in Italy and in Greece it was the distant views of mountain peaks that led him to give expression to his delight in the beauty of Nature.

A different kind of distraction was obtained after his return by occasional visits to Esher, where he was the guest of Mrs. Sanderson, sister of Mr. Prinsep, and where he spent many a happy day riding to hounds. For games he had no training, and little inclination, though he loved in his old age to watch and encourage the village cricket in Surrey; but riding gave him great pleasure. His love for the horse may in part be due to this pastime, in part to his early study of the Parthenon frieze with its famous procession of horsemen. Certainly this animal plays a notable part in his work. Two great equestrian statues occupied him for many years. 'Hugh Lupus', the ancestor of the Grosvenors, was cast in bronze in 1884 and set up at Eaton Hall in the Duke of Westminster's park. 'Physical Energy' was the name given to a similar figure conceived on broader and more ideal lines. At this Watts continued to work till the year of his death, though he parted with the first version in response to Lord Grey's appeal when it was wanted to adorn the monument to Cecil Rhodes. Its original destination was the tomb in the Matoppo hills; but it was proved impracticable to convey such a colossal work, without injury, over the rough country surrounding them; and it was set up at Cape Town. The statue has become better known to the English public since a second version has been set up in Kensington Gardens. The rider, bestriding a powerful horse, has flung himself back and is gazing eagerly into the distance, shading with uplifted hand his eyes against the fierce sunlight which dazzles them. The allegory is not hard to interpret, though the tame landscape of a London park frames it less fitly than a wide stretch of wild and solitary veld.

Horses of many different kinds figure in his pictures. In one, whose subject is taken from the Apocalypse, we see the war-horse, his neck 'clothed with thunder'; in another his head is bowed, the lines harmonizing with the mood of his master, Sir Galahad. 'The Midday Rest', unheroic in theme but grand in treatment, shows us two massive dray horses, which were lent to him as models by Messrs. Barclay and Perkins, while 'A patient life of unrewarded toil' renders sympathetically the weakness of the veteran discharged after years of service, waiting patiently for the end. One instance of a more imaginative kind shows us 'Neptune's Horses' as the painter dimly discerned them, with arched necks and flowing manes, rising and leaping in the crest of the wave.

His portraits of great men generally took the form of half-lengths with the simplest backgrounds. His subjects were of all kinds—Tennyson and Browning, Rossetti and Burne-Jones, Gladstone, Mill, Motley, Joachim, Thiers, and Anthony Panizzi.[34] His object was a national one, and the foreigners admitted to the company were usually closely connected with England. Sometimes the pose of the body and the hands helps the conception, as in Lord Lytton and Cardinal Manning; more often Watts trusts to the simple mass of the head or to the character revealed by the features in repose. No finer examples for contrast can be given than the portraits of the two friends, Burne-Jones and William Morris, painted in 1870. In the former we see the spirit of the dreamer, in the latter the splendid vitality and force of the craftsman, who was impetuous in action as he was rich in invention. The room at the National Portrait Gallery where this collection is hung speaks eloquently to us of the Victorian Age and the varied genius of its greatest men; and in some cases we have the additional interest of being able to compare portraits of the same men painted by Watts and by other artists. Well known is the contrast in the case of Carlyle. Millais has painted a picturesque old man whose talk might be racy and his temper uncertain; but the soul of the seer, tormented by conflicts and yet clinging to an inner faith, is revealed only by the hands of Watts. Again Millais gives us the noble features, the extravagant 'hure'[35] of the Tennyson whom his contemporaries saw, alive, glowing with force; Watts has exalted this conception to a higher level and has portrayed the thinker whom the world will honour many centuries hence. Some will perhaps prefer the more objective treatment; and it is certain that Watts's ambition led him into difficult paths. Striving to represent the soul of his sitter, he was conscious at times that he failed—that he could not see or realize what he was searching for. More than once he abandoned a commission when he felt this uncertainty in himself. But when the accord between artist and sitter was perfect, he achieved a triumph of idealization, combined with a firm grasp on reality, such as few artists since Giorgione and the young Titian have been able to achieve.

Apart from portraits there was a rich variety in the subjects which the painter handled, some drawn from Bible stories, some from Greek legends or mediaeval tales, some for which we can find no source save in his own imagination. He dealt with the myths in a way natural to a man who owed more to Greek art and to his own musings than to the close study of Greek literature. His pictures of the infancy of Jupiter, of the deserted Ariadne, of the tragedy of Orpheus and Eurydice, have no elaborate realism in detail.

The Royal Academy walls showed, in those days, plenty of marble halls, theatres, temples, and classic groves, reproduced with soulless pedantry. Watts gave us heroic figures, with strong masses and flowing lines, simply grouped and charged with emotion—the yearning love of Diana for Endymion, the patient resignation of Ariadne, the passionate regret of Orpheus, the cruel bestiality of the Minotaur. Some will find a deeper interest, a grander style, in the designs which he made for the story of our first parents in the Book of Genesis. Remorse has rarely been expressed so powerfully as in the averted figure of Eve after the Fall, or of Cain bowed under the curse, shut out from contact with all creation. In one of his masterpieces Watts drew his motive from the Gospel story. The picture entitled 'For he had great possessions' shows us the young ruler who has come to Christ and has failed in the supreme moment. His back, his bowed neck and averted head, with the gesture of indecision in his right hand, tell their tale with consummate eloquence.

In his more famous allegories the same is true; by simple means an impression of great power is conveyed. The popularity of 'Love and Death' and its companion picture shows how little the allegory needs explanation. These themes were first handled between 1860 and 1870; but the pictures roused such widespread admiration that the painter made several replicas of them. Versions are now to be found in the Dominions and in New York, as well as in London and Manchester. Photographs have extended their renown and they are so familiar to-day that there is no need to describe them. Another masterpiece dealing with the subject of Death is the 'Sic transit', where the shrouded figure of the dead warrior is impressive in its solemnity and stillness. 'Dawn' and 'Hope' show what different notes Watts could strike in his treatment of the female form. At the other extreme is 'Mammon', the sordid power which preys on life and crushes his victims with the weight of his relentless hand. The power of conscience is shown in a more mystic figure called 'The Dweller in the Innermost'. Judgement figures in more than one notable design, the most familiar being that which now hangs in St. Paul's Cathedral with the title of 'Time, Death, and Judgement'. Its position there shows how little we can draw the line between the different classes of subjects as they were handled by Watts. A courtier like Rubens could, after painting with gusto a rout of Satyrs, put on a cloak of decorum to suit the pageantry of a court, or even simulate fervour to portray the ecstasy of a saint. He is clearly acting a part, but in Watts the character of the man is always seen. Whether his subjects are drawn from the Bible or from pagan myths, they are all treated in the same temper of reverence and purity.

It is impossible to avoid the question of didactic art in writing of these pictures, though such a wide question, debated for half a century, can receive no adequate treatment here. We must frankly allow that Watts was 'preaching sermons in paint', nor would he have repudiated the charge, however loud to-day are the protests of those who preach the doctrine of 'art for art's sake'. But the latter, while stating many principles of which the British public need to be reminded, seem to go beyond their rights. It is, of course, permissible for students of art to object to technical points of handling—Watts himself was among the first to deplore his own failures due to want of executive ability; it is open to them to debate the part which morality may have in art, and to express their preference for those artists who handle all subjects impartially and conceive all to be worthy of treatment, if truth of drawing or lighting be achieved. But when they make Watts's ethical intention the reason for depreciating him as an artist they are on more uncertain ground. There is no final authority in these questions. Ruskin was too dogmatic in the middle years of his life and only provoked a more violent reaction. Twenty years later the admirers of Whistler and Manet were equally intolerant, and assumed doctrines which may hold the field to-day but are certain to be questioned to-morrow.

Watts was most reluctant to enter into controversy and had no ambition to found a school; in fact so far was he from imposing his views on others, that he scarcely ever took pupils, and was content to urge young artists to follow their own line and to be sincere. But he could at times be drawn into putting some of his views on paper, and in 1893 he wrote down a statement of the relative importance which he attached to the qualities which make a painter. Among these Imagination stands first, Intellectual idea next to it. After this follow Dignity of form, Harmony of lines, and Colour. Finally, in the sixth place comes Realism, the idol of so many of the end of the century, both in literature and art.

Some years earlier, in meeting criticism, Watts had said, 'I admit my want of dexterity with the brush, in some cases a very serious defect,' but at the same time he refused to accept the authority of those 'who deny that art should have any intellectual intention'. In general, he pleaded that art has a very wide range over subject and treatment; but he did not set himself up as a reformer in art, nor inflict dogmas on the public gratuitously. He found that some of his more abstract themes needed handling in shadowy and suggestive fashion: if this gave the impression of fumbling, or displayed some weakness in technique, even so perhaps the conception reaches us in a way that could not be attained by dexterity of brushwork. As he himself said, 'there were things that could only be done in art at the sacrifice of some other things'; but the points which Watts was ready to sacrifice are what the realists conceive to be indispensable, and his aims were not as theirs. But his life was very little troubled by controversy; and he would not have wished his own work to be a subject for it.

External circumstances also had little power to alter the even tenor of his way. Late in life, at the age of 69, he married Miss Fraser Tytler, a friend of some fifteen years' standing, who was herself an artist, and who shared all his tastes. After the marriage he and his wife spent a long winter in the East, sailing up the Nile in leisurely fashion, enjoying the monuments of ancient Egypt and the colours of the desert. It was a time of great happiness, and was followed by seventeen years of a serene old age, divided between his London house in Melbury Road and his new home in Surrey. Staying with friends in Surrey, Watts had made acquaintance with the beautiful country lying south of the Hog's Back; and in 1889 he chose a site at Compton, where he decided to build a house. To this he gave the name of Limnerslease. Thanks to the generosity of Mrs. Watts, who has built a gallery and hung some of his choicest pictures there, Compton has become one of the three shrines to which lovers of his work resort.[36]

But for many years he met with little recognition from the world at large. It was only at the age of 50 that he received official honours from the Royal Academy, though the success of his cartoons had marked him out among his contemporaries twenty-five years earlier. About 1865 his pictures won the enthusiastic admiration of Mr. Charles Rickards, who continued to be the most constant of his patrons, and gave to his admiration the most practical form. Not only did he purchase from year to year such pictures as Watts was willing to sell, but twenty years later he organized an exhibition of Watts's work at Manchester, which did much to spread his fame in the North. In London Watts came to his own more fully when the Grosvenor Gallery was opened in 1877. Here the Directors were at pains to attract the best painters of the day and to hang their pictures in such a way that their artistic qualities had full effect. No one gained more from this than Watts and Burne-Jones; and to a select but growing circle of admirers the interest of the annual exhibitions began and ended with the work of these two kindred spirits. The Directors also arranged in 1881 for a special exhibition devoted to the works of Watts alone, when, thanks to the generosity of lenders, 200 of his pictures did justice to his sixty years of unwearied effort. This winter established his fame, and England now recognized him as one of her greatest sons. But when his friends tried to organize a dinner to be held at the Gallery in his honour, he got wind of the plot, and with his usual fastidious reserve begged to be spared such an ordeal. The *élite* of London society, men famous in politics, literature, and other departments of public life, were only too anxious to honour him; but he could not endure to be the centre of public attention. To him art was everything, the artist nothing. Throughout his life he attended few banquets, mounted fewer platforms, and only wished to be left to enjoy his work, his leisure, and the society of his intimate friends.

His interest in the progress of his age was profound, though it did not often take shape in visible form. He believed that the world might be better, and was not minded to acquiesce in the established order of things. He sympathized with the Salvation Army; he was a strong supporter of women's education; he was ardent for redressing the balance of riches and poverty, and for recognizing the heroism of those who, labouring under such grim disadvantages, yet played a heroic part in life. The latter he showed in practical form. In 1887 he had wished to celebrate the Queen's Jubilee by erecting a shrine in which to preserve the records of acts of self-sacrifice performed by the humblest members of the community. The scheme failed at the time to win support; but in 1899, largely through his help, a memorial building arose in the churchyard of St. Botolph, near Aldersgate, better known as the 'Postmen's Park'.

In private life his kindliness and courtesy won the hearts of all who came near him, young and old, rich and poor. He was tolerant towards those who differed from him in opinion: he steadily believed the best of other men in passing judgement on them. No mean thought, no malicious word, no petty quarrel marred the purity of his life. He had lost his best friends: Leighton in 1896, Burne-Jones three years later; but he enjoyed the devotion of his wife and the tranquillity of his home. Twice he refused the offer of a Baronetcy. The only honour which he accepted was the Order of Merit, which carried no title in society and was reserved for intellectual eminence and public service. At the age of 80 he presented to Eton College his picture of Sir Galahad, a fit emblem of his own lifelong quest. His last days of active work were spent on the second version of the great statue of 'Physical Energy', which had occupied him so long, and in which he ever found something new to express as he dreamed of the days to come and the future conquests of mankind. In 1904 his strength gradually failed him, and on July 1 he died in his Surrey home. Like his great exemplar Titian, whom he resembled in outward appearance and in much of the quality of his painting, he outlived his own generation and was yet learning, as one of the young, when death took him in the 88th year of his life.

JOHN COLERIDGE PATTESON

1827-71

1827.	Born in London, April 1.
1838-45.	At school at Eton.
1841.	Selwyn goes out to New Zealand as Bishop.
1845-9.	Undergraduate at Balliol College, Oxford.
1850-1.	Visits Germany.
1852-3.	Fellow of Merton College, Oxford.
1853.	Curate at Alphington, near Ottery.
1854.	Accepted by Bishop Selwyn for mission work.
1855.	Sails for New Zealand, March. Head-quarters at Auckland.
1856.	First cruise to Melanesia.
1860.	First prolonged stay (3 months) in Mota.
1861.	Consecrated first Bishop of Melanesia, February.
1864.	Visit to Australia to win support for Mission (repeated 1855). Serious attack on his party by natives of Sta. Cruz.
1867.	Removal of head-quarters to Norfolk Island.
1868.	Selwyn goes home to become Bishop of Lichfield.
1869.	Exploitation of native labour becomes acute.
1870.	Severe illness: convalescence at Auckland.
1871.	Last stay at Mota. Cruise to Sta. Cruz. Death at Nukapu, September 20.

JOHN COLERIDGE PATTESON
MISSIONARY

New Zealand, discovered by Captain Cook in 1769, lay derelict for half a century, and like others of our Colonies it came very near to passing under the rule of France. From this it was saved in 1840 by the foresight and energy of Gibbon Wakefield, who forced the hand of our reluctant Government; and its steady progress was secured by the sagacity of Sir George Grey, one of our greatest empire-builders in Australia, South Africa, and New Zealand. Thanks to them and to others, there has arisen in the Southern Pacific a state which, more than any other, seems to resemble the mother country with its sea-girt islands, its temperate climate, its mountains and its plains. A population almost entirely British, living in these conditions, might be expected to repeat the history of their ancestors. In politics and social questions its sons show the same independence of spirit and even greater enterprise.

JOHN COLERIDGE PATTESON
From a drawing by William Richmond

The names of two other men deserve recognition here for the part they played in the history of these islands. In 1814, before they became a British possession, Samuel Marsden came from Australia to carry the Gospel to their inhabitants, and formed settlements in the Northern districts, in days when the lives of settlers were in constant peril from the Maoris. But nothing could daunt his courage; and whenever they came into personal contact with him, these childlike savages felt his power and responded to his influence, and he was able to lay a good foundation. In 1841 the English Church sent out George Augustus Selwyn as first Missionary Bishop of New Zealand, giving him a wide province and no less wide discretion. He was the pioneer who, from his base in New Zealand, was to spread Christian and British influences even farther afield in the vast stretches of the Pacific Ocean.

Selwyn was educated at Eton and King's College, Cambridge, and these famous foundations have never sent forth a man better fitted to render services to his country. In a small sphere, as curate of Windsor, he had already, by his energy, patience, and practical sagacity, achieved remarkable results; and it was providential that, in the strength of early manhood, he was selected for a responsible post which afforded scope for the exercise of his powers. In the old country he might have been hampered by routine and tradition; in a new land he could mark out his own path. The constitution of the New Zealand Church became a model for other dioceses and other lands, and his wisdom has stood the test of time.

What sort of man he was can best be shown by quoting a story from his biography.[37] When the Maori War broke out he joined the troops as chaplain and shared their perils in the field. Against the enterprising native fighters these were not slight, especially as the British troops were few and badly led. He was travelling without escort over routes infested by Maoris, refusing to have any special care taken of his own person, and his chief security lay in rapid motion. Yet twice he dismounted on the way, at peril of his life, once under an impulse of humanity, once from sheer public spirit. The first time it was to pull into the shade a drunken soldier asleep on duty and in danger of sunstroke; the second to fill up the ruts in a sandy road, where it seemed possible that the transport wagons which were following might be upset. Many other incidents could be quoted which show his unconventional ways and his habitual disregard for his own comfort, dignity, or safety. In New Zealand he found plenty of people to appreciate these qualities in a bishop.

Though Selwyn was the master and perhaps the greater man, yet a peculiar fame has attached to his disciple John Coleridge Patteson, owing to the sweetness of his disposition, the singleness of his aim, and the consummation of his work by a martyr's death. Born in London in 1827, he was more truly a son of Devon, to which he was attached by many links. His mother's brother, Justice Coleridge, and many other relatives, lived close round the old town of Ottery St. Mary; and his father, an able lawyer who was raised to the Bench in 1830, bought an estate at Feniton and came to live in the same district before the boy was fifteen years old. It was at Ottery, where the name of Coleridge was so familiar, that the earliest school-days of 'Coley' Patteson were passed; but before he was eleven years old he was sent to the boarding-house of another Coleridge, his uncle, who was a master at Eton. Here he spent seven happy years working in rather desultory fashion, so that he had his share of success and failure. His chief distinctions were won at cricket, where he rose to be captain of the XI; but with all whose good opinion was worth having he won favour by his cheerful, frank, independent spirit. If he was idle at one time, at another he could develop plenty of energy; if he was one of the most popular boys in the school, he was not afraid to risk his popularity by protesting strongly against moral laxity or abuses which others tolerated. It is well to remember this, which is attested by his school-fellows, when reading his letters, in which at times he blames himself for caring too much for the good opinion of others.

His interest in the distant seas where he was to win fame was first aroused in 1841. Bishop Selwyn was a friend of his family, and coming to say good-bye to the Pattesons before sailing for New Zealand, he said, half sportively, to the boy's mother, 'Will you give me "Coley"?' This idea was not pursued at the time; but the name of Selwyn was kept before him in his school-days, as the Bishop had left many friends at Eton and Windsor, and Edward Coleridge employed his nephew to copy out Selwyn's letters from his diocese in order to enlist the sympathy of a wider audience. But this connexion dropped out of sight for many years and seems to have had little influence on Patteson's life at Oxford, where he spent four years at Balliol. He went up in 1845 as a commoner, and this fact caused him some disquietude. He felt that he ought to have won a scholarship, and, conscious of his failure, he took to more steady reading. He was also practising self-discipline, giving up his cricket to secure more hours for study. He did not scorn the game. He was as fond as ever of Eton, and of his school memories. But his life was shaping in another direction, and the new interests, deepening in strength, inevitably crowded out the old.

After taking his degree he made a tour of the great cities of Italy and wrote enthusiastically of the famous pictures in her galleries. He also paid more than one visit to Germany, and when he had gained a fair knowledge of the German language, he went on to the more difficult task of learning Hebrew and Arabic. This pursuit was due partly to his growing interest in Biblical study, partly to the delight he took in his own linguistic powers. He had an ear of great delicacy; he caught up sounds as by instinct; and his retentive memory fixed the impression. Later he applied the reasoning of the philologist, classified and tabulated his results, and thus was able, when drawn into fields unexplored by science, to do original work and to produce results of great value to other students. But he was not the man to make a display of his power; in fact he apologizes, when writing to his father from Dresden, for making a secret of his pursuit, regarding it rather as a matter of self-indulgence which needed excuse. Bishop Selwyn could have told him that he need have no such fears, and that in developing his linguistic gifts he was going exactly the right way to fit himself for service in Melanesia.

Patteson's appointment to a fellowship at Merton College, which involved residence in Oxford for a year, brought no great change into his life. Rather he used what leisure he had for strengthening his knowledge of the subjects which seemed to him to matter, especially the interpretation of the Bible. He returned to Greek and Latin, which he had neglected at school, and found a new interest in them. History and geography filled up what time he could spare from his chief studies. Resuming his cricket for a while, he mixed in the life of the undergraduates and made friends among them. At College meetings, for all his innate conservatism, he found himself on the side of the reformers in questions affecting the University; but he had not time to make his influence felt. At the end of the year he was ordained and took a curacy at Alphington, a hamlet between Feniton and Ottery. His mother had died in 1842, and his object was to be near his father, who was growing infirm and found his chief pleasure in 'Coley's' presence and talk. His interest in foreign missions was alive again, but at this time his first duty seemed to be to his family; and in a parish endeared to him by old associations he quickly won the affection of his flock. He was happy in the work and his parishioners hoped to keep him for many years; but this was not to be. In 1854 Bishop Selwyn and his wife were in England pleading for support for their Church, and their visit to Feniton brought matters to a crisis. Patteson was thrilled at the idea of seeing his hero again, and he at once seized the opportunity for serving under him. There was no need for the Bishop to urge him; rather he had to assure himself that he could fairly accept the offer. To the young man there was no thought of sacrifice; that fell to the father's lot, and he bore it nobly. His first words to the Bishop were, 'I can't let him go'; but a moment later he repented and cried, 'God forbid that I should stop him'; and at parting he faced the consequences unflinchingly. 'Mind!' he said, 'I give him wholly, not with any thought of seeing him again.'

In the following March, the young curate, leaving his home and his parish where he was almost idolized, where he was never to be seen again, set his face towards the South Seas. Once the offer had been made and accepted, he felt no more excitement. It was not the spiritual exaltation of a moment, but a deliberate applying of the lessons which he had been learning year by year. He had put his hand to the plough and would not look back.

The first things which he set himself to learn, on board ship, were the Maori language and the art of navigation. The first he studied with a native teacher, the second he learnt from the Bishop, and he proved an apt pupil in both. In a few months he became qualified to act as master of the Mission ship, and the speaking of a new language was to him only a matter of weeks. His earliest letters show how quickly he came to understand the natives. He was ready to meet any and every demand made upon him, and to fulfil duties as different from one another as those of teacher, skipper, and storekeeper. His head-quarters, during his early months in New Zealand, were either on board ship or else at St. John's College, five miles from Auckland. But, before he had completed a year, he was called to accompany the Bishop on his tour to the Islands and to make acquaintance with the scene of his future labours.

Bishop Selwyn had wisely limited his mission to those islands which the Gospel had not reached. The counsels of St. Paul and his own sagacity warned him against exposing his Church to the danger of jealous rivalry. So long as Christ was preached in an island or group of islands, he was content; he would leave them to the ministry of those who were first in the field. Many of the Polynesian groups had been visited by French and English missionaries and stations had been established in Samoa, Tahiti, and elsewhere; but north of New Zealand there was a large tract of the Pacific, including the New Hebrides and the Solomon Islands, where the natives had never heard the Gospel message. These groups were known collectively as Melanesia, a name hardly justified by facts,[38] as the inhabitants were by no means uniform in colour. If the Solomon Islanders had almost black skins, those who lived in the Banks Islands, which Patteson came to know so well, were of a warm brown hue such as may be seen in India or even in the south of Europe. Writing in the very last month of his life, Patteson tells his sisters how the colour of the people in Mota 'is just what Titian and the Venetian painters delighted in, the colour of their own weather-beaten boatmen'.

Selwyn had visited these islands intermittently since 1849, and had thought out a plan for spreading Christianity among them. With only a small staff of helpers and many other demands on his time, he could not hope to get into direct contact with a large population, so widely scattered. His work must be done through natives selected by himself, and these must be trained while they were young and open to impressions, while their character was still in the making. So every year he brought back with him from his cruise a certain number of Melanesian boys to spend the warmer months of the New Zealand year under the charge of the missionaries, and restored them to their homes at the beginning of the next cruise. At Auckland, with its soldiers, sailors, and merchants, the boys became familiar with other sides of European life beyond the walls of the Mission School; and their interest was stimulated by a close view of the strength to be drawn from European civilization. By this system Selwyn hoped that they on their return would spread among the islanders a certain knowledge of European ways, and that their relatives, seeing how the boys had been kindly treated, would feel confidence in the missionaries and would give them a hearing. This policy commended itself to Patteson by its practical efficacy; and though he modified it in details, he remained all his life a convinced adherent of the principle. Slow progress through a few pupils, selected when young, and carefully taught, was worth more than mere numbers, though too often in Missionary reports success is gauged by figures and statistics.

These cruises furnished the adventurous part of the life. Readers of Stevenson and Conrad can picture to themselves to-day the colour, the mystery, and the magic of the South Seas. Patteson, with his reserved nature and his dread of seeming to throw a false glamour over his practical duties, wrote but sparingly of such sights; but he was by no means insensitive to natural beauty and his letters give glimpses of coral reefs and lagoons, of palms and coco-nut trees, of creepers 100 feet long trailing over lofty crags to the clear water below.

He enjoyed being on board ship, with his books at hand and some leisure to read them, with the Bishop at his side to counsel him, and generally some of his pupils to need his help. They had many delightful days when they received friendly greeting on the islands and found that they were making real progress among the natives. But the elements of discomfort, disappointment, and danger were rarely absent for long. For a large part of each voyage they had some forty or fifty Melanesian boys on board, on their way to school or returning to their homes. The schooner built for the purpose was as airy and convenient as it could be made; yet there was little space for privacy. The natives were constitutionally weak; and when illness broke out, no trained nurses were at hand and Patteson would give up his own quarters to the sick and spend hours at their bedsides. Sometimes they found, on revisiting an island, that their old scholars had fallen away and that they had to begin again from the start. Sometimes they had to abstain from landing at all, because the behaviour of the natives was menacing, or because news had reached the Mission of some recent quarrel which had roused bitter feeling. The traditions of the Melanesians inclined them to go on the war-path only too readily, and both Selwyn and Patteson had an instinctive perception of the native temperament and its danger.

However lightly Patteson might treat these perils in his letters home, there was never complete security. To reassure his sisters he tells them of 81 landings and only two arrows fired at them in one cruise; and yet one poisoned arrow might be the cause of death accompanied by indescribable agony. Even when a landing had been effected and friendly trading and talk had given confidence to the visitors, it might be that an arrow was discharged at them by some irresponsible native as they made for their boats.

These voyages needed unconventional qualities in the missioner; few of the subscribers in quiet English parishes had an idea how the Melanesian islanders made their first acquaintance with their Bishop. When the boat came near the shore, the Bishop, arrayed in some of his oldest clothes, would jump into the sea and swim to land, sometimes being roughly handled by the breakers which guarded the coral bank. It was desirable not to expose their precious boat to the cupidity of the natives or to the risk of it being dashed to pieces in the surf, so the Bishop risked his own person instead. He would then with all possible coolness walk into a gathering of savages, catch up any familiar words which seemed to occur in the new dialect, or, failing any linguistic help, try to convey his peaceful intentions by gesture or facial expression. When an island had been visited before, there was less reason to be on guard; but sometimes the Bishop had to break to relatives the sad news that one of the boys committed to his care had fallen a victim to the more rigorous climate of New Zealand or to one of the diseases to which these tribes were so liable. Then it was only the personal ascendancy won by previous visits that could secure him against a violent impulse to revenge.

All practical measures were tried to establish friendly relations with the islanders; and when people at home might fancy the Bishop preaching impressively to a decorous circle of listeners, he was really engaged in lively talk and barter, receiving yams and other articles of food in return for the produce of Birmingham and Sheffield, axe-heads which he presented to the old, and fish-hooks with which he won the favour of the young. But such brief visits as could be made at a score of islands in a busy tour did not carry matters far, and the memory of a visit would be growing dim before another chance came of renewing intercourse with the same tribe. Selwyn felt it was most desirable that he should have sufficient staff to leave a missionary here and there to spend unbroken winter months in a single station, where he could reach more of the people and exercise a more continuous influence upon them. Patteson's first experience of this was in 1858, when he spent three months at Lifu in the Loyalty Islands, a group which was later to be annexed by the French.

A sojourn which was to bear more permanent fruit was that which he made at Mota in 1860. This was one of the Banks Islands lying north of the New Hebrides, in 14° South Latitude. The inhabitants of this group showed unusual capacity for learning from the missionaries, and sufficient stability of character to promise lasting success for the work carried on among them. Mota, owing to the line of cliffs which formed its coast, was a difficult place for landing; so it escaped the visits of white traders who could not emulate the swimming feats of Selwyn and Patteson, and was free from many of the troubles which such visitors brought with them. Once the island was reached, it proved to be one of the most attractive, with rich soil, plenty of water, and a kindly docile population. Here, on a site duly purchased for the mission, under the shade of a gigantic banyan tree, on a slope where bread-fruit and coco-nuts (and, later, pine-apples and other importations) flourished, the first habitation was built, with a boarded floor, walls of bamboo canes, and a roof of coco-nut leaves woven together after the native fashion so as to be waterproof. Here, in the next ten years, Patteson was to spend many happy weeks, taking school, reading and writing when the curiosity of the natives left him any peace, but in general patiently conversing with all and sundry who came up, with the twofold object of gathering knowledge of their dialect and making friends with individuals. While he showed instinctive tact in knowing how far it was wise to go in opposing the native way of life, he was willing to face risks whenever real progress could be made. After he had been some days in Mota a special initiation in a degrading rite was held outside the village. Patteson exercised all his influence to prevent one of his converts from being drawn in; and when an old man came up and terrorized his pupils by planting a symbolic tree outside the Mission hut, Patteson argued with him at length and persuaded him to withdraw his threatening symbol. But apart from idolatry, from internecine warfare, and from such horrors as cannibalism, prevalent in many islands, he was studious not to attack old traditions. He wanted a good Melanesian standard of conduct, not a feeble imitation of European culture. He was prepared to build upon the foundation which time had already prepared and not to invert the order of nature.

In writing home of his life in the island Patteson regularly depreciates his own hardships, saying how unworthy he feels himself to be ranked with the pioneers in African work. But the discomforts must often have been considerable to a man naturally fastidious and brought up as he had been.

Food was most monotonous. Meat was out of the question except where the missioners themselves imported live stock and kept a farm of their own; variety of fruit depended also on their own exertions. The staple diet was the yam, a tuber reaching at times in good soil a weight far in excess of the potato. This was supplied readily by the natives in return for European goods, and could be cooked in different ways; but after many weeks' sojourn it was apt to pall. Also the climate was relaxing, and apt sooner or later to tell injuriously on Europeans working there. Dirt, disease, and danger can be faced cheerfully when a man is in good health himself; but a solitary European suffering from ill-health in such conditions is indeed put to an heroic test. Perhaps the greatest discomfort of all was the perpetual living in public. The natives became so fond of Patteson that they flocked round him at all times. His reading was interrupted by a stream of questions; when writing he would find boys standing close to his elbow, following his every movement with attention. The mere writing of letters seems to have been a relief to him, though they could not be answered for so long. His journal, into which he poured freely all his hopes and fears, all his daily anxieties over the Mission, was destined for his family. But he had other correspondents to whom he wrote more or less regularly, especially at Eton and Winchester. At Eton his uncle was one of his most ardent supporters and much of the money which supported the Mission funds came to Patteson through the Eton Association. Near Winchester was living his cousin Charlotte Yonge, the well-known authoress, who afterwards wrote his Life, and through her he established friendly communications with Keble at Hursley and Bishop Moberly, then Head Master of Winchester College. To them he could write sympathetically of Church questions at home, in which he maintained his interest.

During the summer months also, spent near Auckland, Patteson suffered from the want of privacy. At Kohimarana, a small bay facing the entrance to the harbour, to which the school was moved in 1859, he had a tiny room of his own, ten feet square; but the door stood open all day long in fine weather, and he was seldom alone. And when there was sickness among the boys, his own bedroom was sure to be given up to an invalid. But these demands upon his time and comfort he never grudged, while he talks with vexation, and even with asperity, of the people from the town who came out to pay calls and to satisfy their curiosity with a sight of his school. His real friends were few and were partners in his work. The two chief among them were unquestionably Bishop Selwyn, too rarely seen owing to the many claims upon him, and Sir Richard Martin, who had been Chief Justice of the Colony. The latter shared Patteson's taste for philology, and had a wide knowledge of Melanesian dialects.

By the middle of 1860, when Patteson had been five years at work, he became aware that the question of his consecration could not be long delayed. New Zealand was taxing the Primate's strength and he wished to constitute Melanesia a separate diocese. He believed that in Patteson, with his single-minded zeal and special gifts, he had found the ideal man for the post, and in February 1861 the consecration took place. The three bishops who laid hands upon him were, like the Bishop-elect, Etonians;[39] and thus Eton has played a very special part in founding the Melanesian Church. What Patteson thought and felt on this solemn occasion may be seen from the letters which he wrote to his father. The old judge, still living with his daughters at Feniton, had been stricken with a fatal disease, and in the last months of his life he rejoiced to know that his son was counted worthy of his high calling. He died in June 1861 and the news reached his son when cruising at sea a few months later. They had kept up a close correspondence all these years, which he now continued with his sisters; nothing shows better his simple affectionate nature. They are filled mostly with details of his mission life. It was this of which his sisters wanted to hear, and it was this which filled almost entirely his thoughts: though he loved his family and his home, he had put aside all idea of a voyage to England as incompatible with the call to work. To the Mission he gave his time, his strength, his money. Eton supplied him with regular subscriptions, Australia responded to appeals which he made in person and which furnished the only occasions of his leaving the diocese; but, without his devotion of the income coming from his Merton fellowship and from his family inheritance, it would have been impossible for him to carry on the work in the islands.

In his letters written just about the time of his consecration there are abundant references to the qualities which he desired to see in Englishmen who should offer to serve with him. He did not want young men carried away by violent excitement for the moment, eager to make what they called the sacrifice of their lives. The conventional phrases about 'sacrifices' he disliked as much as he did the sensational appeals to which the public had been habituated in missionary meetings. He asked for men of common sense, men who would take trouble over learning languages, men cheerful and healthy in their outlook, 'gentlemen' who could rise above distinctions of class and colour and treat Melanesians as they treated their own friends. Above all, he wanted men who would whole-heartedly accept the system devised by Selwyn, and approved by himself. He could not have the harmony of the Mission upset by people who were eager to originate methods before they had served their apprenticeship. If he could not get the right recruits from England, he says more than once, he would rather depend on the materials existing on the spot: young men from New Zealand would adapt themselves better to the life and he himself would try to remedy any defects in their education. Ultimately he hoped that by careful education and training he would draw his most efficient help from his converts in the islands, and to train them he spared no pains through the remaining ten years of his service.

His way of life was not greatly altered by his consecration. He continued to divide his year between New Zealand and his ocean cruise. He had no body of clergy to space out over his vast diocese or to meet the urgent demands of the islands. In 1863 he received two valuable recruits—one the Rev. R. Codrington, a Fellow of Wadham College, Oxford, who shared the Bishop's literary tastes and proved a valued counsellor; the other a naval man, Lieut. Tilly, who volunteered to take charge of the new schooner called the *Southern Cross*, just sent out to him from England. Till then his staff consisted of three men in holy orders and two younger men who were to be ordained later. One of these, Joseph Atkin, a native of Auckland, proved himself of unique value to the Mission before he was called to share his leader's death. But the Bishop still took upon himself the most dangerous work, the landing at villages where the English were unknown or where the goodwill of the natives seemed to be doubtful. This he accepted as a matter of course, remarking casually in his letters that the others are not good enough swimmers to take his place. But caution was necessary long after the time when friendship had begun. In the interval between visits anything might have happened to render the natives suspicious or revengeful; and it is evident that, month after month, the Bishop carried his life in his hand.

The secret of his power can be found in his letters, which are quite free from heroics. His religion was based on faith, simple and sincere; and he never hesitated to put it into practice. From the Bible, and especially from the New Testament, he learned the central lessons, the love of God and the love of man. Nothing was allowed to come between him and his duty; and to it he devoted the faculties which he had trained. His instinct often stood him in good stead, bidding him to practise caution and to keep at a distance from treacherous snares; but there were times when he felt that, to advance his work, he must show absolute confidence in the natives whatever he suspected, and move freely among them. In such cases he seemed to rise superior to all nervousness or fear. At one time he would find his path back to the boat cut off by natives who did not themselves know whether they intended violence or not. At another he would sit quietly alone in a circle of gigantic Tikopians, some of whom, as he writes, were clutching at his 'little weak arms and shoulders'. 'Yet it is not', he continued, 'a sense of fear, but simply of powerlessness.' No amount of experience could render him safe when he was perpetually trying to open new fields for mission work and when his converts themselves were so liable to unaccountable waves of feeling.

This was proved by his terrible experience at Santa Cruz. He had visited these islands (which lie north of the New Hebrides) successfully in 1862, landing at seven places and seeing over a thousand natives, and he had no reason to expect a different reception when he revisited it in 1864. But on this occasion, after he had swum to land three times and walked freely to and fro among the people, a crowd came down to the water and began shooting at those in the boat from fifteen yards away, while others attacked in canoes. Before the boat could be pulled out of reach, three of its occupants were hit with poisoned arrows, and a few days later two of them showed signs of tetanus, which was almost invariably the result of such wounds. They were young natives of Norfolk Island, for whom the Bishop had conceived a special affection, and their deaths, which were painful to witness, were a very bitter grief to him. The reason for the attack remained unknown. The traditions of Melanesia in the matter of blood-feuds were like those of most savage nations; and under the spur of fear or revenge the islanders were capable of directing their anger blindly against their truest friends.

The most notable development in the first year of Patteson's episcopate was the forming of a solid centre of work in the Banks Islands. Every year, while the Mission ship was cruising, some member of the Mission, often the Bishop himself, would be working steadily in Mota for a succession of months. For visitors there was not much to see. At the beginning, hours were given up to desultory talking with the natives, but perseverance was rewarded. Those who came to talk would return to take lessons, and some impression was gradually made even on the older men attached to their idolatrous rites. Many years after Patteson's death it was still the most civilized of the islands with a population almost entirely Christian.

A greater change was effected in 1867 when the Bishop boldly cut adrift from New Zealand and made his base for summer work at Norfolk Island, lying 800 miles north-east of Sydney.[40] The advantages which it possessed over Auckland were two. Firstly, it was so many hundred miles nearer the centre of the Mission work; secondly, it had a climate much more akin to that of the Melanesian islands and it would be possible to keep pupils here for a longer spell without running such risks to their health. Another point, which to many would seem a drawback, but to Patteson was an additional advantage, was the absence of all distraction. At Auckland the clergy implored him to preach, society importuned him to take part in its gatherings; and if he would not come to the town, they pursued him to his retreat. He was always busy and grudged the loss of his time. A contemporary tells us that he worked from 5 a.m. to 10 p.m. and later; and besides his philological interests, he needed time for his own study of the Bible. In the former he was a pioneer and had to mark out his own path; in the latter he welcomed the guidance of the best scholars whenever he could procure their books. He spoke with delight of his first acquaintance with Lightfoot's edition of St. Paul's Epistles; he wrote home for such new books as would be useful to him, and he read Hebrew daily whenever he could find time. Into this part of his life he put more conscientious effort the older he grew, and was always trying to learn. It may have seemed to many a dull routine to be followed year after year by a man who might have filled high place and moved in brilliant society at home; but from his letters it is clear that he was satisfied with his life and that no thought of regret assailed him.

The year 1868 brought a severe loss when Bishop Selwyn was called home to take charge of the Diocese of Lichfield. It was he who had drawn Patteson to the South Seas: his presence had been an abiding strength to the younger man, however rare their meetings; and Patteson felt his departure as he had felt nothing since his father's death. But he went on unfalteringly with his work, ever ready to look hopefully into the future. At the moment he was intensely interested in the ordination of his first native clergyman, George Sarawia, who had now been a pupil for nine years and had shown sufficient progress in knowledge and strength of character to justify the step. Eager though he was to enrol helpers for the work, Patteson was scrupulously careful to ensure the fitness of his clergy, and to lay hands hastily on no man. In little matters also he was careful and methodical. His scholars in Norfolk Island were expected to be punctual, his helpers to be content with the simple life which contented him. All were to give their work freely; between black and white there was to be equality; no service was to be considered degrading.

He did not wish to hurry his converts into outward observance of European ways. More important than the wearing of clothes was the true respect for the sanctity of marriage; far above the question of Sunday observance was the teaching of the love of God.

Foreign missions have come in for plenty of criticism. It is sometimes said that our missionaries have occasioned strife leading to intervention and annexation by the British Government, and have exposed us abroad to the charge of covetousness and hypocrisy. But there are few instances in which this charge can be maintained, least of all in Australasian waters. A more serious charge, often made in India, is that missioners destroy the sanctions of morality by undermining the traditional beliefs of the natives, and that the convert is neither a good Asiatic nor a passable European. This depends on the methods employed. It may be true in some cases. Patteson fully realized the danger, as we can see from his words, and built carefully on the foundation of native character. He took away no stone till he could replace it by better material. He was never content merely to destroy.

Another set of critics are roused by the extravagance of some missionary meetings and societies: their taste is offended or (we are bound to admit) their sense of humour roused. It was time for Dickens to wield this weapon when he heard Chadbands pouring forth their oily platitudes and saw Mrs. Jellybys neglecting their own children to clothe the offspring of 'Borrioboola Gha'. Such folly caught the critic's eye when the steady benevolence of others, unnoticed, was effecting work which had a good influence equally at home and abroad. Against the fanciful picture of Mrs. Jellyby let us put the life-story of Charlotte Yonge, who, while discharging every duty to her family and her village, in a way which won their lasting affection, was able to put aside large sums from the earnings of her pen to supply the needs of the Melanesian Mission.

Let us remember, too, that much of the bitterest criticism has come from those who have a direct interest in suppressing missions, who have made large profits in remote places by procedure which will not bear the light of day. Patteson would have been content to justify his work by his Master's bidding as quoted in the Gospel. His friends would have been content to claim that the actual working of the Mission should be examined. If outside testimony to the value of his work is wanted, one good instance will refute a large amount of idle calumny. Sir George Grey, no sentimentalist but the most practical ruler of New Zealand, gave his own money to get three native boys, chosen by himself, educated at Patteson's school, and was fully satisfied with the result.

But this simple regular life was soon to be perturbed by new complications, which rose from the European settlers in Fiji. As their plantations increased, the need for labour became urgent and the Melanesian islands were drawn upon to supply it. In many ways Patteson felt that it was good for the Melanesians to be trained to agricultural work; but the trouble was that they were being deceived over the conditions of the undertaking. Open kidnapping and the revival of anything like a slave trade could hardly be practised under the British flag at this time; nor indeed did the Fiji settlers, in most cases, wish to do anything unfair or brutal. It was to be a matter of contracts, voluntarily signed by the workmen; but the Melanesian was not educated up to the point where he could appreciate what a contract meant. When they did begin to understand, many were unwilling to sign for a period long enough to be useful; many more grew quickly tired of the work, changed their mind and broke their engagements. As the trade grew, some islands were entirely depopulated, and it became necessary to visit others, where the natives refused to engage themselves. The trade was in jeopardy; but the captains of merchant vessels, who found it very lucrative, were determined that the supply of hands should not run short. So when they met with no volunteers, they used to cajole the islanders on board ship under pretence of trade and then kidnap them; when this procedure led to affrays, they were not slow to shoot. The confidence of the native in European justice was shaken, and the work of years was undone. Security on both sides was gone, and the missionary, who had been sure of a welcome for ten years, might find himself in face of a population burning with the desire to revenge themselves on the first white man who came within their reach.

Patteson did all that he could, in co-operation with the local officials, to regulate the trade. There was no case for a crusade against the Fiji planters, who were doing good work in a humane way and were ignorant of the misdeeds practised in Melanesia. The best method was to forbid unauthorized vessels to pursue the trade and to put the authorized vessels under supervision; but, to effect this in an outlying part of the vast British Empire, it was necessary to educate opinion and to work through Whitehall. This he set himself to do; but meanwhile he was so distressed to find the islanders slipping out of his reach, that in the last months of his life he was planning a campaign in Fiji, where he intended to visit several of the plantations in turn and to carry to the expatriated workers the Gospel which he had hoped to preach to them in their homes.

But before he could redress this wrong he was himself destined to fall a victim to the spirit of hostility evoked. His best work was already done when in 1870 he had a prolonged illness, and was forced to spend some months at Auckland for convalescence. In the judgement of his friends his exertions had aged him considerably, and the climate had contributed to break down his strength. Though he was back at work again before the end of the summer he was far more subject to weariness. His manner became peaceful and dreamy, and his companions found that it was difficult to rouse him in the ordinary interchange of talk. His thoughts recurred more often to the past; he would write of Devonshire and its charms in spring, read over familiar passages in Wordsworth, or fall into quiet meditation, yet he would not unbuckle his armour or think of leaving the Mission in order to take a holiday in England.

In April 1871, when the time came for him to leave Norfolk Island for his annual cruise, his energy revived. He spent seven weeks at Mota, leaving it towards the end of August to sail for the Santa Cruz group. On September 20, as he came in sight of the coral reef of Nukapu, he was speaking to his scholars of the death of St. Stephen. Next morning he had the boat lowered and put off for shore accompanied by Mr. Atkin and three natives. He knew that feeling had lately become embittered in this district over the Labour trade, but the thought of danger did not shake his resolution. To show his confidence and disarm suspicion he entered one of the canoes, alone with the islanders, landed on the beach and disappeared among the crowd. Half an hour later, for no apparent reason, an attack was started by men in canoes on the boat lying close off the shore; and before the rowers could pull out of range, Joseph Atkin and two of the natives had been wounded by poisoned arrows which, some days later, set up tetanus with fatal effect. They reached the ship; but after a few hours, when their wounds had been treated, Mr. Atkin insisted on taking the boat in again to learn the Bishop's fate. This time no attack was made upon them; but a canoe was towed out part of the way and then left to drift towards the boat. In it was the dead body of the Bishop tied up in a native mat. How he died no one ever knew, but his face was calm and no anguish seems to have troubled him in the hour of death. 'The placid smile was still on the face: there was a palm leaf fastened over the breast, and, when the mat was opened, there were five wounds, no more. The strange mysterious beauty, as it may be called, of the circumstances almost make one feel as if this were the legend of a martyr of the Primitive Church.'[41]

Miss Yonge, from whom these lines are quoted, goes on to show that the five wounds, of which the first probably proved fatal, while the other four were deliberately inflicted afterwards, were to be explained by native custom. In the long leaflets of the palm five knots had been tied. Five men in Fiji were known to have been stolen from this island, and there can be little doubt that the relatives were exacting, in native fashion, their vengeance from the first European victim who fell into their power. The Bishop would have been the first to make allowance for their superstitious error and to lay the blame in the right quarter. His surviving comrades knew this, and in reporting the tragedy they sent a special petition that the Colonial Office would not order a bombardment of the island. Unfortunately, when a ship was sent on a mission of inquiry, the natives themselves began hostilities and bloodshed ensued. But at last the Bishop had by his death secured what he was labouring in his life to effect. The Imperial Parliament was stirred to examine the Labour trade in the Pacific and regulations were enforced which put an end to the abuse.

'Quae caret ora cruore nostro?' The Roman poet puts this question in his horror at the wide extension of the civil wars which stained with Roman blood all the seas known to the world of his day.

Great Britain has its martyrs in a nobler warfare yet more widely spread. Not all have fallen by the weapons of war. Nature has claimed many victims through disease or the rigour of unknown climes. The death of some is a mystery to this day. India, the Soudan, South and West Africa, the Arctic and Antarctic regions, speak eloquently to the men of our race of the spirit which carried them so far afield in the nineteenth century. Thanks to its first bishop, the Church of Melanesia shares their fame, opening its history with a glorious chapter enriched by heroism, self-sacrifice, and martyrdom.

SIR ROBERT MORIER
From a drawing by William Richmond

SIR ROBERT D. B. MORIER, G.C.B., P.C.

1826-93

1826. Born at Paris, March 31.

1832-9. Childhood in Switzerland.

1839-44. With private tutors.

1845-9. Balliol College, Oxford.

1850. Clerk in Education Office.

1853. Attaché at Vienna Embassy.

1858. Attaché at Berlin.

1861. Marriage with Alice, daughter of General Jonathan Peel.

1865. Commissioner at Vienna. Commercial Treaty. C.B. Chargé d'Affaires at Frankfort.

1866-71. Chargé d'Affaires at Darmstadt.

1870. Tour in Alsace to test national feeling.

1871. Chargé d'Affaires at Stuttgart.

1872-6. Chargé d'Affaires at Munich.

1875. Danger of second Franco-German War.

1876. Minister at Lisbon.

1881. Minister at Madrid. 1882. K.C.B.

1884. Bismarck vetoes Morier as Ambassador to Berlin.

1885-93. Ambassador at St. Petersburg.

1886. Bulgaria, Batum, and Black Sea troubles.

1887. G.C.B. 1889. D.C.L., Oxford.

1891. Appointed Ambassador at Rome: retained at St. Petersburg.

1893. Death at Montreux. Funeral at Batchworth.

ROBERT MORIER

Diplomatist

Diplomacy as a profession is a product of modern history. As Europe emerged from the Middle Ages, the dividing walls between State and State were broken down, and Governments found it necessary to have trained agents resident at foreign courts to conduct the questions of growing importance which arose between them. Churchmen were at first best qualified to undertake such duties, and Nicholas Wotton, Dean of Canterbury, who enjoyed the confidence of four Tudor sovereigns, came to be as much at home in France or in the Netherlands as he was in his own Deanery. It was his great nephew Sir Henry (who began his days as a scholar at Winchester, and ended them as Provost at Eton) who did his profession a notable disservice by indulging his humour at Augsburg when acting as envoy for James I, defining the diplomatist as 'one who was sent to lie abroad for his country'.[42] Since then many a politician and writer has let fly his shafts at diplomacy, and fervent democrats have come to regard diplomats as veritable children of the devil. But this prejudice is chiefly due to ignorance, and can easily be cured by a patient study of history. In the nineteenth century, in particular, English diplomacy can point to a noble roll of ambassadors, who worked for European peace as well as for the triumph of liberal causes, and none has a higher claim to such praise than Sir Robert Morier, the subject of this sketch.

The traditions of his family marked out his path in life. We can trace their origin to connexions in the Consular service at Smyrna, where Isaac Morier met and married Clara van Lennep in the latter half of the eighteenth century. Swiss grandfather and Dutch grandmother became naturalized subjects of the British Crown and brought up four sons to win distinction in its service. Of these the third, David, married a daughter of Robert Burnet Jones—a descendant of the famous Bishop Burnet, and himself a servant of the Crown—and held important diplomatic appointments for over thirty years at Paris and Berne. So it was that his only son Robert David Burnet Morier was born in France, spent much of his childhood in Switzerland, and acquired early in life a remarkable facility in speaking foreign languages. To his schooling in England he seems to have owed little of positive value. His father and uncles had been sent to Harrow; but perhaps it was as well that the son did not, in this, follow in his father's footsteps. However much he neglected his studies with two easy-going tutors, he preserved his freshness and originality and ran no danger of being drilled into a type. If he had as a boy undue self-confidence, no one was better fitted to correct it than his mother, a woman of wide sympathies and strong intellectual force. The letters which passed between them display, on his part, mature powers of expression at an early age, and show the generous, affectionate nature of both; and till her death in 1855 she remained his chief confidante and counsellor. In trying to matriculate at Balliol College he met with a momentary check, due to the casual nature of his education; but, after retrieving this, he rapidly made good his deficiency in Greek and Latin, and ended by taking a creditable degree. His time at Oxford, apart from reading, was well spent. He made special friends with two of the younger dons: Temple, afterwards Archbishop of Canterbury, and Jowett, the future Master of Balliol. The former was carried by rugged force and sheer ability to the highest position in the Church; the latter won a peculiar place, in Oxford and in the world outside, by his gifts of judging character and stimulating intellectual interest. Morier became his favourite pupil and lifelong friend. F. T. Palgrave, the friend of both, tells us how 'Morier went up to Balliol a lax and imperfectly educated fellow; but Jowett, seeing his great natural capacity, took him in the Long Vacation of 1848 and practically "converted" him to the doctrine of work. This was the turning-point in Morier's life.' Together the two friends spent many a holiday in Germany, Scotland, and elsewhere, and must have presented a strange contrast to one another: Jowett, small, frail, quiet and precise in manner, Morier big in every way, exuberant and full of vitality. It was with Jowett and Stanley (afterwards Dean of Westminster) that Morier went to Paris in 1848, eager to study the Revolutionary spirit in its most lively manifestations. Stanley describes him as 'a Balliol undergraduate of gigantic size, who speaks French better than English, is to wear a blouse, and to go about disguised to the clubs'.

He took his degree in November 1849, and a month later he was visiting Dresden and Berlin, making German friends and initiating himself in German politics and German ways of thought. Though his British patriotism was fervid and sustained, he was capable of understanding men of other nations and recognizing their merits; and in knowledge of Germany he acquired a position among Englishmen of his day rivalled only by Odo Russell, afterwards Ambassador at Berlin. Morier's father had for many years represented Great Britain in Switzerland and could guide him both by precept and by example. Free intercourse with the most liberal minds in Oxford had developed the lessons which he had learnt at home. But his own energy and application effected more than anything. He was not satisfied till he had mastered a problem; and books, places, and people were laid under contribution unsparingly. He started on his tour carrying letters of introduction to some of the famous men in Germany, including the great traveller and scientist, Alexander von Humboldt. Of a younger generation was the philologist Max Müller, who was a frequent companion of Morier in Berlin, and gave up his time to nursing him back to health when he was taken ill with quinsy. He found friends in all professions, but chiefly among politicians. A typical instance is von Roggenbach, who rose to be Premier of Baden in the years 1861 to 1865, when the destinies of Germany were in the melting-pot. Baden was in some ways the leading state in South Germany at that time, combining liberal ideals with a fervent advocacy of national union, and the views of Roggenbach on political questions attracted Morier's warmest sympathy. Another state in which Morier felt genuinely at home was the Duchy of Coburg, from which Prince Albert had come to wed our own Queen Victoria. The Prince's brother, the reigning Duke, treated Morier as a personal friend; and here, too, he found Baron Stockmar, a Nestor among German Liberals, who had spent his political life in trying to promote goodwill between England and Germany. He received Morier into his family circle and adopted him as the heir to his policy. This intimacy led to further results; and, thanks in part to Morier's subsequent friendship with the Crown Prince and Princess of Prussia, generous ideals and a liberal spirit were to be found surviving in a few places even after 1870, though Bismarck had poisoned the minds of a whole generation by the material successes which he achieved.

In 1849 the doors of the Foreign Office were closed to Morier. The Secretary of State, Lord Palmerston, had treated his father unfairly, as he thought, some years before, and Morier would ask no favours of him. He continued his education, keeping in close touch with Jowett and Temple, and, when he saw a chance of studying politics at first hand, he eagerly availed himself of it. The troubles of Schleswig-Holstein, too intricate to be explained briefly, had been brewing for some time. In 1850, the dispute, to which Prussia, Denmark, and the German Diet were all parties, came to a head. The Duchies were overrun by Prussian troops, while the Danish Navy held the sea. Morier rushed off to see for himself what was happening, and spent some interesting days at Kiel, talking to those who could instruct him, and forming his own judgement. This was adverse to the wisdom of the Copenhagen Radicals, who were trying to assert by force their supremacy over a German population. In the circumstances, as Prussia gave way to the wishes of other powers, no satisfactory decision could be reached; but ten years later the issue was in the ruthless hands of Bismarck, and was settled by 'blood and iron'.

In 1850 Morier accepted a clerkship in the Education Office at £120 a year. The work was not to his taste, but at least it was public service, and he saw no hope of employment in the Foreign Office. He found some distractions in London society. He kept up relations with his old friends, and he took a leading part in establishing the Cosmopolitan Club, which later met in Watts's studio, but began its existence in Morier's own rooms. He enjoyed greatly a meeting with Tennyson and Browning, and wrote with enthusiasm of the former to his father, as 'one who gave men an insight into the real Hero-world, as one from whom he could catch reflected something of the Divine'. But Morier's spirits were mercurial, and between moments of elation he was apt to fall into fits of melancholy, when he could find no outlet for his energies. Waiting for his true profession tried him sorely, and he was even resigning himself to the prospect of a visit to Australia as a professional journalist, when fortune at last smiled upon him. Palmerston retired from the Foreign Office, and when Clarendon succeeded him, Morier's name was placed on the list of candidates for an attachéship. At Easter 1853 he started for another visit to the Continent, full of hope and more than ever determined to qualify himself for the profession which he loved.

He was rewarded for his zeal a few weeks later, when he paid a visit to Vienna, won the favour of the Ambassador, Lord Westmorland, and was commended to the Foreign Office. At the age of twenty-seven he was appointed to serve Her Majesty as unpaid attaché, having already acquired a knowledge of European politics which many men of sixty would have envied. In figure he was tall, with a tendency already manifested to put on flesh, good-looking, genial and sympathetic in manner, a *bon vivant*, passionately fond of dancing and society, an excellent talker or listener as the occasion demanded. His intelligence was quick, his powers of handling details and of grasping broad principles were alike remarkable. He wrote with ease, clearness, and precision; he knew what hard work meant and revelled in it. Unfortunately he was subject already to rheumatic gout, which was to make him acquainted with many watering-places, and was to handicap him gravely in later life. But at present nothing could check his ardour in his profession, and during his five years at Vienna he took every chance of studying foreign lands and of making acquaintance with the chief figures in the diplomatic world. He enjoyed talks with Baron Jellaçiç, who had saved the monarchy in 1848, and with Prince Metternich, whose political career ended in that year of revolutions and who was now only a figure in society. After the Crimean War Morier obtained permission to make a tour through South-east Hungary and to study for himself the mixture of Slavonic, Magyar, and Teutonic races inhabiting that district. He followed this up by another tour of three months, which carried him from Agram southwards into Bosnia and Herzegovina, having prepared for it by working ten to twelve hours a day for some weeks at the language of the southern Slavs. Incidentally he enjoyed some hunting expeditions with Turkish pashas, and obtained some insight into the weakness of the British consular system. All his life he believed strongly in the value of such tours to obtain first-hand information; and thirty years later, as Ambassador, he encouraged his secretaries to familiarize themselves with the outlying districts of the Russian empire.

In 1858, at the age of thirty-two, Morier passed from Vienna to Berlin. It was the year in which the Princess Royal, the eldest daughter of Queen Victoria, married the Crown Prince of Prussia.[43] Her father, the Prince Consort, was very anxious that Morier should be at hand to advise the young couple, and the appointment to Berlin was his work. Then it was that Morier became involved in the struggle between Bismarck and the Liberal influences in Germany, which had no stronger rallying-point than the Coburg Court. This conflict only showed itself later, and at first the young English attaché must have seemed a sufficiently unimportant person; but before 1862 Bismarck, coming home to Berlin from the St. Petersburg Embassy, and discerning the nature of Morier's character, had declared that it was desirable to remove such an influence from the path of his party, who were determined to bring Liberal Germany under the yoke of a Prussia which had no sympathy for democratic ideals.

For the moment the ship of State was hanging in the wind; light currents of air were perceptible; sails were filling in one parliamentary boat or another; but the chief movement was to be seen not in parliamentary circles but in the excellent civil service, which preserved that honesty and efficiency which it had acquired in the days of Stein. There were marked tendencies towards Liberalism and towards unification in different parts of Germany; and, if the Liberal party could have produced one man of firmness and decision, these forces might have triumphed over the reactionary Prussian clique. In this conflict Morier was bound to be a passionate sympathiser with the parties which included so many of his personal friends and which advocated principles so dear to his heart. With the triumph of his friends, too, were associated the prospects of a good understanding between England and Germany, for which Morier himself was labouring; and he was accused of having meddled indiscreetly with local politics. When King William broke with the Liberals over the Army Bill, caution was doubly necessary. Bismarck became Minister in 1862, and, great man though he was, he was capable of any pettiness when he had once declared war on an opponent. From that time the policy of working for an Anglo-Prussian *entente* was a losing game, not only because Bismarck detested the parliamentarism which he associated with England, but also because, on our side too, extremists were stirring up ill-feeling. In his letters Morier makes frequent reference to the 'John Bullishness' of *The Times*. When this journal, to which European importance attached during the editorship of Delane, was not openly flouting Prussia, it was displaying reckless ignorance of a people who were making the most solid contributions to learning and raising themselves by steady industry from the losses due to centuries of Continental warfare.

From time to time he paid visits to friends at Dresden, at Baden, and elsewhere. One year he was sent to Naples on a special mission, another year he was summoned to attend on Queen Victoria, who was visiting Coburg. In 1859 he is lamenting the monotony of existence at Berlin, which he calls 'a Dutch mud canal of a life, without even the tulip beds on the banks'. But when later in that year Lord John Russell, who knew and appreciated his talents, became Foreign Secretary and called on him for frequent reports on important subjects, Morier found solace in work. He was only too willing to put his wide knowledge of the country in which he was serving at the disposal of his superiors at home. He wrote with equal ability on political, agrarian, and financial subjects. That he could take into account the personal factor is shown by the long letter which he wrote in 1861 to Sir Henry Layard, then Political Under-Secretary of State.[44] It contained a masterly analysis of the character and upbringing of King William, showing how his intellectual narrowness had hampered Liberal Governments, while his professional training in the army had made him a most efficient instrument in promoting the aims of Junker politicians and ministers of war.

On Schleswig-Holstein, above all, Morier exerted himself to convey a right view of the question to those who guided opinion in London, whether newspaper editors or responsible ministers. He appealed to the same principle which had won support for the Lombards against Austria. The inhabitants of the disputed Duchies were for the most part Germans, and the Danish Government had done violence to their national sentiment. If England could have extended its sympathy to its northern kinsmen in time, the question might have been settled peacefully before 1862, and Bismarck could never have availed himself of such a lever to overthrow his Liberal opponents. As it was, Prussia ignored the Danish sympathies displayed abroad, especially in the English press, went her own way and invaded the Duchies, dragging in her train Austria, her confederate and her dupe. Palmerston, who controlled our foreign policy at the time, waited till the last moment, blustered, found himself impotent to move without French support, and left Denmark smarting with a sense of betrayal which lasted till 1914. By such bungling Morier knew that we were incurring enmity on both sides and lowering our reputation for courage as well as for statesmanship.

In 1865 he was chosen as one of the Special Commissioners to negotiate a treaty of commerce between Great Britain and Austria. He had always been a Free-trader, and he was convinced that such economic agreements could do much to improve the world and to strengthen the bonds of peace. So he was ready and willing to do hard work in this sphere, and finding a congenial colleague in Sir Louis Mallet, one of the best economists of the day, he spent some months at Vienna in fruitful activity and won the good opinion of all associated with him. For his services he received the C.B. and high commendation from London.

This same year brought promotion in rank, though for long it was uncertain where he would go. In August he accepted the offer of First Secretary to the Legation in Japan, most reluctantly, because he saw his peculiar knowledge of Germany would be wasted there. Ten days later this offer was changed for a similar position at the Court of Greece, which was equally uncongenial; but at the end of the year the Foreign Office decided that he would be most useful in the field which he had chosen for himself, and after a few months at Frankfort he was sent in the year 1866 as chargé d'affaires to the Grand Ducal Court of Hesse-Darmstadt.

From these posts he was destined to be a spectator of the two great conflicts by which Bismarck established the union of North Germany and its primacy in Europe. Morier detested the means by which this end was achieved, but he had consistently maintained that this union ought to be, and could only be, achieved by Prussia, and he remained true to his beliefs. It is a great tribute to his intellectual force that he was able to control his personal sympathies and antipathies, and to judge passing events with reference to the past and the future. He had liked the statesmen whom he had met at Vienna, and he recognized their good faith in the difficult negotiations of 1865. But for the good of Europe, he thought the Austrian Government should now look eastwards. It could not do double work at Vienna and at Frankfort. The impotence of the Frankfort Diet could be cured only by the North Germans, and the aspirations of good patriots, from Baden to the Baltic, had been for long directed towards Prussia. But it was no easy task to make people in England realize the justice of this view or the certainty that Prussia was strong enough to carry through the work. Led by *The Times*, the British Press had grown accustomed to use a contemptuous tone towards Prussia; and when in the decisive hour this could no longer be maintained, and British sentiment, as is its nature, declared for Austria as the beaten side, this sentiment was attributed at Berlin to the basest envy. Relations between the two peoples steadily grew worse during these years, despite the efforts of Morier and other friends of peace.

The Franco-German war brought even greater bitterness between Prussia and Great Britain. The neutrality, which the latter power observed, was misunderstood in both camps; and the position of a British diplomat abroad became really unpleasant. Morier in particular, as a marked man, knew that he was subject to spying and misrepresentation, but this did not deter him from doing his duty and more than his duty. He took measures to safeguard those dependent on him, in case Hesse came into the theatre of war. He organized medical aid for the wounded on both sides. He took a journey in September into Alsace and Lorraine to ascertain the feeling of the inhabitants, that he might give the best possible advice to his Government if the cession of these districts became a European question. He came to the conclusion that Alsace was not a homogeneous unit—that language, religion, and sentiment varied in different districts, and that it was desirable to work for a compromise. But Bismarck was determined in 1870, as in 1866, that the settlement should remain in his own hands and that no European congress should spoil his plans. Morier found that he was being talked of at Berlin as 'the enemy of Prussia', and atrocious calumnies were circulated. One of these was revived some years later when Bismarck wished to discredit him, and Bismarckian journals accused him of having betrayed to Marshal Bazaine military secrets which he discovered in Hesse. Morier obtained from the Marshal a letter which clearly refuted the charge, and he gave it the widest publicity. The plot recoiled on its author, and Morier was spoken of in France as 'le grand ambassadeur qui a roulé Bismarck'. Yet all the while, with his wife a strong partisan of France, with six cousins fighting in the French Army, with his friends in England only too ready to quarrel with him for his supposed pro-German sentiments, he was appealing for fair judgement, for reason, for a wise policy which should soften the bitterness of the settlement between victors and vanquished. Facts must be recognized, he pleaded, and the French claim for peculiar consideration and their traditional *amour propre* must not be allowed to prolong the miseries of war. At the same time Morier did not close his eyes to the danger arising from the overwhelming victories of the German armies. No one saw more clearly the deterioration which was taking place in German character, or depicted it in more trenchant terms. But it was his business to work for the future and not to let sentiment bring fresh disasters upon Europe.

Apart from this critical period, life at Darmstadt bored him considerably. His presence there was valued highly by Queen Victoria, one of whose daughters had married the Grand Duke; but Morier felt himself to be in a backwater, far from the main stream of European politics, and society there was dull. So he welcomed in 1871 his transference first to Stuttgart, and a few months later to Munich, the capital of the second state in the new Empire and a great centre of literary culture. Here lived Dr. Döllinger, historian and divine, a man suspected at Rome for his liberal Catholicism even before his definite severance from the Roman Church, but honoured everywhere else for the width and depth of his knowledge. With him Morier enjoyed many conversations on Church councils and other subjects which interested them both; and in 1874, lured by the prospect of such society, Gladstone paid him a visit of ten days. Morier did not admire Gladstone's conduct of foreign policy, but he was open-minded enough to recognize his great gifts and to enjoy his company, and he writes home with enthusiasm about his conversational powers. A still more welcome visitor in 1873 was Jowett, his old Oxford friend, who never lost his place in Morier's affections.

Among these delights he retained his vigilance in political matters, and there was often need for it, since the German Government was now developing that habit of 'rattling its sword', and threatening its neighbours with war, which disquieted Europe for another forty years. The worst crisis came in 1875, when Morier heard on good authority that the military clique at Berlin were gaining ground, and seemed likely to persuade the Emperor William to force on a second war, expressly to prevent France recovering its strength.

In general the credit for checking this sinister move is given to the Tsar; but English influences played a large part in the matter. Morier managed to catch the Crown Prince on his way south to Italy and had a long talk with him in the railway train. The Crown Prince was known to be a true lover of peace, but capable of being hoodwinked by Bismarck; once convinced that the danger was real (and he trusted Morier as he trusted no German in his entourage), he returned to Berlin and threw all his weight into the scale of peace. Queen Victoria also wrote from London; and, in face of a possible coalition against them, the Germans decided that it was wisest to abstain from all aggression.

A new period opened in his life when he left German courts, never to return officially, and became the responsible head of Her Majesty's Legation at the Portuguese Court. His five years spent at Lisbon cannot be counted as one of his most fruitful periods, despite 'the large settlement of African affairs', which Lord Granville tells us that Morier had suggested to his predecessors in Whitehall. For the big schemes which he planned he could get no continuous backing at home, either in political or commercial circles. For the petty routine England hardly needed a man of such outstanding ability. Of necessity his work consisted often in tedious investigation of claims advanced by individual Englishmen, whether they were suffering from money losses or from summary procedure at the hands of the Portuguese police. Of the diplomatic questions which arose many proved to be shadowy and unreal. Something could be done, even in remote Portugal, to improve Anglo-Russian relations by a minister who had friends in so many European capitals. The politics of Pio Nono and the Papal Curia often find an echo in his correspondence. Here, too, as elsewhere, the intrigues of Germany had to be watched, though Morier was sensible enough to discriminate between the deliberate policy of Bismarck and the manœuvres of those whom he 'allowed to do what they liked and say what they liked—or rather to do what they thought *he* would like done, and say what they thought *he* would like said—and then suddenly sent them about their business to ponder in poverty and disgrace on the mutability of human affairs'. In a passage like this Morier's letters show that he could distinguish between a lion and his jackals, between 'policy' and 'intrigue'.

Had it not been for Germany and German suggestions, Portuguese politicians would perhaps have been free from the fears which loomed darkest on their horizon—the fears of an 'Iberian policy' which Spain was supposed to be pursuing. In reality the leading men at Madrid knew that they had little to gain by letting loose the superior Spanish army against Portugal and trying to form the whole peninsula into a single state. Morier, at any rate, made it clear that England would throw the whole weight of her power against such treatment of her oldest ally. But alarmist politicians were perpetually harping on this string, and Morier, in a letter written in 1876, compares them to 'children telling ghost-stories to one another who have got frightened at the sound of their own voices, and mistake the rattling of a mouse behind the wainscot for the tramping of legions on the march'.

To Morier it seemed that the important part of his work concerned South Africa, in which, at the time, Portugal and Great Britain were the European powers most interested. It was in 1877 that Sir Theophilus Shepstone annexed the Transvaal, and many people, in Europe and Africa, were talking as if this must lead to the expropriation of the Portuguese at Delagoa Bay. Morier himself was as far as possible from the imperialism which would ride rough-shod over a weaker neighbour. In fact, he pleaded strongly for British approval of the pride which Portugal felt in her traditions and of her desire to cling to what she had preserved from the past. Once break this down, he said, and we should see Portuguese dominions put up for auction, and England might not always prove to be the highest bidder. Friendly co-operation, joint development of railways, and commercial treaties commended themselves better to his judgement, and he was prepared to spend a large part even of his holidays in England in working out the details of such treaties. He studied the people among whom he was, and did his best to lead them gently towards reforms, whether of the slave-trade or other abuses, on lines which could win their sympathy. He appealed to his own Foreign Office to abstain from too many lectures, and to make the most of cases in which the Portuguese showed promise of better things. 'This diet of cold gruel', he says in 1878, 'must be occasionally supplemented by a cup of generous wine, or all intimacy must die out.' Again in 1880, he asks for a K.C.M.G. to be awarded to a Governor-General of Mozambique, who had done his best to observe English wishes in checking the slave-trade. 'Perpetual admonition', he says, 'and no sugar plums is bad policy'—a maxim too often neglected when our philanthropy outruns our discretion.

When Morier was promoted in 1881 to Madrid, he used the same tact and geniality to lighten the burden of his task. No seasoned diplomatist took the politics of Madrid too seriously. Though the political stage was bigger, it was often filled by actors as petty and grasping as those of Lisbon. The distribution to their own friends of the 'loaves and fishes' was, as Morier says, the one steady aim of all aspirants to power; and measures of reform, much needed in education, in commerce, in law, were doomed to sterility by the factiousness of the men who should have carried them out. In the absence of principles Morier had to study the strife of parties, and his correspondence gives us lively pictures of the eloquent Castelar, the champion of a visionary Republic, the harsh, domineering Romero y Robledo, at once the mainstay and the terror of his Conservative colleagues, and the cold, egotistic Liberal leader Sagasta, whose shrewdness in the manipulation of votes had always to be reckoned with. The constitution given in 1876 had entirely failed to establish Parliament on a democratic basis. For this the bureaucracy was responsible. The Home Office abused its powers shamelessly, and by the votes of its functionaries, and of those who hoped to receive its favours, it could always secure a big majority for the Government of the moment. For the three years which Morier spent at Madrid, he recounts surprising instances of the reversal of electoral verdicts within a short space of time.

The King was popular and deserved to be so, for his personal qualities of courage, intelligence, and public spirit; but his position was never secure. There was a bad tradition by which at intervals the army asserted its power and upset the constitution. Some intriguing general issued a *pronunciamiento*, the troops revolted, and the Central Government at Madrid, having no effective force and no moral ascendancy, gave way. Parliament had little stability. Cabinets rose and vanished again; the same eloquent but empty speeches were made, and the same abuses remained unchanged.

But before now a spark from Spain had set the Continent ablaze. The past had bequeathed some questions which, awkwardly handled, might cause explosions elsewhere, and it was well to know the character of those who had the key to the powder magazine. More than once Morier was approached on the delicate question of the admission of Spain to the council of the Great Powers. In Egypt, where so many foreign interests were involved, and where Great Britain suffered, in the 'eighties, from so many diplomatic intrigues, Spain might easily find an opening for her ambitions. She might advance the plea that the Suez Canal was the direct route to her colonies in the Philippines. Germany, for ulterior ends, was encouraging Spanish pretensions; but, to the British, Spain with its illiberal spirit scarcely seemed likely to prove a helpful fellow-worker. Morier had to try to convince Spanish ministers that Great Britain was their truer friend while refusing them what they asked for; and in such interviews he had to know his men and to touch the right chord in appealing to their prejudices or their patriotism. The English tenure of Gibraltar was also a perpetual offence to Spanish pride. Irresponsible journalists loved to expatiate on it when they had no more spicy subject to handle. On this, as on all questions affecting prestige only, Morier was tactful and patient. When they should come within the range of practical politics, he could take a different tone. But he knew that more serious dangers were arising in Morocco, where the weakness of the Sultan's rule was tempting European powers to intervene, and he laboured to maintain peace and goodwill not only between his own country and Spain, but also between Spain and France. The common accusation that the English are not 'good Europeans' was pre-eminently untrue in his case. He realized that the interests of all were bound up together, and used his influence, which soon became considerable, to remove all occasions of bitterness in the European family, being fully aware that at Berlin there was another active intelligence working by hidden channels to keep open every festering sore.

Morier was fertile in expedients when ministers consulted him, as we see notably on the occasion of King Alfonso's tour in 1883. Before the King started, the newspapers had been writing of it as a 'visit to Berlin', though it was intended to be a compliment to the heads of various states. To allay the sensitiveness of the French, Morier suggested to the Foreign Secretary that the King should make a point of visiting France first; but, owing to the ineptitude of President Grévy, this suggestion was rendered impracticable. When the King did visit Paris, after a sojourn at Berlin, where he received the usual compliment of being made titular colonel of a Prussian regiment, a terrible scene ensued by which Morier's sagacity was justified. The King was greeted with cries of 'à bas le Colonel d'Uhlans', and was hissed as he passed along the streets; only his personal tact and restraint saved the two Governments from an undignified squabble. He was able to give a lesson in deportment to his hosts and also to satisfy the resentful pride of his fellow-countrymen. The whole episode shows how individuals can control events when the masses can only become excited; kings and diplomats may still be the best mechanics to handle the complicated machinery on which peace or war depends. Alfonso XII died in November 1885, soon after Morier's departure for another post, but not before he had testified to the high esteem in which our Minister had been held in Spain.

From Madrid he might have passed to Berlin. The British Government had only one man fit to replace Lord Ampthill (Lord Odo Russell), who died in 1884. Inquiries were made in Berlin whether it was possible to employ Morier's great knowledge at the centre of European gravity, but Bismarck made it quite clear that such an appointment would be displeasing to his sovereign. It was believed by a friend and admirer of both men that, if Bismarck and Morier could have come to know one another, mutual respect and liking would have followed; but magnanimity towards an old enemy, or one whom he had ever believed to be such, was not a Bismarckian trait, and it is more probable that all Morier's efforts would have been thwarted by misrepresentation and malignity.

Instead he was sent to St. Petersburg, where he took up his duties as Ambassador in November 1885. Here he had to deal with bigger problems. The affray at Penjdeh, when the Russians attacked an Afghān outpost and forcibly occupied the ground, had, after convulsing Europe, been settled by Mr. Gladstone's Government. Feeling did not subside for some years, but for the moment Asiatic questions were not so serious as the conflict of interests in the Balkan peninsula. The principality of Bulgaria created by the Congress of Berlin was the focus of the 'Eastern question'—that is, the question whether Russia, Austria, or a united Europe led by the Western powers, was to preside over the dissolution of Turkey. Bulgaria certainly owed its existence to Russian bayonets; in her cause Russian lives had been freely given; and this formed a real bond between the two nations, more lasting than the effect of Mr. Gladstone's speeches, to which English sentimentalists attached such importance. But the Bulgarians have often shown an obstinate tendency to go their own way, and their politicians were loath to be kept in Russian leading-strings. Their last act, in 1885, had been to annex the Turkish province of Eastern Roumelia without asking the consent of the Tsar. At the moment they could safely flout the Sultan of Turkey, their nominal suzerain; but diplomatists doubted whether they could, with equal safety, ignore the Treaty of Berlin and the wishes of their Russian protector. The path was full of pitfalls. The Austrian Government was on the watch to embarrass its great Slavonic rival; English statesmen were too anxious to humour Liberal sentiment as expressed at popular meetings; Russian agents on the spot committed indiscretions; Russian opinion at home suspected that Bulgaria was receiving encouragement elsewhere, and the air was full of rumours of war.

Across this unquiet stage may be seen to pass, in the lively letters which Morier sent home, the figures of potential and actual princes of Bulgaria, of whom only two deserve mention to-day. The first, Alexander of Battenberg, member of a family which enjoyed Queen Victoria's special favour, had been put forward at the Berlin Congress, and justified his choice in 1885 by repelling the Serbian Army and winning a victory at Slivnitza. He had won the attachment of his subjects but had incurred the hatred of the Tsar, and the tone of his speeches in 1886 offended Russian sentiment. Two years after Slivnitza, in face of intrigues and violence, he abandoned the contest and abdicated. The second is Ferdinand of Coburg, whose tortuous career, begun in 1887, only ended with the collapse of the Central Powers in 1918. He was put forward by Austria and supported by Stambuloff, the dictatorial chief of the Bulgarian ministry. For years the Russian Government refused to recognize him, and it was not till 1896 that he came to heel, at the bidding of Prince Lobanoff, and made public submission to the Tsar. But, first and last, he was only an astute adventurer of no little vanity and of colossal egotism, and such sympathies as he had for others beside himself went to Austria-Hungary, where he owned landed property, and had served in the army. He was also displeasing to orthodox Russia as a Roman Catholic, and in Morier's letters we see clearly the mistrust and contempt which Russians felt for him.

With an autocrat like Alexander III, secretive and obstinate, these personal questions became very serious. Ambitious generals might anticipate his wishes, Russian regiments might be on the march before the Ministers knew anything, and Europe might awake to find itself over the edge of the precipice.

Morier's own attitude can best be judged from the letters which he exchanged with Sir William White, our able ambassador to the Porte, who was frankly anti-Russian in his views. At first he put his trust in strict observance of the Treaty of Berlin, and wished that Prince Alexander would consent to restore the *status quo ante* (i.e. before the change in Eastern Roumelia); but although a stout upholder of treaties, he admitted as a second basis for settlement 'les vœux des populations', on which the modern practice of plebiscites is founded. The peasants of Eastern Roumelia were clearly glad to transfer their allegiance from the Sultan to the Prince. Also the successes achieved by Prince Alexander in so soon welding together Bulgaria and Eastern Roumelia had to be recognized as altering the situation. In fact, Morier's position was nearer to that of 1919 than to the old traditions in vogue a century earlier, and would commend itself to most English Liberals. But, as an ambassador paid to watch over British interests, he was guided by expediency rather than by sentiment. These interests, he was convinced, were more vitally affected in Central Asia than in the Balkans. He believed that, if British statesmen would recognize Russia's peculiar position in Bulgaria, the advance of Russian outposts towards India might be stayed, and the two great powers might work together all along the line. But, to effect this, national jealousies must be allayed and an understanding established. Morier had to interpret at St. Petersburg speeches of English politicians, which often sounded more offensive there than in London: he also had to watch and report to London the unofficial doings and sayings of the aggressive Pan-Slavist party, who might at any moment undermine the Ministry.

Foreign policy was in the hands of de Giers, an enlightened, pacific minister, who lacked, however, the courage to face his master's prejudices and had little authority over many of his own subordinates. De Nelidoff, at Constantinople, dared even to make himself the centre of diplomatic intrigue directed against the policy of his chief. Still less was de Giers able to control the strong Pan-Slavist influences which ruled in the Church, the Home Office, and the Press. Morier gives interesting portraits of Pobedonóstsev, the bigoted procurator of the Holy Synod, of Tolstoy the reactionary Minister of the Interior, of Katkoff the truculent editor of the *Moscow Gazette*. These were the most notable of the men who flouted the authority, thwarted the work, and undermined the position of the Tsar's nominal adviser, and often they carried the day in determining the attitude of the Tsar himself. Yet Morier was bound by his own honesty and by the traditions of British diplomacy to do business with de Giers alone, to receive the assurances of one who was being betrayed by his own ambassadors, to make his protests to one who could not effectively remedy the grievances. His difficulty was increased by de Giers's manner—'when getting on to slippery ground he has a remarkable power of speaking only half intelligibly and swallowing a large proportion of his words'. Morier was often conscious that he was building on sand; but in quiet weather it was possible to stem the flood for a while even with dikes of sand. Perhaps a little later the tide of Balkan troubles might be setting in another direction and the danger might be past. In Russia, where so much was incalculable, it was wise to make the most of such help as presented itself. Meanwhile the Russian Ambassador in London, Baron de Staäl, co-operated as loyally with Lord Salisbury as Morier with de Giers; and thanks to their diplomatic skill, rough places were smoothed away and bases of agreement were found. In the course of 1887, the smouldering fires of Anglo-Russian antagonism died down, and Russia adopted a waiting attitude in Bulgaria.

But this happy result was not attained till after Asiatic problems had given rise to serious alarms. The worst moment was in July 1886, when the Tsar suddenly proclaimed, contrary to the Treaty of Berlin, that the port of Batum was closed to foreign trade. His point of view was characteristic. His father had, autocratically, expressed in 1878 his intention to open the port; this had been done, and it had proved in practice a failure; as a purely administrative act, he (Alexander III) now declared the port closed, *et tout était dit*. But naturally foreign merchants resented the injury to their trade, and insisted on the sanctity of treaties. The Berlin Government, as usual, left to Great Britain all the odium incurred in making a protest, and the other Continental powers were equally silent. Morier asserted the British case so strongly that he roused even de Giers to vehemence; but when he saw that protests would avail nothing, he advised his Government to cut the loss and to avoid further bitterness. He reminded them that Russia had given way in Bulgaria, where the British point of view had prevailed, and that they must not expect her to submit to a second diplomatic defeat. Besides, a quarrel between Russia and Great Britain would only benefit a third party, ready enough to avail himself of it. Harmony was preserved, but the risk of a breach had been very great, and feeling was not improved by Russian activity at Sebastopol, where the Pan-Slavists were acclaiming the new birth of the Black Sea fleet. The death of Katkoff in 1887, and of Tolstoy in 1889, with the advent of more Liberal ministers, strengthened de Giers's hands; and during his later years, though he often needed great vigilance and tact, Morier was not troubled by any crisis so severe.

The Grand Cross of the Bath, which he received in 1887, was a fitting reward for the services he had rendered to England and to Europe in this anxious time. He never lost heart or despaired of a peaceful solution.

At bottom, as he often repeats, Russia was not ready for big adventures—was, in fact, still suffering from lassitude after the war of 1878, 'like an electric eel which, having in one great shock given off all its electricity, burrows in the mud to refill its battery, desiring nothing less than to come again too soon into contact with organic tissue'.

Apart from *la haute politique* and the conflicts between governments, Morier's own compatriots were giving him plenty to do. A few instances will illustrate the variety of the applications which reached the Embassy. Captain Beaufort requests a special permit to visit Kars and its famous fortifications. Mr. Littledale asks for a Russian guide to help him in an ascent of Mount Ararat. Father Perry, S.J. (the Jesuits were specially obnoxious to the Holy Synod), wishes to observe a solar eclipse only visible in Russia. Another traveller, Mr. Fairman, is summarily arrested near Rovno where the Tsar's visit is making the police unduly brisk for the moment. Morier procures him a prompt apology; but, not content with this, the Englishman now thinks himself entitled to a personal audience with the Tsar and the gift of some decoration to compensate him, which suggestion draws a curt reply from the much-vexed ambassador. But he was always ready to help a genuine explorer, whether it was Mr. de Windt in Trans-Caucasia or Captain Wiggins in the Kara Sea. To the latter, in his efforts to establish trade between Great Britain and Siberia by the Yenisei river, Morier lent most valuable aid, and he is proud to report the concessions which he won for our merchants in a new field of commerce.

Meanwhile he found occasion to cultivate friendships with Russians and foreign diplomats of all kinds. Of the more important he sends home interesting sketches to his superiors in Whitehall, Vischnegradsky, the 'wizard of finance', who raised the value of the rouble 30 per cent., became one of his intimate friends. When that ambiguous figure, Witte, his rival and successor, tried to discredit him, Morier vindicated with warmth the honesty and patriotism of his friend. Baron Jomini of the Foreign Office was of a different kind, witty, volatile, audaciously outspoken, more like a character in Thackeray's novels. Pobedonóstsev, the Procurator of the Holy Synod, remained 'somewhat of an enigma'—as we can easily believe when we hear that this bigoted Churchman, the terror of the Jews, had been a friend of Dean Stanley, and was still fond of English literature and English theology.

Still more amusing are the stories which he tells of foreign visitors of high station—of the Duke of Orleans playing truant without the knowledge of his parents and being snubbed by his Grand Ducal relatives; of Dalīp Singh touring the provinces with a disreputable entourage and trying to make trouble for the British at Moscow; of the Prince of Montenegro and his beautiful daughters, whom Morier heartily admires—'tall and massive, strong-limbed and comely, the true type of the mothers of heroes in the Homeric sense'.

With the Court his relations were excellent. His intimacy with members of our own royal family helped him, and his geniality and unconventional, natural manner won favour with the Romanoffs, who retained in their high station a great deal of simplicity. More than once Morier seized an opportunity for an act of special courtesy to the Tsar; and Alexander appreciated this from a man whose character was too well known for him to be suspected of obsequiousness.

But the life in St. Petersburg was not all pleasure, even when diplomatic waters were quiet. The work was hard, the climate was very exacting with its extremes of temperature, and epidemics were rife. In November 1889 he reports the appearance of 'Siberian Catarrh, more usually described under the general name of Influenza', which was working havoc in girls' schools and guardsmen's barracks, and had laid low simultaneously Emperor, Empress, and half the imperial family. Morier himself became increasingly liable to attacks of ill-health, and found difficulty in discharging his duties regularly. It required a keen sense of duty for him to stay at his post; and when in December 1891 he was appointed to the Embassy at Rome, he was very willing to go. But public interest stood in the way. He had made for himself an exceptional place at St. Petersburg. No one could be found to replace him adequately, and the Tsar expressed a desire that his departure should be postponed. He consented to stay on, and the next two years of work in that climate, together with the death in 1891 of his only son, broke his spirit and his strength. Too late he went in search of health, first to the Crimea and then to Switzerland. Death came to him as the winter of 1893 was approaching, when he was at Montreux on the Lake of Geneva, close to the home of his ancestors.

The impression which he made on his friends and colleagues is clear and consistent, and the ignorance of the general public about men of his profession justifies a few quotations. Sir Louis Mallet brackets him with Sir James Hudson,[45] and Lord Cromer as 'the most admirable trio of public servants he had known'. Sir William White speaks of him and Odo Russell as 'two giants of the diplomatic service'. Lord Acton, who knew Europe as well as any Foreign Minister, and weighed his words, refers to him in 1884 as 'our only strong diplomatist', and again 'as a strong man, resolute, ready, well-informed and with some amount of real resource'. More than one Foreign Secretary has borne testimony to the value of Morier's dispatches; and Sir Charles Dilke, who, without holding the portfolio himself, often shaped our foreign policy and was an expert in European questions, is still more emphatic about his intellectual powers, though he thinks that Morier's imperious temper made him 'impossible in a small place'. Sir Horace Rumbold,[46] in his *Recollections*, has many references to him, especially as he was in earlier years. He speaks of Morier's 'prodigious fund of spirits that made him the most entertaining, but not always the safest, of companions'; 'of his imperious, not over-tolerant disposition'; 'of the curious compound that he was of the thoughtless, thriftless Bohemian and the cool, calculating man of the world'; of his 'exceptionally powerful brain and unflagging industry'. Elsewhere he recalls Morier's journeys among the Southern Slavs, in which he opened up a new field of knowledge, and adds, 'since then he has made himself a thorough master of German politics, and is, I believe, one of the few men whom Prince Bismarck fears and correspondingly detests'.

Jowett's testimony may perhaps be discounted as that of an intimate friend; yet he was no flatterer, and as he often criticized Morier severely, it is of interest to read his deliberate verdict, given in 1873, that 'if he devoted his whole mind to it, he could prevent a war in Europe'. Four years earlier Jowett had been told by a diplomatist whom he respected, 'Morier is the first man in our profession'.

By those who still remember him, Morier is described as a diplomatist of 'the old school'. His noble presence, his courtly manner, and the dignity which he observed on all ceremonial occasions, would have qualified him to adorn the court of Maria Theresa or Louis Quatorze. This dignity he could put off when the need for it was past. Among his friends his manner was vivacious, his talk racy, his criticism free. He was of the old school, too, in being self-confident and independent, and in believing that he would do his best work if there were no telegraph to bring frequent instructions from Whitehall. But he had not the natural urbanity of Odo Russell, nor the invariable discretion of Lord Lyons. He had hard work to discipline his imperious temper, and by no means always succeeded in masking his own feelings. Perhaps too high a value has been set on impenetrable reserve by those who have modelled themselves on Talleyrand. By their very candour and openness some British diplomatists have gained an advantage over rivals who confound timidity with reserve, and have won a peculiar position of trust at foreign courts. In dealing with de Giers, Morier at any rate found no need to mumble or swallow his words. He was sure of himself and of his honourable intentions. On one occasion, after reading to that minister the exact words of the dispatch which he was sending to London, he stated his policy to him categorically. 'I always went', he said, 'upon the principle, whenever it could be done, of clearing the ground of all possible misunderstandings at the earliest date.' Probably we shall never see the end of 'secret diplomacy', whether under Tory, Liberal, or Labour governments; but this is not the tone of one who loves secrecy for its own sake.

In many ways Morier combined the qualities of the old and the new schools. Though personally a favourite with kings and queens, he was fully alive to the changes in the Europe of the nineteenth century, where, along with courts and cabinets, other more unruly forces were at work. His visit to Paris in 1848 showed his early interest in popular movements, and he maintained a catholic width of view in later life. He knew men of all sorts and kept himself acquainted with unofficial currents of opinion. He could talk freely to journalists or to merchants, could put them at their ease and get the information which he wanted. His comprehensiveness was remarkable. The strife of politicians in the foreground did not blur the distant landscape. In Russia, behind Balkan intrigues and Black Sea troubles he could see the cloud of danger overhanging the Pamirs. In Spain or Portugal he was watching and forecasting the possibilities of the white races in Africa. So his dispatches, varied and vivacious as they were, proved of the greatest value to Foreign Secretaries at home, and furnish excellent reading to-day.

In these dispatches a few Gallicisms occur; and in writing to an old friend like Sir William White he uses a free mixture of French and English with other ingredients for seasoning. But in general the literary style is admirable. He has a rare command of language, a most inventive use of metaphor, a felicitous touch in sketching a character or an incident. Towards those working under him he was exacting, setting up a high standard of industry, but he was generous in his praise and very ready to take up the cudgels for them when they needed support. In commending one of them, he selects for special praise 'his old-fashioned conscientiousness about public work and his subordination of private comfort'. He inherited this tradition from his own family and his faithfulness to it cost him his life.

Above all, we feel in reading these letters and memoranda that here is a man whose aim is truth rather than effect—not thinking of commending a programme to thousands of half-informed readers or hearers, in order to win their votes, but giving counsel to his peers, Odo Russell or Sir William White, Lord Granville or Lord Salisbury, on events and tendencies which affect the grave issues of peace and war and the lives of thousands of his fellow-countrymen. This generation has learnt how unsafe it is to treat these in a parliamentary atmosphere where men force themselves to believe what they wish and close their eyes to what is uncomfortable. While human nature remains the same, democracy cannot afford to deprive itself of such counsel or to belittle such a profession.

JOSEPH LISTER

1827-1912

1827.	Born at West Ham, April 5.
1844-52.	University College, London.
1851.	Acting House Surgeon under Erichsen.
1852.	First research work published.
1853.	Goes to Edinburgh. House Surgeon under Syme.
1855.	Assistant Surgeon and Lecturer at Edinburgh Infirmary.
1856.	Marries Agnes Syme.
1860.	Appointed Professor of Clinical Surgery at Glasgow.
1865.	Makes acquaintance with Pasteur's work.
1866-7.	Antiseptic treatment of compound fractures and abscesses.
1867.	Papers on antiseptic method in the *Lancet*.
1869.	Appointed Professor of Surgery at Edinburgh.
1872-5.	Conversion of leading scientists in Germany to Antisepticism.
1875.	Lister's triumphal reception in Germany.
1877.	Accepts professorship at King's College, London.
1879.	Medical congress at Amsterdam. Acceptance of Lister's methods by Paget and others in London.
1882.	von Bergmann develops Asepticism in Berlin.
1883.	Lister created a Baronet.
1891.	British Institute of Preventive Medicine incorporated.
1892.	Lister attends Pasteur celebration in Paris.
1893.	Death of Lady Lister.
1895-1900.	President of Royal Society.
1897.	Created a Peer.

1902.   Order of Merit.

1907.   Freedom of City of London: last public appearance.

1912.   Dies at Walmer, February 10.

JOSEPH LISTER
Surgeon

In a corner of the north transept of Westminster Abbey, almost lost among the colossal statues of our prime ministers, our judges, and our soldiers, will be found a small group of memorials preserving the illustrious names of Darwin, Lister, Stokes, Adams, and Watt, and reminding us of the great place which Science has taken in the progress of the last century. Watt, thanks partly to his successors, may be said to have changed the face of this earth more than any other inhabitant of our isles; but he is of the eighteenth century, and between those who developed his inventions it is not easy to choose a single representative of the age. Stokes and Adams command the admiration of all students of mathematics who can appreciate their genius, but their work makes little appeal to the average man. In Darwin's case no one would dispute his claim to represent worthily the scientists of the age, and his life is a noble object for study, single-hearted as he was in his devotion to truth, persistent as were his efforts in the face of prolonged ill-health. No better instance could be found to show that the highest intellectual genius may be found united with the most endearing qualities of character. Kindly and genial in his home, warmly attached to his friends, devoid of all jealousy of his fellow scientists, he lived to see his name honoured throughout the civilized world; and many who are incapable of appreciating his originality of mind can find an inspiring example in the record of his life. There is no need to make comparisons either of fame, of mental power, or of character; but the choice of Lister may be justified by the fact that his science, the science of Health and Disease, is one of absorbing interest to all men, and that with his career is bound up the history of a movement fraught with grave issues of life and death from which few families have been exempt.

About these issues bitter controversies have raged; but it is to the lesser men that the bitterness is due. By his family traditions, as well as by his natural disposition, Lister was a man of peace; and though he left the Society of Friends at the time of his marriage, he retained a respect for their views which accorded well with his own nature. When he had to speak or write on behalf of what he believed to be the truth, it was from no motive of self-assertion or combativeness. He had the calm contemplative mind of the student, whereas Bright, the Quaker tribune, the champion of Repeal, had all the fervour of the man of action. Lister's family had been Quakers since the beginning of the eighteenth century; and at this time too they moved from Yorkshire to London, where his grandfather and father were engaged in business as wine merchants. But Joseph Jackson Lister, who married in 1818, and became in 1827 the father of the famous surgeon, was much more than a merchant. He had taught himself the science of optics, had made improvements in the microscope, and had won his way within the sacred portals of the Royal Society. Letters have been preserved which show us how keen his interest in science always remained, and with what full appreciation he entered into the researches which his son was making as professor at Glasgow in the middle of the century. A father like this was not likely to grudge money on the boy's education; but for the Friends many avenues to knowledge were still closed, including the Universities of Oxford and Cambridge. He had to be content to go successively to Quaker schools at Hitchin and Tottenham, and from the latter to proceed, at the age of seventeen, to University College, London, which was non-sectarian. There the teaching was good, the atmosphere favourable to industry, and Lister was not conscious of hardship in missing the delights of youth that fell to his more fortunate contemporaries.

His father lived in a comfortable house at Upton, some six miles east of London Bridge, in a district now completely swamped by the growth of the vast borough of West Ham. He kept up close relations with other Quaker families living in the neighbourhood, especially the Gurneys of Plashets. In their circle the most striking figure was Elizabeth Fry, who from 1813 to her death in 1843 devoted herself unsparingly to the cause of prison reform. From his home the father continued to exercise a strong influence over his son, who was industrious and serious beyond his years.

From his father Lister learned as a boy to delight in the use of the microscope. He learned also to use his own power of observation, and to make hand and eye work together to minister to his studies. The power of drawing, which the future surgeon thus early developed, stood him in good stead later in life; and it is interesting to contrast his enjoyment of it with the laments made by his great contemporary Darwin, who felt keenly what he lost through his inability to use a pencil and to preserve the record of what he saw in nature or in the laboratory. Lister's school-days were over when he was seventeen years old and there is nothing remarkable to tell of them; but his period at University College was unusually prolonged. He was a student there for seven years and continued an eighth year, after he had taken his degree, as Acting House Surgeon. In 1848, half-way through his time, a physical breakdown was brought on by overwork, just as he was finishing his general studies; but a long holiday enabled him to recover his strength, and before the end of the year he had begun the course of medical studies which was to be his life-work.

At school his record had been good but not brilliant, nor did he come quickly to the front in London. His mind was not of the sort which can be forced to produce untimely fruit in the hot-house of examinations. But his education was both extensive and thorough; it formed an excellent general training for the mind and a good basis for the special studies in which he was later to distinguish himself. He had been at University College for two years before he gained his first medal; but by 1850 he had made his name as the best man of his year, capable of upholding the credit of his College against any rival in the metropolis. Among his fellow students the best known in later years was Sir Henry Thompson, whose portrait by Millais hangs in our National Gallery. Among his professors one stands out pre-eminent, alike for his character and for his influence on Lister's life. This was William Sharpey, Professor of Physiology, an original man with a keen eye for originality in others. In days when most English professors were content with a narrow empirical training, he had trudged with his knapsack over half Europe in quest of knowledge, had studied in France, Switzerland, Italy, and Austria, and had made himself acquainted at first hand with the best that was taught in their schools. He was a first-rate lecturer, clear and simple, and took much pains to get to know his pupils. When Lister had held for a short time the post of Acting House Surgeon at University College Hospital, and needed to make definite plans for his career, it was Sharpey who advised him to go north for a while and attend some classes in Edinburgh before deciding on his course. Thus it was Sharpey who introduced him to Scotland and to Syme.

Before we speak of the latter, a few words must be given to the year 1851, when Lister completed his studentship and became for a time an active member of the hospital staff. This year was important as introducing him to the practice of his art under the direction of Erichsen, an Anglo-Dane and one of the foremost surgeons in London. It also led to a change in his way of living, to his being thrown into closer relations with men of his own age, and to his taking a more lively part in social gatherings. What we hear of the essays that he wrote at school, what we can read of his early letters, all harmonizes with our conception of a Quaker upbringing. There is a staid primness about him, which contrasts strangely with the pictures of medical students presented to us in the pages of Dickens. Capable though he was of enjoying a holiday, or of expanding among congenial associates, Lister was not quick to make friends. He was apt to keep too much to himself; and he seems to have inspired respect and even a certain awe among men of his own age. In his youth men noticed the same grave mien, steadfast eyes, and lofty intellectual forehead which are conspicuous in his later portraits. He was steady in conduct, serious in manner, precise in his way of expressing himself;

and while these qualities helped him in the mental application which was so necessary if he was to profit by his student days, he needed a little shaking up in order to adapt himself to the ways of other men in the sphere of active life. This was given him by the constant activities of the hospital, and by the demands which the various societies made upon him; but he did not allow them to interfere with his own researches, for which he could find time when others were overwhelmed by the routine of their daily tasks.

His first bit of original research is of special interest because it connects him with his father's work. He made special observations with the microscope of the muscular tissue of the iris of the eye, illustrated his paper by delicate drawings of his own, and published it in the leading microscopical journal. This and a subsequent paper on the phenomena of 'Goose-skin' attracted some attention among physiologists at home and abroad, and brought him into friendly relations with a German professor of world-wide reputation. They also gave great satisfaction to his father and to his favourite teacher Sharpey.

But Lister's development henceforth was to take place on Scottish ground, and his visit to Edinburgh in 1853 shaped the whole course of his career. James Syme, under whose influence he thus came, was the most original and brilliant surgeon then living in the British Isles, perhaps in all Europe. His merits as a lecturer were somewhat overshadowed by his extraordinary skill as an operator; but he was a remarkable man in all ways, and the fact that Lister was admitted, first to his lecture-room and operating theatre, and then to his home, was without doubt the happiest accident in his life.

The atmosphere of Edinburgh with its large enthusiastic classes in the hospitals, its cultivated and intellectual society outside, supplied just what was wanted to foster the genius of a young man on the threshold of his career. In London, centres of culture were too widely diffused, indifference and apathy too prevalent, conservatism in principles and methods too strongly entrenched. In his new home in the north Lister could watch the boldest operator in his own profession, and could daily meet men scarcely less distinguished in other sciences, and as a visitor to Syme's house he was from time to time thrown among able men following widely different lines in life. Above all, here he met one who was peculiarly qualified to be his helper; and three years later, at the age of twenty-nine, he was married to Agnes Syme, the daughter of his chief, to whom he had been attracted, as can be seen from the letters which passed between Edinburgh and Upton, soon after his arrival in the north. Before this event, he had already made his mark as Resident House Surgeon, as assistant operator to Syme, and also as an independent lecturer under the liberal system which gave an opening to all who could establish by merit a claim to be heard. He had also begun those researches into the early stages of inflammation which, ten years later, were to bear such wonderful fruit. It was a full and busy life, and the distraction of courtship must have made it impossible for him at times to meet all demands; but after 1856 his mind was set at rest and his strength doubled by the sympathy which his wife showed in his work, and by the help which she was able to render him in writing to his dictation.

For their honeymoon they took a long journey on the Continent in the summer of 1856; but half, even of this rare holiday, was given to science, and, after some weeks' enjoyment of the beauties of Italy, husband and wife made the tour of German universities, as he was desirous to see something, if possible, of the leading surgeons and the newest methods. Vienna, Dresden, Berlin, Munich, Frankfort, Heidelberg, and Stuttgart were all included in the tour. They were well received, and at Vienna the most eminent professor of Pathology in the University gave more than three hours of his time to showing his museum to Lister, and also invited the young couple to dine at his house. Though he had not yet made a name for himself, Lister's earnestness and intelligence always made a favourable impression; and as he had taken pains with foreign languages in his youth, he was able, now and later in life, to address French and German friends, and even public meetings, in their native tongue. He came back to find work waiting for him which would tax his energies to the full. In October 1856 he was elected Assistant Surgeon to the Infirmary, and now, in addition to lecturing, he had to conduct public operations himself, whereas he had hitherto only acted as Syme's assistant. This was at first a severe trial for his nerves. That it affected him differently from most experienced surgeons is shown by the fact that he used always, all his life, to perspire freely when starting to operate; but he learnt to overcome this nervousness by concentrating his attention on his work. He was not a man who had religious phrases on his lips; but in letters to his family, quoted by Sir Rickman Godlee, he gives us the secret of his confidence and his power. 'Yesterday', he says in a letter written to his father on February 26, 'I made my début at the hospital in operating before the students. I felt very nervous before beginning; but when I had got fairly to work, this feeling went off entirely, and I performed both operations with entire comfort.' A week later, in a letter to his sister, he returns to the subject. 'The theatre was again well filled; and though I again felt a good deal before the operation, yet I lost all consciousness of the presence of the spectators during its performance, and did it exactly as if no one had been looking on. Just before the operation began I recollected that there was only one Spectator whom it was important to consider, one present alike in the operating theatre and in the private room; and this consideration gave me increased firmness.' Interest in the work for its own sake, forgetfulness of himself, these were to be the key-notes of his life-work.

As yet, to a superficial observer, there were not many signs of a brilliant career ahead of him. His private practice was small and did not grow extensively for many years. The attendance at his earlier course of lectures was discouragingly meagre. This would have been more discouraging still, had not his dressers, from personal affection for him, made a point of attending regularly to swell the number of the class. Indeed, in view of the exacting demands made on him by the hospital, Lister might have been content to follow the ordinary routine of his profession. With his wife at his side and friends close at hand, he had every chance of living a useful and happy life. But he still found time to conduct experiments and to think for himself. His researches were continued along the line which he had opened up in 1855, and in 1858 he appeared before an Edinburgh Surgical Society to read a paper on Spontaneous Gangrene.

This gave Mrs. Lister an opportunity to show her value. All his life Lister was prone to unpunctuality and to being late with preparations for his addresses, not because he was indifferent to the convenience of others or careless about the quality of his teaching, but because he became so engrossed in the work of the moment that he could not tear himself away from it so long as any improvement seemed possible. This same quality made him slow over his hospital rounds and often over operations, with the result that his own mealtimes were most irregular and his assistants often had trouble to stay the pangs of hunger. This handicapped him in private practice and in some measure as a lecturer. He gave plenty of thought to his subjects, but rarely began to put thoughts in writing sufficiently in advance of his engagement. When he was in time with his written matter the credit was chiefly due to his wife. On the occasion of this paper she wrote for seven hours one day and eight hours the next, and her heroic industry saved the situation.

Towards the end of 1859 Lister decided to be a candidate for the Surgical Professorship at Glasgow, which appointment was in the gift of the Crown; and in spite of some intrigues to secure the patronage for a local man, the post was offered by the Home Secretary, Sir George Lewis, to the young Edinburgh surgeon. Syme's opinion and influence no doubt counted for much. Lister's appointment dated from January 1860, but it was not till a year and a half later that his position in Glasgow was assured by his being elected Surgeon to the Royal Infirmary. Before this he could preach his principles in the lecture-room, but he had little influence on the practice of his students and colleagues. Thanks to the reputation which he brought from Edinburgh, his first lecture drew a full room, and his class grew year by year till it reached the unprecedented figure of 182, and each year the enthusiasm seemed to rise. But in the hospital he had an uphill task, as any one will know who has studied the history of these institutions in the first half of the century.

To-day the modern hospital is an object of general admiration, with its high standard of cleanliness and efficiency; and few of us would have any hesitation if a doctor advised us to go into hospital for an operation. Seventy or a hundred years ago the case was very different; and when we read the statistics of the early nineteenth century, gathered by the surgeons who had known its horrors, it is hard to believe that we are not back among the worst abuses of the Middle Ages. Such terrible scourges as pyaemia and hospital gangrene were rife in all of them. In the chief hospital of Paris, which for centuries claimed pre-eminence for its medical faculty, the latter disease raged for 200 years without intermission: 25 per cent. of those entering its doors were found to have died, and the mortality after certain operations was more than double this figure. Erichsen, who published in 1874 the statistics of deaths after operations, quoted 25 per cent. in London as satisfactory, and referred to the 60 per cent. of Paris as not surprising. In military practice the number of deaths might reach the appalling figure of 80 or 90 per cent. What was so tragic about this situation was that it was precisely hospitals, built to be the safeguard of the community, which were the most dangerous places in the case of wounds and amputations. In 1869 Sir James Simpson, the famous discoverer of chloroform, collected statistics of amputations. He took over 2,000 cases treated in hospitals, and the same number treated outside. In the former 855 patients (nearly 43 per cent.) died, as it seemed, from the effects of the operation; in the latter only 266 cases (over 13 per cent.) ended fatally. He went so far as to condemn altogether the system of big hospitals; and under his influence a movement began for breaking them up and substituting a system of small huts, which, whether tending to security or not, was in other ways inconvenient and very expensive. About the same time certain other reforms, obvious as they seem to us since the days of Florence Nightingale, were tried in various places, tending to more careful organization and to greater cleanliness; but till the cause of the mischief could be discovered, only varying results could be obtained, and no real victory could be won. Hence a radical policy like Simpson's met with considerable support. In days when many surgeons submitted despairingly to what they regarded as inevitable, it was an advantage to have any one boldly advocating a big measure; and Simpson had sufficient prestige in Edinburgh and outside to carry many along with him. But before 1869 another line of attack had been initiated from Glasgow, and Lister was already applying principles which were to win the battle with more certainty of permanent success.

Glasgow was no more free from these troubles than other great towns; in fact it suffered more than most of them. With its rapid industrial development it had already in 1860 a population of 390,000. Its streets were narrow, its houses often insanitary. In the haste to make money its citizens had little time to think of air and open spaces. The science of town-planning was unborn. Its hospital, far from having any special advantage of position, was exposed to peculiar dangers. It lay on the edge of the old cathedral graveyard, where the victims of cholera had received promiscuous pit-burial only ten years before. The uppermost tier of a multitude of coffins reached to within a few inches of the surface. These horrors have long been swept away; but, when Lister took charge of his wards in the Infirmary, they were infected by the poisonous air generated so close at hand, and in consequence they presented a gruesome appearance. The patients came from streets which often were foul with dirt, smoke, and disease, and were admitted to gloomy airless wards, where pyaemia or gangrene were firmly established. In such an environment certain death seemed to await them.

Though his heart must have sunk within him, Lister set himself bravely to the task of fighting these grim adversaries. For two years, indeed, he was chiefly occupied with routine work and practical improvements; but he continued his speculations, and in 1861 an article on amputations which he contributed to the *System of Surgery*, a large work in four volumes published in London, showed that he had not lost his power of surveying questions broadly and examining them with a fresh and original insight. He was not in danger of letting his mind be swamped with details, but could put them in their place and subordinate them to principles; and his article is chiefly directed to a philosophical survey which would enable his readers to go through the same process of education which he had followed out for himself. Sir Hector Cameron, the most constant of his Glasgow disciples, once illustrated this philosophic spirit from a passage in Cicero contrasting the many scientists who 'render themselves familiar with the strange' (not realizing that it is strange or needs explanation) with the few who 'render themselves strange to the familiar'—who stand away from the phenomena to which every one has become too accustomed and examine them afresh for themselves. In Lister he recognized the peculiar gift which enabled him to rise superior to his subject, and to interpret what was to his colleagues a sealed book. In these days, among the too familiar scourges of the hospital, his work was perpetually putting questions to him; to a man whose mind was open the answer might come at any moment and from any quarter.

As a fact, already, far from his own circle and for a long while out of his ken, there was working in France the most remarkable scientist of the century, Louis Pasteur, who more than once put his scientific ability at the disposal of a stricken industry, and in his quiet laboratory revived the industrial life of a teeming population. A manufacturer who was confronted with difficulties in making beetroot-alcohol and was threatened with financial ruin, appealed for his help in 1856; and Pasteur spent years on the study of fermentation, making countless experiments to test the action of the air in the processes of putrefaction, and coming to the conclusion that the oxygen of the air was not responsible for them, as was widely believed. He went further and reached a positive result. He satisfied himself that putrefaction was set up by tiny living organisms carried in the dust of the air, and that the process was due to what we now familiarly term 'germs' or 'microbes'. The existence of these infinitesimal creatures was known already to scientists, but their importance was not grasped till Pasteur, in the years 1862 to 1864, expounded the results of his long course of studies. He himself was no expert in medicine, but his discovery was to bear wonderful fruit when it was properly applied to the science of health and disease. Lister's study of open wounds, his observation of the harm done to the tissues in them when vitality was impaired, and of the value of protective scabs when they formed, enabled him to see the way and to point it out to others. When in 1865 he first read the papers which Pasteur had been publishing, he found the principle for which he had so long been searching. With what excitement he read them, with what suddenness of conviction he accepted the message, we do not know; he has left no record of his feelings at the time: but it was the most important moment in his career, and the rest of his life was spent in applying these principles to his professional work.

With his mind thus fortified by the knowledge of the true source of the mischief, realizing that he had to assist in a battle between the deadly germs carried in the air and the living tissues trying to defend themselves, Lister returned afresh to the study of methods. He knew that he had to reckon with germs in the wound itself, if the skin was broken, with germs on the hands and instruments of the operator, and with germs on the dust in the air. He must find some defensive power which was able to kill the germs, at least in the first two instances, without exercising an irritating effect on the tissues and weakening their vitality. The relative importance of these various factors in the problem only time and experience could tell him. Carbolic acid had been discovered in 1834 and had already been tried by surgeons with varying results. At Carlisle it had been used by the town authorities to cope with the foul odour of sewage, and Lister visited the town to study its operation. In its cruder form carbolic proved only too liable to irritate a wound and was difficult to dissolve in water. Lister tried solutions of different strengths, and finally arrived at a form of carbolic acid which proved to be soluble in oil and to have the 'antiseptic' force which he desired—that is, to check the process of sepsis or putrefaction inside the wound. He also set himself to devise some 'protective' which would enable Nature to do her healing work without further interference from without. Animals have the power to form quickly a natural scab over a wound, which is impermeable and at the same time elastic. The human skin, after a slight wound, in a pure atmosphere, may heal quickly; but a serious wound may continue open for a long time, discharging 'pus' at intervals, while decomposition is slowly lowering the vitality of the patient. Lister made numerous experiments with layers of chalk and carbolic oil, with a combination of shellac and gutta-percha, with everything of which he could think, to imitate the work of nature. His inexhaustible patience stood him in good stead in all these practical details. Rivals might speak contemptuously of the 'carbolic treatment' and the 'putty method' as if he were the vender of a new quack medicine; but at the back of these details was a scientific principle, firmly grasped by one man, while all others were groping in the dark.

LORD LISTER
From a photograph by Messrs. Barraud

During 1866 and 1867 we see from his letters how he set himself to apply the new principle first to cases of compound fracture and then to abscesses, how closely and anxiously he watched the progress of his patients, and how slow he was to claim a victory before his confidence was assured. In July 1867, when he was just forty years old, he felt it to be his duty to communicate what he had learnt and to put his experience at the disposal of his fellow workers. He wrote then to *The Lancet* describing in detail eleven cases of compound fracture under his care, in which one patient had died, one had lost a limb, and the other nine had been successfully cured. This ratio of success to failure was far in advance of the average practice of the time; but, for all that, it is not surprising that he met with the common fate which rewards pioneers in new fields of study. It is true that other reforms were helping to reduce the number of fatal cases. Florence Nightingale had led the way, and much had been learnt about hospital management. It was possible to maintain that good results had been achieved by other methods, and that Lister's proofs were in no way decisive. But there was no need for critics to misapprehend the nature of his claims or to introduce the personal element and accuse him of plagiarism. Sir James Simpson revived the memory of a Frenchman, Lemaire, who had used carbolic acid and written about it in 1860, and refused to give Lister any credit for his discoveries. As a fact Lister had never heard of Lemaire or his work; and, besides, the Frenchman had never known the principles on which Lister based his work, nor did he succeed in converting others to his practice. How little the personal question need be raised between men of the highest character is shown by the relations of Darwin and Wallace, who arrived independently and almost simultaneously at their theory of the origin of species, Wallace put his notes, the fruit of many years of work, at the disposal of Darwin; and both continued to labour at the establishment of truth, each giving generous recognition to the other's part in the work.

Unmoved then by this and other attacks, Lister continued his experiments and spent the greatest pains, for years in succession, in improving the details of his treatment. It would take too long to narrate his struggles with carbolized silk and catgut in the search for the perfect ligature, which should be absorbed by the living tissues without setting up putrefaction in the wound; or his countless experiments to find a dressing which should be antiseptic without bringing any irritating substance near the vital spot. These latter finally resulted in the choice of the cyanide gauze, which with its delicate shade of heliotrope is now a familiar object in hospital and surgery. But one story is of special interest because it shows us clearly how Lister, while clinging to a principle, was ready to modify the details of treatment by the lessons which experience taught him. It was on the advice of others that he first introduced a carbolic spray in order to purify the air in the neighbourhood of an operation. At first he used a small spray worked by hand, but this was, for practical reasons, changed into a foot-spray and afterwards into one worked by steam. One objection to this was that the steam-engine was a cumbrous bit of apparatus to carry about with him to operations; and Lister all his life loved simplicity in his methods. Another was that the carbolic solution, falling on the hands of the operator, might chill them and impair his skill in handling his instruments. Lister himself suffered less in this way than most other surgeons; with some men it was a grave handicap. The spectators at a demonstration found it inconvenient, and in one instance at least we know that the patient was upset by the carbolic vapour reaching her eyes. This was no less a person than Queen Victoria, upon whom Lister was called to operate at Balmoral in 1870. About the use of this apparatus, which was an easy mark for ridicule, Lister had doubts for some time; but it was not the ridicule which killed it, but his growing conviction that it did not afford the security which was claimed for it. He was hesitating in 1881; in 1887 he abandoned the use of the spray entirely; in 1890 he expressed publicly at Berlin his regret for having advocated what had proved to be a needless complication and even a source of trouble in conducting operations. In adopting it he had for once been ready to listen to the advice of others without his usual precaution of first-hand experiments; in abandoning it he showed his contempt for merely outward consistency in practice and his willingness to admit his own mistakes.

It was at Glasgow that Lister made his initial discoveries and conducted his first operations under the new system. It was in the Glasgow Infirmary that he worked cures which roused the astonishment of his students, however incredulous the older generation might be. He had formed a school and was happy in the loyal service and in the enthusiasm of those who worked under him, and he had no desire to leave such a fruitful field of work. But when in 1869 his father-in-law, owing to ill-health, resigned his professorship, and a number of Edinburgh students addressed an appeal to Lister to become a candidate for the post, he was strongly drawn towards the city where he had married and spent such happy years. No doubt too he and his wife wished to be near Syme, who lived for fourteen months after his stroke, and to cheer his declining days. Lister was elected in August 1869 and moved to Edinburgh two months later. For a while he took a furnished house, but early in 1870 he made his home in Charlotte Square, from which he had easy access to the gardens between Princes Street and the Castle, 'a grand place' for his daily meditations, as he had it all to himself before breakfast. Altogether, Edinburgh was a pleasant change to him, and refreshing; and the one man who was likely to stir controversy, Sir James Simpson, died six months after Lister's arrival. Among his fellow professors were men eminent in many lines, perhaps the most striking figures being old Sir Robert Christison of the medical faculty, Geikie the geologist, and Blackie the classical scholar. The hospital was still run on old-fashioned lines; but the staff were devoted to their work, from the head nurse, Mrs. Porter, a great 'character' whose portrait has been sketched in verse by Henley,[47] to the youngest student; and they were ready to co-operate heartily with the new chief. The hours of work suited Lister better than those at Glasgow, where he had begun with an early morning visit to the Infirmary and had to find time for a daily lecture. Here he limited himself to two lectures a week, visited the hospital at midday, and was able to devote a large amount of time to bacteriological study, which was his chief interest at this time.

He stayed in Edinburgh eight years, and it was during his time here that he saw the interest of all Europe in surgical questions quickened by the Franco-German war, and had to realize how incomplete as yet was his victory over the forces of destruction. Some enterprising British and American doctors, who volunteered for field-service, came to him for advice, and he wrote a series of short instructions for their guidance; but he soon learnt how difficult it was to carry out his methods in the field, where appliances were inadequate and where wounds often got a long start before treatment could be applied. The French statistics, compiled after the war, are appalling to read: 90 out of 100 amputations proved fatal, and the total number of deaths in hospital worked out at over 10,000. The Germans were in advance of the French in the cleanliness of their methods, and some of their doctors were already beginning to accept the antiseptic theory; but it was not till 1872 that this principle can be said to have won the day. The hospitals on both sides were left with a ghastly heritage of pyaemia and other diseases, raging almost unchecked in their wards; but, in the two years after the war, two of the most famous professors in German Universities[48] had by antiseptic methods obtained such striking results among their patients that the superiority of the treatment was evident; and both of them generously gave full credit to Lister as their teacher. When he made a long tour on the Continent in 1875, finishing up with visits to the chief medical schools in Germany, these men were foremost in greeting him, and he enjoyed a conspicuous triumph also at Leipzig. Sir Rickman Godlee, commenting on the indifference of his countrymen, says that Lister's teaching was by them 'accepted as a novelty, when it came back to England, refurbished from Germany'. But this was not till after he had left Edinburgh, to carry the torch of learning to the south.

In Edinburgh his colleagues, with all their opportunities for learning at first hand, seemed strangely indifferent to Lister's presence in their midst, even when foreigners began to make pilgrimages to the central shrine of antiseptics. The real encouragement which he got came, as before, from his pupils, who thronged his lecture-room to the number of three or four hundred, with sustained enthusiasm. In some ways it is difficult to account for the popularity of his lectures. He made no elaborate preparations, but was content to devote a quiet half-hour to thinking out the subject in his arm-chair. After this he needed no notes, having his ideas and the development of his thought so firmly in his grasp that he could follow it out clearly and could hold the attention of his audience. His voice, though musical, was not of great power. He was often impeded by a slight stammer, especially at the end of a session. He was not naturally an eloquent man, and attempted no flights of rhetoric. But it seems impossible to deny the possession of special ability to a man who consistently drew such large audiences throughout a long career; and if it was the matter rather than the manner which wove the spell, surely that is just the kind of good speaking which Scotsmen and Englishmen have always preferred.

And so it needed an even greater effort than at Glasgow for Lister to strike his tent and adventure himself on new ground. It is true that London was his early home; London could give him wider fame and enable him to make a larger income by private practice; yet it is very doubtful whether these motives combined could have induced him to migrate again, now that he had reached the age of fifty. But he was a man with a mission. Some of his few converts in London held that only his presence there could shake the prevailing apathy, and he himself felt that he must make the effort in the interests of science.

The professorial chair to which he was invited in 1877 was at King's College, which was relatively a small institution; its hospital was not up to the Edinburgh standard; the classes which attended his lectures were small. Owing to an unfortunate incident he was handicapped at the start. When receiving a parting address from 700 of his Edinburgh students he made an informal speech in the course of which he compared the conditions of surgical teaching then prevailing at Edinburgh and London, in terms which were not flattering to the southern metropolis. Some comparison was natural in the circumstances; Lister was not speaking for publication and had no idea that a reporter was present. But his remarks appeared in print, with the result that might be expected. The sting of the criticism lay in its truth, and many London surgeons were only too ready to resent anything which might be said by the new professor. When he had been living some time in London, Lister succeeded in allaying the ill feeling which resulted; but at first, even in his own hospital, he was met by coldness and opposition in his attempt to introduce new methods. In fact, had he not laid down definite conditions in accepting the post, he could never have made his way; but he had stipulated for bringing with him some of the men whom he had trained, and he was accompanied by four Edinburgh surgeons, the foremost of whom were John Stewart, a Canadian, and Watson Cheyne, the famous operator of the next generation. Even so he found his orders set at naught and his work hampered by a temper which he had never known elsewhere. In some cases the sisters entrenched themselves behind the Secretary's rules and refused to comply, not only with the requests of the new staff, but even with the dictates of common sense and humanity. Another trouble arose over the system of London examinations which tempted the students to reproduce faithfully the views of others and discouraged men from giving time to independent research. Lister's method of lecturing was designed to foster the spirit of inquiry, and he would not deign to fill his lecture-room by any species of 'cramming'. Never did his patience, his hopefulness, and his interest in the cause have to submit to greater trials; but the day of victory was at hand.

The most visible sign of it was at the International Medical Congress held at Amsterdam in 1879 and attended by representatives of the great European nations. One sitting was devoted to the antiseptic system; and Lister, after delivering an address, received an ovation so marked that none of his fellow-countrymen could fail to see the esteem in which he was held abroad. Even in London many of his rivals had by now been converted. The most distinguished of them, Sir James Paget, openly expressed remorse for his reluctance to accept the antiseptic principle earlier, and compared his own record of failures with the successes attained by his colleague at St. Bartholomew's Thomas Smith, the one eminent London surgeon who had given Listerism a thorough trial. Other triumphs followed, such as the visits in 1889 to Oxford and Cambridge to receive Honorary Degrees, the offer of a baronetcy in 1883, and the conferring on him in 1885 of the Prussian 'Ordre pour le merite'.[49] But a chronicle of such external matters is wearisome in itself; and before the climax was reached, the current of opinion was, by a strange turn of fortune, already setting in another direction.

This was due to the introduction of the so-called aseptic theory so widely prevalent to-day, of which the chief prophet in 1885 was Professor von Bergmann of Berlin. Into the relative merits of systems, on which the learned disagree, it is absurd for laymen to enter; nor is it necessary to make such comparisons in order to appreciate the example of Lister's life. The new school believe that they have gained by the abandonment of carbolic and other antiseptics which may irritate a wound and by trusting to the agency of heat for killing all germs. But Lister himself took enormous pains to keep his antiseptic as remote as possible from the tissues to whose vitality he trusted, and went half-way to meet the aseptic doctrine. If he retained a belief in the need for carbolic and distrusted the elaborate ritual of the modern hospital, with its boiling of everybody and everything connected with an operation, it was not either from blindness or from pettiness of mind. As in the case of abandoning the spray, it was his love of simplicity which influenced him. If the detailed precautions of the complete aseptic system are found practicable and beneficial in a hospital, they are difficult to realize for a country surgeon who has to work in a humbler way, and Lister wished his procedure to be within reach of every practitioner who needed it.

One more point must be considered before pronouncing Listerism to be superseded. In time of war there are occasions when necessity dictates the treatment to be followed. Wounded men, picked up on the field of battle some hours after they were hit, are not fit subjects for a method that needs a clear field of operation. It is then too late for aseptic precautions, as the wound may already be teeming with bacteria. Only the prompt use of carbolic can stay the ravages of putrefaction; and Lister's method, so often disparaged, must have saved the lives of thousands during the late War.

In any case there is much common ground between the two schools: each can learn from the other, and those professors of asepticism who have acknowledged their debt to Lister have been wiser than those who have made contention their aim. This was never the spirit in which he approached scientific problems.

An earlier controversy, in which his name was involved, was that which raged round the practice of vivisection. Here Lister had practically the whole of his profession behind him when he boldly supported the claims of science to have benefited humanity by the experiments conducted on animals and to have done so with a minimum of suffering to the latter. And it was well that science had a champion whose reputation for gentleness and moderation was so well established. Queen Victoria herself showed a lively interest in this fiercely-debated question; and in 1871, when Lister was appealed to by Sir Henry Ponsonby, her private secretary, to satisfy her doubts on the subject, he wrote an admirable reply, calm in tone and lucid in statement, in which he showed how unfounded were the charges brought against his profession.

In 1892 his professional career was drawing to a close. In that year he received the heartiest recognition that France could give to his work, when he went there officially to represent the Royal Society at the Pasteur celebration. A great gathering of scientists and others, presided over by President Carnot, came together at the Sorbonne to honour Pasteur's seventieth birthday. It was a dramatic scene such as our neighbours love, when the two illustrious fellow workers embraced one another in public, and the audience rose to the occasion. To be acclaimed with Pasteur was to Lister a crowning honour; but a year later fortune dealt him a blow from which he never recovered. His wife, his constant companion and helper, was taken ill suddenly at Rapallo on the Italian Riviera, and died in a few days; and Lister's life was sadly changed.

He was still considerably before the public for another decade. He did much useful work for the Royal Society, of which he became Foreign Secretary in 1893 and President from 1895 to 1900. He visited Canada and South Africa, received the freedom of Edinburgh in 1898 and of London in 1907, and in 1897 he received the special honour of a peerage, the only one yet conferred on a medical man. He took an active interest in the discoveries of Koch and Metchnikoff, preserving to an advanced age the capacity for accepting new ideas. He was largely instrumental in founding the Institute of Preventive Medicine now established at Chelsea and called by his name. But his work as a surgeon was complete before death separated him from his truest helper. In 1903 his strength began to fail, and for the last nine years of his life, at London or at Walmer, he was shut off from general society and lived the life of an invalid.

WILLIAM MORRIS
From the painting by G. F. Watts in the National Portrait Gallery

In 1912 he passed away by almost imperceptible degrees, in his home by the sea, and by his own request was buried in the quiet cemetery of West Hampstead where his wife lay. A public service was held in Westminster Abbey, and a portrait medallion there preserves the memory of his features. The patient toil, the even temper, the noble purpose which inspired his life, had achieved their goal—he was a national hero as truly as any statesman or soldier of his generation; and if, according to his nature he wished his body to lie in a humble grave, he deserved full well to have his name preserved and honoured in our most sacred national shrine.

WILLIAM MORRIS

1834-96

1834. Born at Walthamstow, March 24.

1848-51. Marlborough College.

1853-5. Exeter College, Oxford.

1856. Studies architecture under Street.

1857. Red Lion Square; influence of D. G. Rossetti.

1858. *Defence of Guenevere.*

1859. Marries Miss Jane Burden.

1860-5. 'Red House', Upton, Kent.

1861. Firm of Art Decorators founded in Queen Square, Bloomsbury. (Dissolved and refounded 1875.)

1867-8. *Life and Death of Jason.* 1868-70. *Earthly Paradise.*

1870. Tenant of Kelmscott Manor House, on the Upper Thames.

1871-3. Visits to Iceland; work on Icelandic Sagas.

1876. *Sigurd the Volsung.*

1878. Tenant of Kelmscott House, Hammersmith.

1881. Works moved to Merton.

1883-4. Active member of Social Democratic Federation.

1884-90. Founder and active member of Socialist League.

1891. Kelmscott Press founded.

1892-6. Preparation and printing of Kelmscott *Chaucer.*

1896. Death at Hammersmith, October 3.

1896. Burial at Kelmscott, Oxfordshire.

WILLIAM MORRIS

Craftsman and Social Reformer

In general it is difficult to account for the birth of an original man at a particular place and time. As Carlyle says: 'Priceless Shakespeare was the free gift of nature, given altogether silently, received altogether silently.' Of his childhood history has almost nothing to relate, and what is true of Shakespeare is true in large measure of Burns, of Shelley, of Keats. Even in an age when records are more common, we can only discern a little and can explain less of the silent influences at work that begin to make the man. There are few things more surprising than that, in an age given up chiefly to industrial development, two prosperous middle-class homes should have given birth to John Ruskin and William Morris, so alien in temper to all that traditionally springs from such a soil. In the case of Morris there is nothing known of his ancestry to explain his rich and various gifts. From a child he seemed to have found some spring within himself which drew him instinctively to all that was beautiful in nature, in art, in books. His earliest companions were the Waverley Novels, which he began at the age of four and finished at seven; his earliest haunt was Epping Forest, where he roamed and dreamed through many of the years of his youth.

His father, who was in business in the City of London, as partner in a bill-broking firm, lived at different times at Walthamstow and at Woodford; and the hills of the forest, in some places covered with thick growth of hornbeam or of beech, in others affording a wide view over the levels of the lower Thames, impressed themselves so strongly on the boy's memory and imagination that this scenery often recurred in the setting of tales which he wrote in middle life.

There was no need of external aid to develop these tastes; and Morris was fortunate in going to a school which did no violence to them by forcing him into other less congenial pursuits. Marlborough College, at the time when he went there in 1848, had only been open a few years. The games were not organized but left to voluntary effort; and during his three or four years at school Morris never took part in cricket or football. In the latter game, at any rate, he should have proved a notable performer on unorthodox lines, impetuous, forcible, and burly as he was. But he found no reason to regret the absence of games, or to feel that time hung heavy on his hands. The country satisfied his wants, the Druidic stones at Avebury, the green water-meadows of the Kennet, the deep glades of Savernake Forest. So strong was the spell of nature, that he hardly felt the need for companionship; and, as chance had not yet thrown him into close relations with any friend of similar tastes, he lived much alone.

It was a different matter at Oxford, to which he proceeded in January 1853. Among those who matriculated at Exeter College that year was a freshman from Birmingham named Edward Burne Jones; and within a few days Morris had begun a friendship with him which lasted for his whole life and was the source of his greatest happiness. For more than forty years their names were associated, and so they will remain for generations to come in Exeter College Chapel, where may be seen the great tapestry of the Nativity designed by one and executed by the other. Burne-Jones had not yet found his vocation as a painter; he came to Oxford like Morris with the wish to take Holy Orders. He was of Welsh family with a Celtic fervour for learning, and a Celtic instinct for what was beautiful, and at King Edward's School he had made friends with several men who came up to Pembroke College about the same time. Their friendship was extended to his new acquaintance from Marlborough. Here Morris found himself in the midst of a small circle who shared his enthusiasm for literature and art, and among whom he quickly learned to express those ideas which had been stirring his heart in his solitary youth. Through the knowledge gained by close observation and a retentive memory, through his impetuosity and swift decision, Morris soon became a leader among them. Carlyle and Ruskin, Keats and Tennyson, were at this time the most potent influences among them; and when Morris was not arguing and declaiming in the circle at Pembroke, he was sitting alone with Burne-Jones at Exeter reading aloud to him for hours together French romances and other mediaeval tales. Young men of to-day, with a wealth of books on their shelves and of pictures on their walls, with popular reproductions bringing daily to their doors things old and new, can little realize the thrill of excitement with which these men discovered and enjoyed a single new poem of Tennyson or an early drawing by Millais or Rossetti. How they were quickened by ever fresh delight in the beauty and strangeness of such things, how they responded to the magic of romance and dreamed of a day when they should themselves help in the creation of such work, how they started a magazine of their own and essayed short flights in prose or verse, can best be read in the volumes which Lady Burne-Jones[50] has dedicated to the memory of her husband. This period is of capital importance in the life of William Morris, and the year 1855 especially was fraught with momentous decisions.

Like Burne-Jones he had gone up to Oxford intending to take Holy Orders in the Church of England; but the last three years had taught him that his interest lay elsewhere. The spirit of faith, of reverence, of love for his fellow men still attracted him to Christianity; but he could not subscribe to a body of doctrine or accept the authority of a single Church. His ideal shifted gradually. At one time he hoped to found a brotherhood which was to combine art with religion and to train craftsmen for the service of the Church; but he was more fitted to work in the world than in the cloister, and the social aspect of this foundation prevailed over the religious. Nor was it mere self-culture to which he aspired. The arts as he understood them were one field, and a wide field, for enlarging the powers of men and increasing their happiness, for continuing all that was most precious in the heritage of the past and passing on the torch to the future; in this field there was work for many labourers and all might be serving the common good.

His own favourite study was the thirteenth century, when princes and merchants, monks and friars, poets and craftsmen had combined to exalt the Church and to beautify Western Europe; and he wished to recreate the nineteenth century in its spirit. And so while Burne-Jones discovered his true gift in the narrower field of painting, Morris began his apprenticeship in the master craft of architecture, and passed from one art to another till he had covered nearly the whole field of endeavour with ever-growing knowledge of principle and restless activity of hand and eye. His father had died in 1847; and when Morris came of age he inherited a fortune of about £900 a year and was his own master. Before the end of 1855 he imparted to his mother his decision about taking Orders. The Rubicon was crossed; but on which road he was to reach his goal was not settled for many years. Twice he had to retrace his steps from a false start and begin a fresh career. The year 1856 saw him still working at Oxford, in the office of Street, the architect. Two more years (1857-8) saw him labouring at easel pictures under the influence of Rossetti, though he also published his first volume of poetry at this time. The year 1859 found him married, and for the time absorbed in the making of a home, but still feeling his way towards the choice of a profession.

Dante Gabriel Rossetti was in some ways the most original man of his generation; certainly he was the only individual whose influence was ever capable of dominating Morris and drawing him to a course of action which he would not have chosen for himself. Rossetti's tragic collapse after his wife's death, and the pictures which he painted in his later life, have obscured the true portrait of this virile and attractive character. Burne-Jones fell completely under his spell, and he tells us how for many years his chief anxiety, over each successive work of art that he finished, was 'what Gabriel would have thought of it'. So decisive was his judgement, so dominating his personality.

Morris's period of hesitation ended in 1861, when the first firm of decorators was started among the friends. Of the old Oxford set it included Burne-Jones and Faulkner; new elements were introduced by Philip Webb the architect and Madox Brown the painter. The leadership in ideas might still perhaps belong to Rossetti; but in execution William Morris proved himself at once the captain. The actual work which he contributed in the first year was more than equal to that produced by his six partners, and future years told the same tale.

In the early part of his married life Morris lived in Kent, at Upton, some twelve miles from Charing Cross, in a house built for him by his friend Webb. The house was of red brick, simple but unconventional in character, built to be the home of one who detested stucco and all other shams, and wished things to seem what they were. Its decoration was to be the work of its owner and his friends.

Here we see Morris in the strength of early manhood and in all the exuberance of his rich vigorous nature, surrounded by friends for whom he kept open house, in high contentment with life, eager to respond to all the claims upon his energy. Here came artists and poets, in the pleasant summer days, jesting, dreaming, discussing, indulging in bouts of single-stick or game of bowls in the garden, walking through the country-side, quoting poets old and new, and scheming to cover the walls and cupboards of the rooms with the legends of mediaeval romance. Visitors of the conventional aesthetic type would have many a surprise and many a shock. The jests often took the form of practical jokes, of which Morris, from his explosive temper, was chosen to be the butt, but which in the end he always shared and enjoyed. Rossetti, Burne-Jones, and Faulkner would conspire to lay booby traps on the doors for him, would insult him with lively caricatures, and with relentless humour would send him to 'Coventry' for the duration of a dinner. Or he would have a sudden tempestuous outbreak in which chairs would collapse and door panels be kicked in and violent expletives would resound through the hall. In all, Morris was the central figure, impatient, boisterous, with his thick-set figure, unkempt hair, and untidy clothing, but with the keenest appreciation and sympathy for any manifestation of beauty in literature or in art. But this idyll was short-lived. Ill-health in the Burne-Jones family was followed by an illness which befell Morris himself; and the demand of the growing business and the need for the master to be nearer at hand forced him to leave Upton. The Red House was sold in 1865; and first Bloomsbury and later Hammersmith furnished him with a home more conveniently placed.

The period of his return to London coincided with the most fruitful period of his poetic work. Already at Oxford he had written some pieces of verse which had found favour with his friends. He soon found that his taste and his talent was for narrative poetry; and in 1856 he made acquaintance with his two supreme favourites, Chaucer and Malory. It is to them that he owes most in all that he produced in poetry or in prose, and notably in the *Earthly Paradise*, which he published between 1868 and 1870. This consists of a collection of stories drawn chiefly from Greek sources, but supposed to be told by a band of wanderers in the fourteenth century. Thus the classic legends are seen through a veil of mediaeval romance. He had no wish to step back, in the spirit of a modern scholar, across the ages of ignorance or mist, and to pick up the classic stones clear-cut and cold as the Greeks left them. To him the legends had a continuous history up to the Renaissance; as they were retold by Romans, Italians, or Provençals, they were as a plant growing in our gardens, still putting out fresh shoots, not an embalmed corpse such as later scholars have taught us to exhume and to study in the chill atmosphere of our libraries and museums. This mediaevalism of his was much misunderstood, both in literature and in art; people would talk to him as if he were imitating the windows or tapestries of the Middle Ages, whereas what he wanted was to recapture the technical secrets which the true craftsmen had known and then to use these methods in a live spirit to carry on the work to fresh developments in the future.

If the French tales of the fourteenth century were an inspiration to him in his earliest poems, a second influence no less potent was that of the Icelandic Sagas. He began to study them in 1869, and a little later, with the aid of Professor Magnusson, he was translating some of them into English. He made two journeys to Iceland, and was deeply moved by the wild grandeur of the scenes in which these heroic tales were set. For many successive days he rode across grim solitary wastes with more enthusiasm than he could give to the wonted pilgrimages to Florence and Venice. When he was once under the spell, only the geysers with their suggestion of modern text-books and *Mangnall's Questions*[51] could bore him; all else was magical and entrancing. This enthusiasm bore fruit in *Sigurd the Volsung*, the most powerful of his epic poems, written in an old English metre, which Morris, with true feeling for craftsmanship, revived and adapted to his theme. His poetry in general, less rich than that of Tennyson, less intense than that of Rossetti, had certain qualities of its own, and owed its popularity chiefly to his gift for telling a story swiftly, naturally and easily, and in such a way as to carry his reader along with him.

His fame was growing in London, which was ready enough in the nineteenth century to make the most of its poets. In Society, if he had allowed it to entertain him, he would have been a picturesque figure, though hardly such as was expected by admirers of his poetry and his art. To some his dress suggested only the prosperous British workman; to one who knew him later he seemed like 'the purser of a Dutch brig' in his blue tweed sailor-cut suit. This was his Socialist colleague Mr. Hyndman, who describes 'his imposing forehead and clear grey eyes with the powerful nose and slightly florid cheeks', and tells us how, when he was talking, 'every hair of his head and his rough shaggy beard appeared to enter into the subject as a living part of himself.' Elsewhere he speaks of Morris's 'quick, sharp manner, his impulsive gestures, his hearty laughter and vehement anger'. At times Morris could be bluff beyond measure. Stopford Brooke, who afterwards became one of his friends, recounts his first meeting with Morris in 1867. 'He didn't care for parsons, and he glared at me when I said something about good manners.

Leaning over the table with his eyes set and his fist clenched he shouted at me, "I am a boor and the son of a boor".' So ready as he was to challenge anything which smacked of conventionality or pretension, he was not quite a safe poet to lionize or to ask into mixed company.

But it was less in literature than in art that he influenced his generation, and we must return to the history of the firm. From small beginnings it had established itself in the favourable esteem of the few, and, thanks to exhibitions, its fame was spreading. Though as many as twelve branches are mentioned in a single copy of its prospectus, there was generally one department which for the moment occupied most of the creative energy of the chief.

Painted glass is named first on the prospectus, and was one of the earlier successes of the firm. As it was employed for churches more often than for private houses, it is familiar to many who do not know Morris's work in their homes; but it is hardly the most characteristic of his activities. For one thing, the material, the 'pot glass', was purchased, not made on the premises. Morris's skill lay in selecting the best colours available rather than in creating them himself. For another, he knew that his own education in figure-drawing was incomplete, and he left this to other artists. Most of the figures were designed by Burne-Jones, and some of the best-known examples of his windows are at St. Philip's, Birmingham, near the artist's birthplace, and at St. Margaret's, Rottingdean, where he died.[52] But no cartoon, by Burne-Jones or any one else, was executed till Morris had supervised the colour scheme; and he often designed backgrounds of foliage or landscape.

To those people of limited means who cannot afford tapestries and embroidery (which follow painted glass on the firm's list), yet who wish to beautify their homes, interest centres in the chintzes and wall-papers. These show the distinctive gifts by which Morris most widely influenced the Victorian traditions. It is not easy to explain why one design stirs our curiosity and quickens our delight, while another has the opposite effect. Critics can prate about natural and conventional art without helping us to understand; but a passage from Mr. Clutton-Brock seems worth quoting as simply and clearly phrased.[53] 'Morris would start', he says, 'with a pattern in his mind and from the first saw everything as a factor in that pattern. But in these early wall-papers he showed a power of pattern-making that has never been equalled in modern times. For though everything is subject to the pattern, yet the pattern itself expresses a keen delight in the objects of which it is composed. So they are like the poems in which the words keep a precise and homely sense and yet in their combination make a music expressive of their sense.' Beginning with the design of the rose-trellis in 1862, Morris laid under contribution many of the most familiar flowers and trees. The daisy, the honeysuckle, the willow branch, are but a few of the best known: each bears the stamp of his inventive fancy and his cunning hand: each flower claims recognition for itself, and reveals new charms in its appointed setting. Of these papers we hear that Morris himself designed between seventy and eighty, and when we add chintzes, tapestry, and other articles we may well be astonished at the fertility of his brain.

Even so, much must have depended on his workmen as the firm's operations extended.

Mr. Mackail tells us of the faith which Morris had in the artistic powers of the average Englishman, if rightly trained. He was ready to take and train the boy whom he found nearest to hand, and he often achieved surprising results. His own belief was that a good tradition once established in the workshops, by which the workman was allowed to develop his intelligence, would of itself produce good work: others believed that the successes would have been impossible without the unique gifts of the master, one of which was that he could intuitively select the right man for each job.

The material as well as the workers needed this selective power. The factories of the day had accustomed the public to second-rate material and second-rate colour, and Morris was determined to set a higher standard. In 1875 he was absorbed in the production of vegetable dyes, which he insisted on having pure and rich in tone. Though madder and weld might supply the reds and yellows which he needed, blue was more troublesome. For a time he accepted prussian blue, but he knew that indigo was the right material, and to indigo he gave days of concentrated work, preparing and watching the vats, dipping the wool with his own hands (which often bore the stain of work for longer than he wished), superintending the minutest detail and refusing to be content with anything short of the best. But these two qualities of industry and of aiming at a high standard would not have carried him so far if he had not added exceptional gifts of nature. With him hand and eye worked together as in few craftsmen of any age; and thus he could carry his experiments to a successful end, choosing his material, mixing his colours, and timing his work with exact felicity. And when he had found the right way he had the rare skill to communicate his knowledge to others and thus to train them for the work.

Queen Square, Bloomsbury, was the first scene of his labours; but as the firm prospered and the demands for their work grew, Morris found the premises too small. At one time he had hopes of finding a suitable spot near the old cloth-working towns at the foot of the Cotswolds, where pure air and clear water were to be found; but the conditions of trade made it necessary for him to be nearer to London. In 1881 he bought an old silk-weaving mill at Merton near Wimbledon, on the banks of the Wandle, and this is still the centre of the work.

To study special industries, or to execute a special commission, he was often obliged to make long journeys to the north of England or elsewhere; but the routine of his life consisted in daily travelling between his house at Hammersmith and the mills at Merton, which was more tiresome than it is to-day owing to the absence of direct connexion between these districts. But his energy overbore these obstacles; and, except when illness prevented him, he remained punctual in his attendance to business and in close touch with all his workers. Towards them Morris was habitually generous. The weaker men were kept on and paid by time, long after they had ceased to produce remunerative work, while the more capable were in course of time admitted as profit-sharers into the business. Every man who worked under him had to be prepared for occasional outbursts of impatient temper, when Morris spoke, we are told, rather as a good workman scornful of bad work, than as an employer finding fault with his men; but in the long run all were sure to receive fair and friendly treatment.

Such was William Morris at his Merton works, a master craftsman worthy of the best traditions of the Middle Ages, fit to hold his place with the masons of Chartres, the weavers of Bruges, and the wood-carvers of Nuremberg. As a manager of a modern industrial firm competing with others for profit he was less successful. The purchasing of the best material, the succession of costly experiments, the 'scrapping' of all imperfect work, meant a heavy drain on the capital. Also the society had been hurriedly formed without proper safeguards for fairly recompensing the various members according to their work; and when in 1875 it was found necessary to reconstitute it, that Morris might legally hold the position which he had from the outset won by his exertions, this could not be effected without loss, nor without a certain friction between the partners. So, however prosperous the business might seem to be through its monopoly of certain wares, it was difficult even for a skilful financier to make on each year a profit which was in any way proportionate to the fame of the work produced. But in 1865 Morris was fortunate in finding a friend ready to undertake the keeping of the books, who sympathized with his aims and whose gifts supplemented his own; and, for the rest, he had read and digested the work of Ruskin, and had learnt from him that the function of the true merchant was to produce goods of the best quality, and only secondarily to produce a profitable balance-sheet.

How it was that from being the head of an industrial business Morris came to be an ardent advocate of Socialism is the central problem of his life. The root of the matter lay in his love of art and of the Middle Ages. He had studied the centuries productive of the best art known to him, and he believed that he understood the conditions under which it was produced. The one essential was that the workers found pleasure in their work. They were not benumbed by that Division of Labour which set the artisan laboriously repeating the same mechanical task; they worked at the bidding of no master jealously measuring time, material, and price against his competitors; they passed on from one generation to another the tradition of work well done for its own sake. He knew there was another side to the picture, and that in many ways the freedom of the mediaeval craftsman had been curtailed. He did not ask history to run backwards, but he felt that the nineteenth century was advancing on the wrong line of progress. To him there seemed to be three types of social framework. The feudal or Tory type was past and obsolete; for the richer classes of to-day had neither the power nor the will to renew it. The Whig or Manchester ideal held the field, the rich employer regarding his workmen as so many hands capable of producing so much work and so much profit, and believing that free bargaining between free men must yield the best economic results for all classes, and that beyond economic and political liberty the State had no more to give, and a man must be left to himself. Against this doctrine emphatic protests had been uttered in widely differing forms by Carlyle and Disraeli, by Ruskin and Dickens; but it was slow to die.

The third ideal was that of the Socialist; and to Morris this meant that the State should appropriate the means of production and should so arrange that every worker was assured of the means of livelihood and of sufficient leisure to enjoy the fruits of what he had made. He who could live so simply himself thought more of the unjust distribution of happiness than of wealth, as may be seen in his *News from Nowhere*, where he gives a Utopian picture of England as it was to be after the establishment of Socialism. Here rather than in polemical speeches or pamphlets can we find the true reflection of his attitude and the way in which he thought about reform.

It was not easy for him to embark on such a crusade. In his early manhood, except for his volunteering in the war scare of 1859, he had taken no part in public life. The first cause which led to his appearing at meetings was wrath at the ill-considered restoration of old buildings. In 1877, when a society was formed for their protection, Morris was one of the leaders, and took his stand by Ruskin, who had already stated the principles to be observed. They believed that the presentation of nineteenth-century masonry in the guise of mediaeval work was a fraud on the public, that it obscured the true lessons of the past, and that, under the pretence of reviving the original design, it marred the development which had naturally gone forward through the centuries. It was from his respect for work and the workman that Morris denounced this pedantry, from his love of stones rightly hewn and laid, of carving which the artist had executed unconsciously in the spirit of his time, and which was now being replaced by lifeless imitation to the order of a bookish antiquary. Against this he was ready to protest at all times, and references to meetings of 'Antiscrape', as he calls the society, are frequent in his letters. He also was rigid in declining all orders to the firm where his own decorations might seem to disturb the relics of the past.

His next step was still more difficult. The plunge of a famous poet and artist into agitation, of a capitalist and employer into Socialism, provoked much wonder and many indignant protests. His severer critics seized on any pamphlet of his in which they could detect logical fallacies and scornfully asked whether this was fit work for the author of the *Earthly Paradise*. Many liberal-minded people indeed regretted the diversion of his activities, but the question whether he was wasting them is one that needs consideration; and to judge him fairly we must look at the problem from his side and postulate that Socialism (whether he interpreted its theories aright or not) did pursue practical ideals. If Aeschylus was more proud of fighting at Marathon than of writing tragedies—if Socrates claimed respect as much for his firmness as a juryman as for his philosophic method—surely Morris might believe that his duty to his countrymen called him to leave his study and his workshop to take an active part in public affairs. He might be more prone to error than those who had trained themselves to political life, but he faced the problems honestly and sacrificed his comfort for the common good.

Criticism took a still more personal turn in the hands of those who pointed out that Morris himself occupied the position of a capitalist employer, and who asked him to live up to his creed by divesting himself of his property and taking his place in the ranks of the proletariat. This argument is dealt with by Mr. Mackail,[54] who describes the steps which Morris took to admit his foremen to sharing the profits of the business, and defends him against the charge of inconsistency. Morris may not have thought out the question in all its aspects, but much of the criticism passed upon him was even more illogical and depended on far too narrow and illiterate a use of the word Socialism. He knew as well as his critics that no new millennium could be introduced by merely taking the wealth of the rich and dividing it into equal portions among the poor.

However reluctant Morris might be to leave his own work for public agitation, he plunged into the Socialist campaign with characteristic energy. For two or three years he was constantly devoting his Sundays to open-air speech-making, his evenings to thinly-attended meetings in stuffy rooms in all the poorer parts of London; and, at the call of comrades, he often travelled into the provinces, and even as far as Scotland, to lend a hand. And he spent time and money prodigally in supporting journals which were to spread the special doctrines of his form of Socialism. Nor was it only the indifference and the hostility of those outside which he had to meet; quarrels within the party were frequent and bitter, though Morris himself, despite his impetuous temper, showed a wonderful spirit of brotherliness and conciliation. For two years his work lay with the Socialist Democratic Federation, till differences of opinion with Mr. Hyndman drove him to resign; in 1885 he founded the Socialist League, and for this he toiled, writing, speaking, and attending committees, till 1889, when the control was captured by a knot of anarchists, in spite of all his efforts. After this he ceased to be a 'militant'; but in no way did he abandon his principles or despair of the ultimate triumph of the cause. The result of his efforts must remain unknown. If the numbers of his audiences were often insignificant, and the visible outcome discouraging to a degree, yet in estimating the value of personal example no outward test can satisfy us. He gave of his best with the same thoroughness as in all his crafts, and no man can do more. But, looking at the matter from a regard to his special gifts and to his personal happiness, we may be glad that his active connexion with Socialism ceased in 1889, and that he was granted seven years of peace before the end.

These were the years that saw the birth and growth of the 'Kelmscott' printing press, so called after his country house. Of illuminated manuscripts[55] he had always been fond, but it was only in 1888 that his attention was turned to details of typography. The mere study of old and new founts did not satisfy him for long; the creative impulse demanded that he should design types of his own and produce his own books. As in the other arts, his lifelong friend Burne-Jones was called in to supply figure drawings for the illustrated books which Morris was himself to adorn with decorative borders and initials. Of his many schemes, not all came to fruition; but after four years of planning, and a year and a half given to the actual process of printing, his masterpiece, the Kelmscott edition of Chaucer, was completed, and a copy was in his hands a few months before his death.

The last seven years of his life were spent partly at Hammersmith and partly at Kelmscott, the old manor house, lying on the banks of the Upper Thames, which he had tenanted since 1878. He had never been a great traveller, dearly though he loved the north of France with its Gothic cathedrals and 'the river bottoms with the endless poplar forests and the green green meadows'. His tastes were very individual. Iceland made stronger appeals to him than Greece or Rome; and even at Florence and Venice he was longing to return to England and its homely familiar scenes. Scotland with its bare hills, 'raw-boned' as he called it, never gave him much pleasure; for he liked to see the earth clothed by nature and by the hand of man. By the Upper Thames, at the foot of the Cotswolds, the buildings of the past were still generally untouched; and beyond the orchards and gardens, with their old-world look, lay stretches of meadows, diversified by woods and low hills, haunted with the song of birds; and he could believe himself still to be in the England of Chaucer and Shakespeare. There he would always welcome the friends whom he loved and who loved him; but to the world at large he was a recluse. His abrupt manner, his Johnsonian utterances, would have made him a disconcerting element in Victorian tea-parties. When provoked by foolish utterances, he was, no less than Johnson, downright in contradiction. There was nothing that he disliked so much as being lionized; and there was much to annoy him when he stepped outside his own home and circle. His last public speech was made on the abuses of public advertisement; and in the last year of his life we hear him growling in Ruskinian fashion that he was ever 'born with a sense of romance and beauty in this accursed age'.

His life had been a strenuous and exhausting one, but he enjoyed it to the last. As he said to Hyndman ten days before the end, 'It has been a jolly good world to me when all is said, and I don't wish to leave it yet awhile'. At least his latter years had been years of peace. He had been freed from the stress of conflict; he had found again the joys of youth, and could recapture the old music.

The days have slain the days, and the seasons have gone by
And brought me the summer again; and here on the grass I lie
As erst I lay and was glad, ere I meddled with right and wrong.

After an illness in 1891 he never had quite the same physical vigour, though he continued to employ himself fully for some years in a way which would tax the energy of many robust men. In 1895 the vital energy was failing, and he was content to relax his labours. In August 1896 he was suffering from congestion of the lungs, and in October he died peacefully at Hammersmith, attended by the loving care of his wife and his oldest friends. The funeral at Kelmscott was remarkable for simplicity and beauty, the coffin being borne along the country road in a farm wagon strewn with leaves; and he lies in the quiet churchyard amid the meadows and orchards which he loved so well.

Among the prophets and poets who took up their parable against the worship of material wealth and comfort, he will always have a foremost place. The thunder of Carlyle, the fiery eloquence of Ruskin, the delicate irony of Matthew Arnold, will find a responsive echo in the heart of one reader or another; will expose the false standards of life set up in a materialistic age and educate them in the pursuit of what is true, what is beautiful, and what is reasonable. But to men who work with their hands there must always be something specially inspiring in the life and example of one who was a handicraftsman and so much beside. And Morris was not content to denounce and to despair. He enjoyed what was good in the past and the present, and he preached in a hopeful spirit a gospel of yet better things for the future. He was an artist in living. Amid all the diversity of his work there was an essential unity in his life. The men with whom he worked were the friends whom he welcomed in his leisure; the crafts by which he made his wealth were the pastimes over which he talked and thought in his home; his dreams for the future were framed in the setting of the mediaeval romances which he loved from his earliest days. Though he lived often in an atmosphere of conflict, and often knew failure, he has left us an example which may help to fill the emptiness and to kindle the lukewarmness of many an unquiet heart, and may reconcile the discords that mar the lives of too many of his countrymen in this age of transition and of doubt.

JOHN RICHARD GREEN
From a drawing by Frederick Sandys

JOHN RICHARD GREEN

1837-83

1837. Born at Oxford, December 12.

1845-52. Magdalen College School, Oxford.

1852-4. With a private tutor.

1855-9. Jesus College, Oxford.

1861-3. Curate at Goswell Road, E.C.

1863-4. Curate at Hoxton.

1864-9. Mission Curate and Rector of St. Philip's, Stepney.

1869. Abandons parochial work. Librarian at Lambeth Palace.

1867-73. Contributor to *Saturday Review*.

1874. *Short History of the English People* published.

1877. Marries Miss Alice Stopford.

1877-80. Four volumes of larger *History of the English People* published.

1880-1. Winter in Egypt.

1882. January, *Making of England* published.

1883. January, *Conquest of England* finished (published posthumously). Last illness. Death, March 7.

JOHN RICHARD GREEN

HISTORIAN

The eighteenth century did some things with a splendour and a completeness which is the despair of later, more restlessly striving generations. Barren though it was of poetry and high imagination, it gave birth to our most famous works in political economy, in biography, and in history; and it has set up for us classic models of imperishable fame. But the wisdom of Adam Smith, the shrewd observation of Boswell, the learning of Gibbon, did not readily find their way into the market-place. Outside of the libraries and the booksellers' rows in London and Edinburgh they were in slight demand. Even when the volumes of Gibbon, Hume, and Robertson had been added to the library shelves, where Clarendon and Burnet reigned before them, too often they only passed to a state of dignified retirement and slumber. No hand disturbed them save that of the conscientious housemaid who dusted them in due season. They were part of the furnishings indispensable to the elegance of a 'gentleman's seat'; and in many cases the guests, unless a Gibbon were among them, remained ignorant whether the labels on their backs told a truthful tale, or whether they disguised an ingenious box or backgammon board, or formed a mere covering to the wall.

The fault was with the public more than with the authors. Those who ventured on the quest would find noble eloquence in Clarendon, lively narrative in Burnet, critical analysis in Hume; but the indolence of the Universities and the ignorance of the general public unfitted them for the effort required to value a knowledge of history or to take steps to acquire it. It is true that the majestic style of Clarendon was puzzling to a generation accustomed to prose of the fashion inaugurated by Dryden and Addison; and that Hume and other historians, with all their precision and clearness, were wanting in fervour and imagination. But the record of English history was so glorious, so full of interest for the patriot and for the politician, that it should have spoken for itself, and the apathy of the educated classes was not creditable to them. Even so Ezekiel found the Israelites of his day, forgetful of their past history and its lessons, sunk in torpor and indifference. He looked upon the wreckage of his nation, settled in the Babylonian plain; in his fervent imagination he saw but a valley of dry bones, and called aloud to the four winds that breath should come into them and they should live.

In our islands the prophets who wielded the most potent spell came from beyond the Border. Walter Scott exercised the wider influence, Carlyle kindled the intenser flame. As artists they followed very different methods. Scott, like a painter, wielding a vigorous brush full charged with human sympathies, set before us a broad canvas in lively colours filled with a warm diffused light. Carlyle worked more in the manner of an etcher, the mordant acid eating deep into the plate. From the depth of his shadows would stand out single figures or groups, in striking contrast, riveting the attention and impressing themselves on the memory. Scott drew thousands of readers to sympathize with the men and women of an earlier day, and to feel the romance that attaches to lost causes in Church and State. Carlyle set scores of students striving to recreate the great men of the past and by their standards to reject the shibboleths of the present. However different were the methods of the enchanters, the dry bones had come to life. Mediaeval abbot and crusader, cavalier and covenanter, Elizabeth and Cromwell, spoke once more with a living voice to ears which were opened to hear.

Nor did the English Universities fail to send forth men who could meet the demands of a generation which was waking up to a healthier political life. The individual who achieved most in popularizing English history was Macaulay, who began to write his famous Essays in 1825, the year after he won his fellowship at Trinity, though the world had to wait another twenty-five years for his History of the English Revolution. Since then Cambridge historians like Acton, or Maitland, have equalled or excelled him in learning, though none has won such brilliant success. But it was the Oxford School which did most, in the middle of the nineteenth century, to clear up the dark places of our national record and to present a complete picture of the life of the English people. Freeman delved long among the chronicles of Normans and Saxons; Stubbs no less laboriously excavated the charters of the Plantagenets; Froude hewed his path through the State papers of the Tudors; while Gardiner patiently unravelled the tangled skein of Stuart misgovernment. John Richard Green, one of the youngest of the school, took a wider subject, the continuous history of the English people. He was fortunate in writing at a time when the public was prepared to find the subject interesting, but he himself did wonders in promoting this interest, and since then his work has been a lamp to light teachers on the way.

In a twofold way Green may claim to be a child of Oxford. Not only was he a member of the University, but he was a native of the town, being born in the centre of that ancient city in the year of Queen Victoria's accession. His family had been engaged in trade there for two generations without making more than a competence; and even before his father died in 1852 they were verging on poverty. Of his parents, who were kind and affectionate, but not gifted with special talents, there is little to be told; the boy was inclined, in after life, to attribute any literary taste that he may have inherited to his mother. From his earliest days reading was his passion, and he was rarely to be seen without a book. Old church architecture and the sound of church bells also kindled his childish enthusiasms, and he would hoard his pence to purchase the joy of being admitted into a locked-up church. So he was fortunate in being sent at the age of eight to Magdalen College School, where he had daily access to the old buildings of the College and the beautiful walks which had been trodden by the feet of Addison a century and a half before. An amusing contrast could be drawn between the decorous scholar of the seventeenth century, handsome, grave of mien, calmly pacing the gravel walk, while he tasted the delights of classic literature, and little 'Johnny Green', a mere shrimp of a boy with bright eyes and restless ways, darting here and there, eagerly searching for anything new or exciting which he might find, whether in the bushes or in the pages of some romance which he was carrying.

But, for all his lively curiosity, Green seems to have got little out of his lessons at school. The classic languages formed the staple of his education, and he never had that power of verbal memory which could enable him to retain the rules of the Greek grammar or to handle the Latin language with the accuracy of a scholar. He soon gave up trying to do so. Instead of aspiring to the mastery of accidence and syntax, he aimed rather at securing immunity from the rod. At Magdalen School it was still actively in use; but there were certain rules about the number of offences which must be committed in a given time to call for its application. Green was clever enough to notice this, and to shape his course accordingly; and thus his lessons became, from a sporting point of view, an unqualified success.

But his real progress in learning was due to his use of the old library in his leisure hours. Here he made acquaintance with Marco Polo and other books of travel; here he read works on history of various kinds, and became prematurely learned in the heresies of the early Church. The views which he developed, and perhaps stated too crudely, did not win approval. He was snubbed by examiners for his interest in heresiarchs, and gravely reproved by Canon Mozley[56] for justifying the execution of Charles I. The latter subject had been set for a prize essay; and the Canon was fair-minded enough to give the award to the boy whose views he disliked, but whose merit he recognized. Partial and imperfect though this education was, the years spent under the shadow of Magdalen must have had a deep influence on Green; but he tells us little of his impressions, and was only half conscious of them at the time. The incident which perhaps struck him most was his receiving a prize from the hands of the aged Dr. Routh, President of the College, who had seen Dr. Johnson in his youth, and lived to be a centenarian and the pride of Oxford in early Victorian days.

Green's school life ended in 1852, the year in which his father died. He was already at the top of the school; and to win a scholarship at the University was now doubly important for him. This he achieved at Jesus College, Oxford, in December 1854, after eighteen months spent with a private tutor; and, as he was too young to go into residence at once, he continued for another year to read by himself. Though he gave closer attention to his classics he did not drop his general reading; and it was a landmark in his career when at the age of sixteen he made acquaintance with Gibbon.

His life as an undergraduate was not very happy and was even less successful than his days at school, though the fault did not lie with him. Shy and sensitive as he was, he had a sociable disposition and was naturally fitted to make friends. But he had come from a solitary life at a tutor's to a college where the men were clannish, most of them Welshmen, and few of them disposed to look outside their own circle for friends. Had Green been as fortunate as William Morris, his life at Oxford might have been different; but there was no Welshman at Jesus of the calibre of Burne-Jones; and Green lived in almost complete isolation till the arrival of Boyd Dawkins in 1857. The latter, who became in after years a well-known professor of anthropology, was Green's first real friend, and the letters which he wrote to him show how necessary it was for Green to have one with whom he could share his interests and exchange views freely. Dawkins had the scientific, Green the literary, nature and gifts; but they had plenty of common ground and were always ready to explore the records of the past, whether they were to be found in barrows, in buildings, or in books. If Dawkins was the first friend, the first teacher who influenced him was Arthur Stanley, then Canon of Christ Church and Professor of Ecclesiastical History. An accident led Green into his lecture-room one day; but he was so much delighted with the spirit of Stanley's teaching, and the life which he imparted to history, that he became a constant member of the class. And when Stanley made overtures of friendship, Green welcomed them warmly.

A new influence had come into his life. Not only was his industry, which had been feeble and irregular, stimulated at last to real effort; but his attitude to religious questions and to the position of the English Church was at this time sensibly modified. He had come up to the University a High Churchman; like many others at the time of the Oxford Movement, he had been led half-way towards Roman Catholicism, stirred by the historical claims and the mystic spell of Rome. But from now onwards, under the guidance of Stanley and Maurice, he adopted the views of what is called the 'Broad Church Party', which suited his moral fervour and the liberal character of his social and political opinions.

Despite, however, the stimulus given to him (perhaps too late) by Dawkins and Stanley, Green won no distinctions at the University, and few men of his day could have guessed that he would ever win distinction elsewhere. He took a dislike to the system of history-teaching then in vogue, which consisted in demanding of all candidates for the schools a knowledge of selected fragments of certain authors, giving them no choice or scope in the handling of wider subjects. He refused to enter for a class in the one subject in which he could shine, and managed to scrape through his examination by combining a variety of uncongenial subjects. This was perverse, and he himself recognized it to be so afterwards. All the while there was latent in him the talent, and the ambition, which might have enabled him to surpass all his contemporaries. His one literary achievement of the time was unknown to the men of his college, but it is of singular interest in view of what he came to achieve later. He was asked by the editor of the *Oxford Chronicle*, an old-established local paper, to write two articles on the history of the city of Oxford. To most undergraduates the town seemed a mere parasite of the University; to Green it was an elder sister. Many years later he complained in one of his letters that the city had been stifled by the University, which in its turn had suffered similar treatment from the Church. To this task, accordingly, he brought a ready enthusiasm and a full mind; and his articles are alive with the essence of what, since the days of his childhood, he had observed, learnt, and imagined, in the town of his birth. We see the same spirit in a letter which he wrote to Dawkins in 1860, telling him how he had given up a day to following the Mayor of Oxford when he observed the time-honoured custom of beating the bounds of the city. He describes with gusto how he trudged along roads, clambered over hedges, and even waded through marshes in order to perform the rite with scrupulous thoroughness. But it was years before he could find an audience who would appreciate his power of handling such a subject, and his University career must, on his own evidence, be written down a failure.

When it was over he was confronted with the need for choosing a profession. It had strained the resources of his family to give him a good education, and now he must fend for himself. To a man of his nature and upbringing the choice was not wide. His age and his limited means put the Services out of the question; nor was he fitted to embark in trade. Medicine would revolt his sensibility, law would chill his imagination, and journalism did not yet exist as a profession for men of his stamp. In the teaching profession, for which he had such rare gifts, he would start handicapped by his low degree. In any case, he had for some time cherished the idea of taking Holy Orders. The ministry of the Church would give him a congenial field of work and, so he hoped, some leisure to continue his favourite studies. Perhaps he had not the same strong conviction of a 'call' as many men of his day in the High Church or Evangelical parties; but he was, at the time, strongly drawn by the example and teaching of Stanley and Maurice, and he soon showed that it was not merely for negative reasons or from half-hearted zeal that he had made the choice. When urged by Stanley to seek a curacy in West London, he deliberately chose the East End of the town because the need there was greater and the training in self-sacrifice was sterner; and there is no doubt that the popular sympathies, which the reading of history had already implanted in him, were nourished and strengthened by nine years of work among the poor. The exertion of parish work taxed his physical resources, and he was often incapacitated for short periods by the lavish way in which he spent himself. Indeed, but for this constant drain upon his strength, he might have lived a longer life and left more work behind him.

Of the parishes which he served, the last and the most interesting was St. Philip's, Stepney, to which he went from Hoxton in 1864. It was a parish of 16,000 souls, lying between Whitechapel and Poplar, not far from the London Docks. Dreary though the district seems to us to-day—and at times Green was fully conscious of this—he could re-people it in imagination with the men of the past, and find pleasure in the noble views on the river and the crowded shipping that passed so near its streets. But above all he found a source of interest in the living individuals whom he met in his daily round and who needed his help; and though he achieved signal success in the pulpit by his power of extempore preaching, he himself cared more for the effect of his visiting and other social work. Sermons might make an impression for the moment; personal sympathy, shown in the moment when it was needed, might change the whole current of a life.

For children his affection was unfailing; and for the humours of older people he had a wide tolerance and charity. His letters abound with references to this side of his work. He tells us of his 'polished' pork butcher and his learned parish clerk, and boasts how he won the regard of the clerk's Welsh wife by correctly pronouncing the magic name of Machynlleth. He gave a great deal of time to his parishioners, to consulting his churchwardens, to starting choirs, to managing classes and parish expeditions. He could find time to attend a morning police court when one of his boys got into difficulties, or to hold a midnight service for the outcasts of the pavement.

When cholera broke out in Stepney in 1866, Green visited the sick and dying in rooms that others did not dare to enter, and was not afraid to help actively in burying those who had died of the disease. At holiday gatherings he was the life and soul of the body, 'shocking two prim maiden teachers by starting kiss-in-the-ring', and surprising his most vigorous helpers by his energy and decision. On such occasions he exhausted himself in the task of leadership, and he was no less generous in giving financial help to every parish institution that was in need.

What hours he could snatch from these tasks he would spend in the Reading Room of the British Museum; but these were all too few. His position, within a few miles of the treasure houses of London, and of friends who might have shared his studies, must have been tantalizing to a degree. To parish claims also was sacrificed many a chance of a precious holiday. We have one letter in which he regretfully abandons the project of a tour with Freeman in his beloved Anjou because he finds that the only dates open to his companion clash with the festival of the patron saint of his church. In another he resists the appeal of Dawkins to visit him in Somerset on similar grounds. His friend may become abusive, but Green assures him emphatically that it cannot be helped. 'I am not a pig,' he writes; 'I am a missionary curate.... I could not come to you, because I was hastily summoned to the cure of 5,000 costermongers and dock labourers.' We are far from the easy standard of work too often accepted by 'incumbents' in the opening years of the nineteenth century.

Early in his clerical career he had begun to form plans for writing on historical subjects, most of which had to be abandoned for one reason or another. At one time he was planning with Dawkins a history of Somerset, which would have been a forerunner of the County Histories of the twentieth century. Dawkins was to do the geology and anthropology; Green would contribute the archaeology and history. In many ways they were well equipped for the task; but the materials had not been sifted and the demands on their time would have been excessive, even if they abstained from all other work. Another scheme was for a series of Lives of the Archbishops of Canterbury. Green was much attracted by the subject. Already he had made a special study of Dunstan and other great holders of the See; and he believed that the series would illustrate, better than the lives of kings, the growth of certain principles in English history. But with other archbishops he found himself out of sympathy; and in the end he was not sorry to abandon the idea, when he found that Dean Hook was already engaged upon it.

A project still nearer to his heart, which he cherished till near the end of his life, was to write a history of our Angevin kings. For this he collected a vast quantity of materials, and it was a task for which he was peculiarly fitted. It would be difficult to say whether Fulc Nerra, the founder of the dynasty, or Black Angers, the home of the race, was more vividly present to him. Grim piles of masonry, stark force of character, alike compelled his admiration and he could make them live again in print. As it proved, his life was too short to realize this ambition and he has only left fragments of what he had to tell, though we are fortunate in having other books on parts of the subject from his wife and from Miss Norgate, which owed their origin to his inspiration.

During his time as a London clergyman Green used to pay occasional visits to Dawkins in Somerset; and in 1862, when he went to read a paper on Dunstan to a society at Taunton, he renewed acquaintance with his old schoolfellow, E. A. Freeman, a notable figure in the county as squire, politician, and antiquarian, and already becoming known outside it as a historian. The following year, as Freeman's guest, he met Professor Stubbs; and about this time he also made friends with James Bryce, 'the Holy Roman', as he calls him in later letters.[57] The friendship of these three men was treasured by Green throughout his life, and it gave rise to much interesting correspondence on historical subjects. They were the central group of the Oxford School; they reverenced the same ideals and were in general sympathy with one another. But this sympathy never descended to mere mutual admiration, as with some literary coteries. Between Freeman and Green in particular there was kept up a running fire of friendly but outspoken criticism, which would have strained the tie between men less generous and less devoted to historical truth. Freeman was the more arbitrary and dogmatic, Green the more sensitive and discriminating. Green bows to

Freeman's superior knowledge of Norman times, acknowledges him his master, and apologizes for hasty criticisms when they give offence; but he boldly rebukes his friend for his indifference to the popular movements in Italian cities and for his pedantry about Italian names.

And he treads on even more delicate ground when he taxes him with indulging too frequently in polemics, urging him to 'come out of the arena' and to cease girding at Froude and Kingsley, whose writings Freeman loved to abuse. Freeman, on the other hand, grumbles at Green for going outside the province of history to write on more frivolous subjects, and scolds him for introducing fanciful ideas into his narrative of events. The classic instance of this was when Green, after describing the capture by the French of the famous Château Gaillard in Normandy, had the audacity to say, 'from its broken walls we see not merely the pleasant vale of Seine, but also the sedgy flats of our own Runnymede'. Thereby he meant his readers to learn that John would never have granted the Great Charter to the Barons, had he not already weakened the royal authority by the loss of Cœur-de-Lion's great fortress beyond the sea, and that to a historian the germs of English freedom, won beside the Thames, were to be seen in the wreckage of Norman power above the Seine. But Freeman was too matter of fact to allow such flights of fancy; and a lively correspondence passed between the two friends, each maintaining his own view of what might or might not be permitted to the votaries of Clio.

But before this episode Green had been introduced by Freeman to John Douglas Cook, founder and editor of the *Saturday Review*, and had begun to contribute to its columns. Naturally it was on historical subjects that his pen was most active; but apart from the serious 'leading articles', the *Saturday* found place for what the staff called 'Middles', light essays written after the manner of Addison or Steele on matters of every-day life. Here Green was often at his best. Freeman growled, in his dictatorial fashion, when he found his friend turning away from the strait path of historical research to describe the humours of his parish, the foibles of district visitors and deaconesses, the charms of the school-girl before she expands her wings in the drawing-room—above all (and this last was quoted by the author as his best literary achievement) the joys of 'Children by the sea'. But any one who turns over the pages of the volume called *Stray Studies from England and Italy*, where some of these articles are reprinted, will probably agree with the verdict of the author on their merits. The subjects are drawn from all ages and all countries. Historical scenes are peopled with the figures of the past, treated in the magical style which Green made his own. Dante is seen against the background of mediaeval Florence; Tintoret represents the life of Venice at its richest, most glorious time. The old buildings of Lambeth make a noble setting for the portraits of archbishops, the gentle Warham, the hapless

Cranmer, the tyrannical Laud. Many of these studies are given to the pleasant border-land between history and geography, and to the impressions of travel gathered in England or abroad. In one sketch he puts into a single sentence all the features of an old English town which his quick eye could note, and from which he could 'work out the history of the men who lived and died there. In quiet quaintly-named streets, in the town mead and the market-place, in the lord's mill beside the stream, in the ruffed and furred brasses of its burghers in the church, lies the real life of England and Englishmen, the life of their home and their trade, their ceaseless, sober struggle with oppression, their steady, unwearied battle for self-government.'

In another he follows the funeral procession of his Angevin hero Henry II from the stately buildings of Chinon 'by the broad bright Vienne coming down in great gleaming curves, under the grey escarpments of rock pierced here and there with the peculiar cellars or cave-dwellings of the country', to his last resting-place in the vaults of Fontevraud. Standing beside the monuments on their tombs he notes the striking contrast of type and character which Henry offers to his son Richard Cœur-de-Lion. 'Nothing', he says, 'could be less ideal than the narrow brow, the large prosaic eyes, the coarse full cheeks, the sensual dogged jaw, that combine somehow into a face far higher than its separate details, and which is marked by a certain sense of power and command. No countenance could be in stronger contrast with his son's, and yet in both there is the same look of repulsive isolation from men. Richard's is a face of cultivation and refinement, but there is a strange severity in the small delicate mouth and in the compact brow of the lion-hearted, which realizes the verdict of his day. To an historical student one glance at these faces, as they lie here beneath the vault raised by their ancestor, the fifth Count Fulc, tells more than pages of history.' Our reviews and magazines may abound to-day in such vivid pen-pictures of places and men; but it was Green and others of his day who watered the dry roots of archaeology and restored it to life.

But from his earliest days as a student Green had looked beyond the figures of kings, ministers, and prelates, who had so long filled the stage in the volumes of our historians. However clearly they stood out in their greatness and in their faults, they were not, and could not be, the nation. And when he came to write on a larger scale, the title which he chose for his book showed that he was aiming at new ideals.

The *Short History of the English People* is the book by which Green's fame will stand or fall, and it occupied him for the best years of his life. The true heroes of it are the labourer and the artisan, the friar, the printer, and the industrial mechanic—'not many mighty, not many noble'. The true growth of the English nation is seen broad-based on the life of the commonalty, and we can study it better in the rude verse of Longland, or the parables of Bunyan, than in the formal records of battles and dynastic schemes.

The periods into which the book is divided are chosen on other grounds than those of the old handbooks, where the accession of a new king or a new dynasty is made a landmark; and a different proportion is observed in the space given to events or to prominent men. The Wars of the Roses are viewed as less important than the Peasants' Revolt; the scholars of the New Learning leave scant space for Lambert Simnels and Perkin Warbecks. Henry Pelham, one of the last prime ministers to owe his position to the king's favour, receives four lines, while forty are given to John Howard, a pioneer in the new path of philanthropy. Besides social subjects, literature receives generous measure, but even here no rigid system is observed. Chaucer, Spenser, and Shakespeare take a prominent place in their epochs; Byron, Wordsworth, and Tennyson are ignored. This is not because Green had no interest in them or undervalued their influence. Far from it. But, as the history of the nation became more complex, he found it impossible, within the limits prescribed by a *Short* History, to do justice to everything. He believed that the industrialism, which grew up in the Georgian era, exercised a wider influence in changing the character of the people than the literature of that period; and so he turned his attention to Watt and Brindley, and deliberately omitted the poets and painters of that day. With his wide sympathies he must have found this rigorous compression the hardest of his tasks, and only in part could he compensate it later. He never lived long enough to treat, as he wished to do, in the fullness of his knowledge, the later periods of English history.

In writing this book Green had many discouragements to contend against, apart from his continual ill-health. Even his friends spoke doubtfully of its method and style, with the exception of his publisher, George Macmillan, and of Stopford Brooke, whose own writings breathe the same spirit as Green's, and who did equally good work in spreading a real love of history and literature among the classes who were beginning to read. It was true that Green's book failed to conform to the usual type of manual; it was not orderly in arrangement, it was often allusive in style, it seemed to select what it pleased and to leave out what students were accustomed to learn. But Green's faith in its power to reach the audience to whom he appealed was justified by the enthusiasm with which the general public received it. This success was largely due to the literary style and artistic handling of the subject. Green claims himself that on most literary questions he is French in his point of view. 'It seems to me', he says, 'that on all points of literary art we have to sit at the feet of French Gamaliels'; and in his best work he has more in common with Michelet than with our own classic historians. But while

Michelet had many large volumes in which to expand his treatment of picturesque episodes, Green was painfully limited by space.

What he can give us of clear and lively portraiture in a few lines is seen in his presentation of the gallant men who laid the foundation of our Empire overseas. By a few lines of narrative, and a happy quotation from their own words, Green brings out the heroism of their sacrifice or their success, the faith which inspired Humphry Gilbert to meet his death at sea, the patience which enabled John Smith to achieve the tillage of Virginian soil.

Side by side with these masterly vignettes are full-length portraits of great rulers such as Alfred, Elizabeth, and Cromwell, and vivid descriptions of religious leaders such as Cranmer, Laud, and Wesley. Strong though Green's own views on Church and State were, we do not feel that he is deserting the province of the historian to lecture us on religion or politics. The book is real narrative written in a fair spirit, the author rendering justice to the good points of men like Laud, whom he detested, and aiming above all at conveying clearly to his readers the picture of what he believed to have happened in the past. As a narrative it was not without faults. The reviewers at once seized on many small mistakes, into which Green had fallen through the uncertainty of his memory for names and words. To these Green cheerfully confessed, and was thankful that they proved to be so slight. But when other critics accused him of superficiality they were in error. On this point we have the verdict of Bishop Stubbs, the most learned and conscientious historian of the day. 'All Green's work', he says, 'was real and original work. Few people beside those who knew him well could see, under the charming ease and vivacity of his style, the deep research and sustained industry of the laborious student. But it was so; there was no department of our national records that he had not studied, and, I think I may say, mastered. Hence, I think, the unity of his dramatic scenes and the cogency of his historical arguments.'

Green himself was as severe a critic of the book as any one. Writing in 1877 to his future wife, he says, 'I see the indelible mark of the essayist, the "want of long breath", as the French say, the jerkiness, the slurring over of the uninteresting parts, above all, the want of grasp of the subject as a whole'. On the advice of some of his best friends, confirmed by his own judgement, in 1874 he gave up contributing to the *Saturday Review*, in order to free his style from the character imparted to it by writing detached weekly articles. The composing of these articles had been a pleasure; the writing of English history was to be his life-work, and no divided allegiance was conceivable to him. But we may indeed be thankful that he resisted the views of other friends who wished to drive him into copying German models. This class Green called 'Pragmatic Historians';[58] and, while acknowledging their solid contributions to history, he maintains his conviction that there is another method and another school worthy of imitation, and that he must 'hold to what he thinks true and work it out as he can'.

Green was a rapid reader and a rapid writer. In a letter to Freeman, written when he was wintering in Florence in 1872, he admits covering the period from the Peasant Revolt to the end of the New Learning (1381-1520) in ten days. But he was writing from notes which represented years of previous study. In another letter, written in 1876, he confesses a tendency to 'wild hitting', and perhaps he was too rapid at times in drawing his inferences. 'With me', he says, 'the impulse to try to connect things, to find the "why" of things, is irresistible; and even if I overdo my political guesses, you or some German will punch my head and put things rightly and intelligibly again.' It is this power of connecting events and explaining how one movement leads to another which makes the stimulating quality of Green's work; and to a nation like the English, too little apt to indulge in general ideas, this quality may be of more value than the German erudition which tends to overburden the intelligence with too great a load of 'facts'. And, after all the labours of Carlyle and Froude, of Stubbs and Freeman, and all the delving into records and chronicles, who shall say what *are* facts, and what is inference, legitimate or illegitimate, from them?

Whatever were the shortcomings of the book, which Green in his letters to Freeman called by the affectionate names of 'Shorts' and 'Little Book', it inaugurated a new method, and won a hearing among readers who had hitherto professed no taste for history; and, financially, it proved so far a success that Green was relieved from the necessity of continuing work that was uncongenial. He had already given up his parish in 1869. Ill-health and the advice of his doctor were the deciding factors; but there is no doubt that Green was also finding it difficult to subscribe to all the doctrines of the Church. He took up the same liberal comprehensive attitude to Church questions as he did to politics, and opposed any attempt to stifle honest inquiry or to punish honest doubt. He was much disturbed by some of the attempts made at this time by the more extreme parties in the Church to enforce uniformity. Also he felt that the Church was not exercising its proper influence on the nation, owing to the prejudice or apathy of the clergy in meeting the social movements of the day. If he had found more support, inside the diocese, for his social and educational work, the breach might have been healed, or at any rate postponed, in the hope of his health mending.

Relieved of parish work, he found plentiful occupation in revising his old books and in planning new; he showed wonderful zest for travelling abroad, and, by choosing carefully the places for his winter sojourn, he fought heroically to combat increasing ill-health and to achieve his literary ambitions. Thus it was that he made intimate acquaintance with San Remo, Mentone, and Capri; and one winter he went as far as Luxor in the hope that the Egyptian climate might help him; but in vain. Under the guidance of his friend Stopford Brooke he visited for shorter periods Venice, Florence, and other Italian towns. He was catholic in his sympathies but not over-conscientious in sight-seeing. When Brooke left him at Florence, Green was openly glad to relapse into vagrant pilgrimage, to put aside his guide-book and to omit the daily visit to the Uffizi Gallery. But, on the other hand, he reproached Freeman for confining his interests entirely to architecture and emperors while ignoring pictures and sculpture, mediaeval guilds, and the relics of old civic life. It was at Troyes that Bryce observed him 'darting hither and thither through the streets like a dog following a scent'—and to such purpose that after a few hours of research he could write a brilliant paper sketching the history of the town as illustrated in its monuments—but in Italy, as in France, he had a wonderful gift for discovering all that was most worth knowing about a town, which other men passed by and ignored.

Capri, which he first visited at Christmas 1872, was the most successful of his winter haunts. The climate, the beauty of the scenery, the simplicity of the life, all suited him admirably. On this occasion he stayed four months in the island, and he has sung its praises in one of the 'Stray Studies'. Within a small compass there is a wonderful variety of scene. Green delights in it all, 'in the boldly scarped cliffs, in the dense scrub of myrtle and arbutus, in the blue strips of sea that seem to have been cunningly let in among the rocks, in the olive yards creeping thriftily up the hill sides, in the remains of Roman sculptures and mosaics, in the homesteads of grey stone and low domes and Oriental roofs'. And he found it an ideal place for literary work, restful and remote, 'where one can live unscourged by Kingsley's "wind of God".' 'The island', he writes, 'is a paradise of silence for those to whom silence is a delight. One wanders about in the vineyards without a sound save the call of the vinedressers: one lies on the cliff and hears, a thousand feet below, the dreary wash of the sea. There is hardly the cry of a bird to break the spell; even the girls who meet one with a smile on the hillside smile quietly and gravely in the Southern fashion as they pass by.' No greater contrast could be found to the conditions under which he began his books; and it is not surprising that in this haven of peace, with no parish business to break in upon his study, he worked more rapidly and confidently—when his health allowed.

From such retreats he would return refreshed in body and mind to continue studying and writing in London and to sketch out new plans for the future. One that bore rich fruit was that of a series of Primers, dealing shortly with great subjects and commending them to the general reader by attractive literary style. They were produced by Macmillan, Green acting as editor; and notable volumes were contributed by Gladstone on Homer, by Creighton on Rome, and by Stopford Brooke on English Literature. Here, again, Green was a pioneer in a path where he has had many followers since; and he would have been the first to edit an English Historical Review if more support had been forthcoming from the public. But for financial reasons he was obliged to abandon the scheme, and it did not see the light of day till Creighton launched it in 1886.

In 1877 he married and found in his wife just the helper that he needed. She too had the historical imagination, the love of research, and the power of writing. Husband and wife produced in co-operation a small geography of the British Isles, well planned, clear, and pleasant to read. But, apart from this, she was content, during the too brief period of their married life, to subordinate her activities to helping her husband, and her aid was invaluable at the time when he was writing his later books. There is no doubt that his marriage prolonged his life. The care which his wife took of him, whether in their home in foggy London, or in primitive lodgings in beautiful Capri, helped him over his worst days; and the new value which he now set on life and its happiness gave him redoubled force of will. There were others who helped him in these days of perpetual struggle with ill-health. His doctors, Sir Andrew Clark and Sir Lauder Brunton, rendered him the devotion of personal friends. The historians gathered round him in Kensington Square, the home of his later years, and cheered him with good talk. Those who were lucky enough to be admitted might hear him at his best, discussing historical questions in a circle which included Sir Henry Maine and Bishop Stubbs, as well as Lecky, Freeman, and Bryce. He had many other interests. Such a man could not be indifferent to contemporary politics. His heroes—and he was an ardent worshipper of heroes—were Gladstone and Garibaldi, and, like many Liberals of the day, he was violent in his opposition to Beaconsfield's policy in Eastern Europe. Hatred of Napoleonic tyranny killed for a while his sympathy with France, and in 1870 he sympathized with the German cause—at least till the rape of the two provinces and the sorrows of disillusioned France revived his old feeling for the French nation. Over everything he felt keenly and expressed himself warmly. As Tennyson said to him at the close of a visit to Aldworth, 'You're a jolly, vivid man; you're as vivid as lightning'.

Particularly dear to him was the close sympathy of Stopford Brooke and that of Humphry Ward, to whose father he had been curate in 1860 and who had himself for years learnt to cherish the friendship of Green and to seek his counsel. Mrs. Ward has told us how she (then Miss Arnold) brought her earliest literary efforts to Green, how kindly was his encouragement but how formidable was the standard of excellence which he set up. She has also pictured for us 'the thin wasted form seated in the corner of the sofa... the eloquent lips... the life flashing from his eyes beneath the very shadow of death'. His latter years, lived perpetually under this grim shadow, were yet full of cheerfulness and of hope. However the body might fail, the active brain was planning and the high courage was bracing him to further effort. Between 1877 and 1880 he published in four volumes a *History of the English People*, which follows the same plan and covers much the same ground as the *Short History*. He was able to revise his views on points where recent study threw fresh light and to include subjects which had been crowded out for want of space. But the book failed to attract readers to the same extent as the *Short History*. The freshness and buoyancy of the earlier sketch could not be recaptured after so long an interval. In the last year of his life he began again on the early history of England, working at a pace which would have been astonishing even in a man of robust health, and he completed in the short period of eleven months the brilliant volume called *The Making of England*. He had thought out the subject during many a day and night of pain and had the plan clear in his head; but he was indefatigable in revising his work, and would make as many as eight or ten drafts of a chapter before it satisfied his judgement. His last autumn and winter were occupied with the succeeding volume, *The Conquest of England*, and he left it sufficiently complete for his wife to edit and publish a few months after his death.

The end came at Mentone early in 1883. Two years of life had been won, as his doctor said, by sheer force of will; but the frail body could no longer obey the soul, and nature could bear no more.

If in the twentieth century history is losing its hold on the thought and feeling of the rising generation, Green is the last man whom we can blame. He gave all his faculties unsparingly to his task—patience, enthusiasm, single-hearted love of truth; and he encouraged others to do the same. No man was more free from the pontifical airs of those historians who proclaimed history as an academic science to be confined within the chilly walls of libraries and colleges. We may apply to his work what Mr. G. M. Trevelyan has said of the English historians from Clarendon down to recent times; it was 'the means of spreading far and wide, throughout all the reading classes, a love and knowledge of history, an elevated and critical patriotism, and certain qualities of mind and heart'.[59] Against the danger which he mentions in his next sentence, that we are now being drilled into submission to German models, Mr. Trevelyan is himself one of our surest protectors.

CECIL RHODES

1853-1902

1853.	Born at Bishop's Stortford, July 5.
1870.	Goes out to Natal.
1871.	Moves to Kimberley.
1873-81.	Intermittent visits to Oxford.
1880.	First De Beers Company started.
1880.	Member for Barkly West.
1883.	Commissioner in Bechuanaland.
1885.	Warren expedition: Bechuanaland annexed by British Government.
1887.	Acute rivalry between Rhodes and Barnato.
1888.	Barnato gives way: De Beers Consolidated founded.
1888.	Lobengula grants concession for mining.
1889.	British South Africa Chartered Company formed.
1890.	Prime Minister of Cape Colony.
1890.	Occupation of Mashonaland.
1893.	Second Rhodes ministry.
1893.	War with Lobengula. Matabeleland occupied.
1895.	'Drifts' question between Cape and Transvaal Government.
1895.	Jameson Raid, December 28.
1896.	January, Rhodes's resignation. Visit to England.
1896.	Rebellion in Rhodesia.
1897.	Inquiry into the Raid by Committee of the House of Commons.
1899.	D.C.L., Oxford.

1899.   Outbreak of Great Boer War.

1902.   Dies at Muizenberg, March 26.

CECIL RHODES
COLONIST

The Rhodes family can be traced back to sturdy English yeoman stock. In the eighteenth century they had held land in North London. Cecil's father was vicar of Bishop's Stortford, a quiet country town in Hertfordshire on the Essex border; he was a man of mark, wealthy, liberal, and unconventional, with the rare gift of preaching ten-minute sermons which were well worth hearing. Of his eldest sons, Herbert went to Winchester, Frank to Eton; Cecil, the fifth son, born on July 5, 1853, was kept at home. He had part of his education at the local Grammar School, but perhaps the better part at the Vicarage from his father himself. The shrewd Vicar soon saw that his fifth son was not fitted for the ordinary routine of professional life at home, and at the age of seventeen he was sent out to visit his brother Herbert, who had emigrated to Natal. Cecil said good-bye to his native land for the first time in 1870, and thus early elected to be a citizen of the Greater Britain beyond the seas.

CECIL RHODES
From the painting by G. F. Watts in the National Portrait Gallery

The brothers had certain points of resemblance, being both original and adventurous; but they had marked differences. The elder was a wanderer pure and simple, a lover of sport and of novelty. He could follow a new track with all the ardour of a pioneer; he could not sit down and develop the wealth which he had opened up. The management of the Natal cotton farm soon fell into the hands of Cecil, now eighteen years old, who noted every detail, and studied his crops, his workmen, and his markets, while Herbert was absent in quest of game and adventure. It was this spirit which led Herbert westward in 1871, among the earliest of the immigrants into the diamond fields: before the end of the year Cecil followed and soon took over and developed his brother's claim. It was no case of Esau and Jacob; the brothers had great affection for one another and fitted in together without jealousy. Each lived his own life and followed his own bent. As Kimberley was the first field in which Cecil showed his abilities, it is worth while to try to picture the scene. It remained a centre of interest to him for thirty years, the scene of many troubles and of many triumphs.

'The New Rush', as Kimberley was called in 1872, was a chaos of tents and rubbish heaps seen through a haze of dust—a heterogeneous collection of tents, wagons, native kraals and debris heaps, each set down with cheerful irresponsibility and indifference to order. The funnel of blue clay so productive of diamonds had been found on a bit of the bare Griqualand Veld, marked out by no geographical advantages, with no charm of woodland or river scenery. Here in the years to come the great pits, familiar in modern photographs, were to grow deeper and deeper, as the partitions fell in between the small claims, or as the more enterprising miners bought up their neighbours' plots. Here the debris heaps were to grow higher and higher, as more hundreds of Kaffirs were brought in to dig, or new machinery arrived, as the buckets plied more rapidly on the network of ropes overhead. In the early 'seventies there were few signs of these marvels to be seen by the outward eye—everything was in the rough—but they were no doubt already existing in the brain of 'a tall fair boy, blue eyed and with somewhat aquiline features, wearing flannels of the school playing-field, somewhat shrunken with strenuous rather than effectual washings, that still left the colour of the red veld dust'.

Here Cecil Rhodes lived for the greater part of ten years, finding time amid his work for dreams: living, in general, aloof from the men with whom he did his daily business, but laying here and there the foundations of a friendship which was to bear fruit hereafter. Rudd,[60] of the Matabeleland concessions, came out in 1873; Beit,[61] the partner in diamond fields and gold fields, the co-founder of the Chartered Company, in 1875; and in 1878 there came out from Edinburgh one whose name was to be linked still more closely with that of Rhodes. Leander Starr Jameson, a skilful doctor, a cheerful companion, gifted with a great capacity for self-devotion, and with unshakeable firmness of will, was now twenty-five years old. Rhodes and he soon drew closely together and for years they were living under one roof. While his casual and rather overbearing manners repelled many of his acquaintances, Rhodes had a genius for friendship with the few; and it was such men as these who shared his work, his pastimes, and his thoughts, and reconciled him to spending many years in the unattractive surroundings of the mines.

But his life at this time had other phases. Not the least wonderful chapter in it was the series of visits which he paid to Oxford between 1873 and 1881. The atmosphere of a mining camp does not seem likely to draw a man towards academic studies and a University life. But Rhodes, who had a great power of absorbing himself in work, had also the power of projecting himself beyond the interests of the moment. Seven times he found opportunity to tear himself away from the busy work of mining and to keep terms at Oxford; and they made a lasting impression upon him. It was not the love of book-learning, still less the love of games, which drew him there. To many he may have seemed to be spending his time unprofitably. He indulged in some rowing and polo, he was master of the drag-hounds, he worried his neighbours by nocturnal practising of the horn. The examinations in the schools, and the more popular athletic contests, knew little of him. But his sojourn in Oxford was a tribute paid by the higher side of his mind to education and to the value of high thinking as compared with material progress; and no one who knew him well in later life could doubt that the traditions of Oxford had deeply influenced his mind. On these things he was by nature reticent, and was often misjudged.

Between the years 1878 and 1888 must be placed the struggle between him and his rivals for predominance in Kimberley. It had begun with small enterprises, the purchasing of adjoining claims, the undertaking of drainage work, the introduction of better machinery. It attracted more attention in 1880 with the founding of the first De Beers Company, named after a Boer who had owned the land on which the mine lay. It culminated in 1887 in the battle with Barnato,[62] his most dangerous competitor, when by dexterous purchasing of shares in his rival's company Rhodes forced him into a final scheme of amalgamation. In 1888 was founded the great corporation of De Beers Consolidated mines. The masterful will of Rhodes dictated the terms of the Trust deed, giving very extensive power to the Directorate for the using of their funds. He was already laying his foundations, though few could then have guessed what imperial work was to be done with the money thus obtained. The process of amalgamation was not popular in Kimberley. It resulted in closing down many of the less profitable claims and in reducing the amount of labour employed. But it brought in better machinery and it saved expenses of management. Above all, it curtailed the output of diamonds and so kept up the market price in Europe and elsewhere. Many people refused to believe that Rhodes could have outmanoeuvred a man of exceptional financial ability without using dishonourable means. But there is no doubt that it was masterful character which won the day, that strength of will which decides the issue at the critical moment. Many others have been prejudiced against him merely from the fact that he spent so much time and energy in the pursuit of 'filthy lucre'. We must remember that Rhodes himself said: 'What's the earthly use of having ideas if you haven't the money to carry them out?' We must also remember that all witnesses of his life agree that the ideas were always foremost, the money a mere instrument to realize them. The story was told to Edmund Garrett by one of Rhodes's old Kimberley associates 'how one day in those scheming years, deep in the sordid details of amalgamation, Rhodes ("always a bit of a crank") suddenly put his hand over a great piece of No Man's Africa on the map and said, "Look here: all that British—that is my dream".'[63]

But long before this struggle was over, Rhodes had embarked on new courses which were to carry him still farther. His dreams of political work began to take shape when Griqualand was created a British province in 1880. Two electoral divisions were formed, Kimberley and Barkly West; and it was for the latter that Rhodes first took his seat in the Cape Parliament in 1880, a seat which he retained till his death. The Prime Minister was Sir Gordon Sprigg, a politician with experience but few ideas, more skilled in retaining office than in formulating a policy. Rhodes was at first reticent about his own projects, and spent his time quietly studying commercial questions, examining the problem of the native races and making friends among the Boers. If these friendships were obscured later by political quarrels, there is no reason to suspect their genuineness. His sympathy with the Dutch farmers had begun in 1872, when he made a long, lonely trek through the Northern Transvaal, and it lasted through life. He was interested in farming, he liked natural men, and was at home in unconventional surroundings. One of the closest observers of his character said that to see the true Rhodes you must see him on the veld. So long as the supremacy of the British flag was assured, there was nothing that he so ardently desired as friendly relations between British and Dutch, a real union of the races, a South African nation. It was for this that he worked so long with Jan Hofmeyr, leader of the Cape Dutch, and earned so many unfair suspicions from the short-sighted politicians of Cape Town.

Hofmeyr was a curious man. He had a great understanding of the Dutch character and a great power of influencing men; but this was not done by parliamentary eloquence. By one satirist he was called 'the captain who never appeared on the bridge'; by another he was nicknamed 'the Mole', because his activity could only be conjectured from the tracks which he left behind him. A third name current in Cape Town, 'the Blind Man,' was an ironical tribute to his exceptional astuteness in politics. His organ was 'the Afrikander Bond', a society formed partly for agricultural, partly for political purposes, a creature which like a chameleon has often changed its colour, sometimes working peacefully beside British politicians, at other times openly conducting an anti-British agitation. He certainly had no enthusiasm for the British flag, but he probably realized the freedom which the Colony enjoyed under it, and was clear of all disloyalty to the Crown. The policy dearest to the farmers of the Afrikander Bond was the protective system for their agricultural produce. If Rhodes would support this, he might induce the Dutch to give him a free hand in his plans for expansion towards the North; and this was needed, because the problem of the North was becoming urgent, and Sprigg and his party were blind to its importance.

A glance at the nineteenth-century map will show that the territories of the Dutch Republic, lying on the less barren side of the continent, tended to block the extension of Cape Colony and Natal towards the north, the more so as the Boers from time to time sent out fresh swarms westward and encroached on native territory in Bechuanaland. The Germans did not annex Namaqualand till 1885, but already their interest in this district was becoming evident to close observers. Rhodes's most cherished dream had been the development of the high-lying healthy inland regions to the north by the British race under the British flag. But in those days, when Whitehall was asleep and officials in Cape Town were indifferent, Rhodes saw that his best chance was to convert the Dutch in the Colony. He hoped to make them realize that, if they supported him, the development of the interior might bring trade through Cape Town, which otherwise would go eastward through Portuguese channels. The building of railways, the settlement of new lands in which Dutch and English would share alike, were practical questions which might interest them, and Rhodes was quite genuine in his desire to see both races going forward together. 'Equal rights for every civilized man south of the Zambezi' was his motto, and to this he steadfastly clung.

To describe all the means by which Rhodes worked towards this end would be impossible. He worked hard at Kimberley to furnish the sinews of war; he used his personal influence and power of persuasion at Cape Town to win support from Hofmeyr and others; and he was ready to go to the frontier at any moment when there was work to be done. His first commission of this sort had been in Basutoland in 1882, when he helped the famous General Gordon to pacify native discontent; but the following year saw him at work on another frontier more directly affecting his programme. The Boers had again been raiding westwards and had started two new republics, called Goshen and Stellaland, on the route from Kimberley to the north. Rhodes travelled to the scene of action, interviewed Mankoroane, the Bechuana chief, and Van Niekerk, the head of the new settlement, and by sheer personal magnetism persuaded them both to accept British control. When the Cape Parliament refused the responsibility, he referred to the Colonial Office in London, and by the help of Sir Hercules Robinson, the High Commissioner, he carried his point. When the new Governor, who was appointed by the Colonial Office, quarrelled with the Boers, it was Rhodes who made up the quarrel, and when in 1885 the Transvaal Dutch interfered and provoked our home Government into sending out an overpowering force under Sir Charles Warren, it was Rhodes once more who acted as the reconciler, and effected a settlement between Dutch and British. When the indignant Delarey,[64] provoked by English blundering, said ominously that 'blood must flow', Rhodes replied, 'No, give me my breakfast, and then we can talk about blood'. He stayed with Delarey a week, came to terms on the points at issue, and even became godfather to Delarey's grandchild. He was never the man to resort to force when persuasion could be employed, and he usually won his end by his own means.

While his great work in 1883-5 was on the northern frontier he was growing to be a familiar figure among politicians at Cape Town. We have an impression of him as he appeared on his entrance into politics. 'He was tall, broad-shouldered, with face and figure of somewhat loose formation. His hair was auburn, carelessly flung over his forehead, his eyes of bluish grey, dreamy but kindly. But the mouth—aye, that was the unruly member of his face—with deep lines following the curve of the moustache, it had a determined, masterful, and sometimes scornful expression.... His style of speaking was straight and to the point. He was not a hard hitter in debate—rather a persuader, reasoning and pleading in a conversational way as one more anxious to convince an opponent than to expose his weakness. He used little gesture: what there was, was most expressive, his hands held behind him, or thrust out, sometimes passed over his brow.'[65] Such success as he had in Parliament he owed less to art than to nature, less to oratorical gifts than to force of character; but this brought him rapidly to the front. As early as 1884 he was in the Ministry, and despite his long absences over his northern work he was judged to be the only man who could become Prime Minister in the parliamentary crisis of 1890. There was, by that year, little question that he was the most influential man in South Africa. He had a large holding in the Transvaal goldfields, discovered in 1886; he was head of the great De Beers Corporation of Kimberley; and he was chairman of the newly-created Chartered Company. To many it seemed impossible that one man could combine these great financial interests with the position of First Minister of the Colony; but at least it was clear that the interests of the companies were subordinated to national aims, that the money which he obtained from mines was spent on imperial ends, and that his political position was never used for the promoting of financial objects.

But it is time to return to the development of the north, the greatest of his schemes and the one dearest to his heart. The year 1885 had secured Bechuanaland to the river Molopo as British territory, while a large stretch farther north was under a British protectorate. One danger had been avoided. The neck of the bottle was not corked up: a way to the interior was now open. The next factor to reckon with was the Matabele nation and its chief, Lobengula. They were a Bantu tribe, fond of fighting and hunting, an offshoot of the Zulus who fought us in 1881. They had a very large country surrounding the Matoppo hills, and Lobengula ruled the various districts through 'indunas' or chiefs, who had 'impis' or armies of fighting men at their disposal. To the north-east of them lay the weaker tribe of the Mashona, who paid tribute to Lobengula and whose country was a common hunting-ground for the Matabele braves. Over the latter, so long as he did not check too much their love of fighting, Lobengula exercised a fairly effective control. He himself was a remarkable man, strong in body and mind. Sir Lewis Michell describes him as he appeared to English visitors: 'A somewhat grotesque costume of four yards of blue calico over his shoulders and a string of tigers' tails round his waist could not make his imposing figure ridiculous. In early days he was an athlete and a fine shot; and though, as years went on, his voracious appetite rendered him conspicuously obese, he was every inch a ruler.... Visitors were much struck by his capacity for government: very little went on in his wide dominions of which he was not instantly and accurately informed.' He was an arbitrary ruler, but not cruel to Europeans, of whom a few, like the famous hunter Selous, visited his capital from time to time. He clearly held the keys to the north, and it was with him that Rhodes had now to deal.

The first step was the mission sent out by Rhodes and Beit early in 1888, headed by their old associate Rudd. He and his two fellow-envoys stayed some months with Lobengula watching for favourable moments and trying to win his favour. They shifted their quarters when the king did so, touring from village to village, plied the king and his indunas with offers and arguments, and finally in October they obtained his signature to a treaty giving full and unqualified rights to the envoys for working minerals in his country. In return they covenanted to give him money, rifles, ammunition, and an armed steamboat.

The next step was to get the support of the British authorities in London for that political extension which was dearer to Rhodes than the richest mines and the biggest dividends. In this he was greatly helped by his consistent supporter, Sir Hercules Robinson, who held office in Africa for many years, studied men and matters at first hand, and had a juster estimate of Rhodes and his value to the Empire than the officials in Whitehall. The method of proceeding was by chartered company, the old Elizabethan method, which still has its value to-day, as it relieves the home Government of the expense of developing new countries, yet reserves to it the right to control policy and to enter into the harvest. The Company was to build railways and telegraphs, encourage colonization and spread trade; the Government was to escape from the diplomatic difficulties which might arise with neighbours if it were acting under its own name.

The third step was to make a way into the country and to start actual work. Lobengula's consent was given conditionally: the first expedition was to avoid his capital, Bulawayo, and to go by the south-east to Mashonaland. The chief knew how difficult it might prove to hold in his impis when, instead of a solitary Selous, some hundreds of Europeans began to cross their hunting-grounds. And so it proved. Lobengula had to pretend later that he had not consented to their passage, and the expedition had to slip through the dangerous zone before they could be recalled authoritatively. By May 1890 a column of nearly one thousand men was ready to start from Khama's country; and in June their equipment was approved by a British officer. On September 11, after a march of four hundred miles through trackless country (some of it unknown even to Selous, their guide), the British flag was hoisted on the site of the modern town of Salisbury. It is a chapter of history well worth reading in detail, but Rhodes himself could not be there: the heroes of the march were Jameson and Selous. The other half of Rhodesia, Matabeleland, was not added till a few years later; but British enterprise had now found the way and overcome the worst difficulties. 'Occupation Day' is still kept as the chief festival of the Colony.

Further extension was inevitable. The Matabele impis would not forgo their old habit of raiding amongst the Mashonas. Jameson's complaints received only partial satisfaction from Lobengula. He himself did not want war, but he failed to control his men, and in September 1893 the Chartered Company was driven to fight. They had on the spot about nine hundred men and some machine-guns. Against these the Matabele with all their bravery could effect little. In two engagements they threw away their lives with reckless gallantry, and then they broke and fled. Lobengula himself was never heard of again. His rearguard cut up a small party of British who were too impetuous in pursuit, but by the end of the year the country was at peace. In 1894 Matabeleland was added to the territory of the Chartered Company, in 1895 the term 'Rhodesia' came into use for postal purposes, and in 1897 it was officially adopted for administrative purposes.

The jealousy of the Portuguese, who claimed the 'Hinterland' behind their East African colony, though they had never occupied it, caused a good deal of ill feeling, and very nearly led to hostilities both in Africa and Europe. The

Boers formed schemes for raiding the new lands before they could be effectively occupied, and had to be headed off. The Matabele impis continued for months in a state of excitement; and their forays made it far too dangerous for Rhodes or for others to go up there for some time. But Rhodes himself said that he had less trouble with natives, with Dutch, and with Portuguese, than he had with compatriots of his own, who claimed to have received concessions from native chiefs and intrigued against him in London. But here his peculiar gifts came out, his patience, his persuasive power, his readiness to pour out money like water for a worthy end. Some he beat, others he bought; and in all cases he maintained his position against his rivals. Robinson, Rudd, Jameson, Selous, had all done their parts well, and Rhodes gave them full credit and generous praise; but the mind and the will that planned and carried out the whole movement, and added a province to the British Empire, was unquestionably his own.

Rhodes was Prime Minister of Cape Colony from 1890 to 1895; and during this time he was obliged to be more often at Cape Town. It was in 1891 that he first leased the property lying on the eastern slopes of Table Mountain where he built 'Groote Schuur', the famous house which he bequeathed to the service of the State. Here he gradually acquired 1,500 acres of land, laying them out with a sure eye to the beauty of the surroundings, and to the pleasure of his fellow-citizens. Here he lived from time to time, and received all kinds of men with boundless hospitality. No one can fully understand him who does not read the varying impressions of the friends and guests who sat with him on the 'stoep', under the trees in his garden, or high up on the mountain side, where he had his favourite nooks. The visitors saw what they had eyes to see. One would note his foibles, his blunt manner, his slovenly dress, his want of skill at billiards, his fondness for special dishes or drinks. Another would be impressed by his library with its teak panelling, by the books which he read and the questions which he asked, by his love for Gibbon and Plutarch, by his interest in Marcus Aurelius and other writers on high themes. Others again tell us of his relations to his fellow-men, how recklessly generous he was to young and old, to British and Dutch, and how his generosity was abused: how his acquaintances preyed upon him; how, for all that, he kept his true friendships few in number and he held them sacred. In fact, loyalty to friends meant more to Rhodes than loyalty to principles. His temper was impatient, especially in the last years of physical pain; he often tried to take short cuts to his ends, believing that his ends were worthy and knowing that life was short. He made many mistakes, but he retrieved them nobly. He was in some ways rough-hewn and unpolished, but he was a great man.

It is impossible to put in a short compass the many important questions with which he dealt. His policy towards the natives was moderate and wise. He wished to educate them and then to trust them; to restrict the sale of liquor among them and to open to them the nobler lessons of civilization; to give them the vote when they were educated enough to use it well, but not before; to apply to them too his motto of 'Equal rights for every civilized man south of the Zambezi'. His policy towards the Dutch was to establish identity of interest between the two nations and so to secure friendly relations with them; to draw them into co-operation in agriculture, in railways, in colonization, in export trade, in imperial politics. He did his best to win over the Orange Free State by a policy of common railways, and even to break down the sullen opposition of the Transvaal. But the latter proved impossible. President Kruger leant more and more upon Dutch counsellors from Holland; he looked more and more to Delagoa Bay and turned his back upon Cape Town: and the antagonism became more acute. In 1895 Mr. Chamberlain initiated a new era at the Colonial Office. He was actively awake to British interests in all parts of the globe; and President Kruger, who had tried to check trade with Cape Town by stopping the Cape railway at his frontier, and then by closing the 'Drifts' or fords over the Vaal, was compelled to give way and to keep to the agreements made with the Suzerain State.

A still more serious question was the treatment of the 'Uitlanders' or alien European settlers in the Transvaal. Though the Boer rulers took an increasingly large share of their earnings, they restricted more and more the grant of the franchise. In taxation, in commerce, in education, there was no prospect between the Vaal and the Limpopo of 'Equal rights for all civilized men' or anything like it. In June 1894 the High Commissioner frankly told Kruger that the Uitlanders had 'very real and substantial grievances'; in 1895 they were no less substantial, and agitation was rife in Johannesburg. On December 28, Jameson at the head of an armed column left Pitsani on the borders and rode into the Transvaal to support a rising against the Boer Government. The Uitlanders were not expecting him; no rising took place, and Jameson's small column was surrounded some miles west of Johannesburg, outnumbered, and forced to surrender. The Jameson Raid, for which Rhodes was generally held responsible, attracted all eyes in Europe as in Africa. How President Kruger used his advantage against the Uitlanders, among whom Col. Frank Rhodes was a leader, can be read in many books: here we need only relate how the event affected the Premier of Cape Colony. He resigned office at once and put himself at the disposal of the Government. Despite his past record he was judged by the Dutch, alike in the Cape and in the Transvaal, to have been the author of the Raid, and all chance of his doing further service in reconciling the two races was at an end. The beginning of 1895 saw him at the height of his ambition. The end of it saw his power shattered beyond repair.

His behaviour in this crisis enables us to know the real man. For a few days he kept aloof, unapproachable, overcome by the ruin of his work. He made no attempt to conciliate opinion: in moments of bitterness he scoffed at the 'unctuous rectitude' of certain politicians who were improving the occasion. But he spoke frankly to those who had the right to question him. He went to London in February and saw Mr. Chamberlain, the Colonial Secretary, and his Directors. He admitted that he was at fault. Believing that Kruger would always yield to a show of force, he had been responsible for putting troops near the border to exercise moral pressure. But neither then nor at any time had he given Jameson orders to invade the Transvaal, or to precipitate an armed conflict, which he believed to be unnecessary. Such was his consistent statement, and he was ready to face, when the time should come, the Parliamentary committees appointed by the British and South African Houses to report on the Raid. Meanwhile he put all brooding away and looked round for some practical work. Fortunately he found it in the most congenial sphere. His colony of Rhodesia, to which he had gone straight from London, was threatened with disaster from a great native outbreak. The causes were various. Rinderpest had spoiled one of the chief native industries, and superstition had invented foolish reasons for it; also the rumours, which were spreading about the Raid, made the natives believe that the British power was shaken. The Mashonas, as well as the Matabele, took part in the revolt which began early in April 1896. To meet it the colonists mustered their full strength, while General Carrington was sent out from home with some regular troops. Several engagements in difficult country followed: the enemies' forces were quickly broken up, and by the end of July the time for negotiation was come.

But the chiefs of the Matabele had retired into their fortresses in the Matoppo hills and could not be reached. To send small columns to track them down might mean needless loss of life: to keep the forces in the field right through the winter was ruinous to the Company's finances. Rhodes offered his own services as negotiator, and they were accepted. The man who could carry his point with Jewish financiers and Dutch politicians might hope to achieve his ends with the simpler native chiefs. But it was a sore trial of patience. He moved his own tent two miles away from the British troops to the foot of the hills, sent native messengers to the chiefs, and waited. During this time he was not idle: he put in a lot of riding and of miscellaneous reading: his mind was actively employed in planning roads and dams for irrigation, in scheming for the future greatness of the country. It was six weeks before a chief responded. Gradually they began to drop in and to hold informal meetings round the tent, putting questions, replying to Rhodes's jokes, relapsing into fits of silence, oblivious as all savages are of the value of time. He would spend hours day after day in this apparently futile way; accustoming them to his presence, coaxing them into the right humour. At last he persuaded them to meet him in a formal 'indaba', which must have been a dramatic scene. Alone he stood facing them, boldly reproaching them with their bad faith and cruel acts. They stated their grievances: some were admitted: satisfaction was promised. In the end peace was proclaimed and the delighted natives greeted him uproariously with the title of Lamula 'm Kunzi (Separator of the Fighting Bulls). The discussions were not over till the end of October, and it was a month later ere Rhodes was able to leave the country and face the Committee in London—a very different gathering in very different surroundings. His work during these two months was perhaps the greatest of his life; and that he should have been able to concentrate all his powers upon it so soon after the shattering blow of the Raid is a great tribute to his essential manliness and patriotism.

The two Committees, sitting in London and Cape Town, agreed to censure, though in modified terms, Rhodes's conduct over the Raid; but he still retained the respect of the bulk of his countrymen, and on his return the citizens of Cape Town gave him an enthusiastic welcome. They and he were looking ahead as well as behind: they felt that his services were still needed for the establishing of a United South Africa under the British flag. But in this respect his work was done. The Cape Dutch were more and more influenced by their sentiment for the Transvaal, and racial feeling ran high. Rhodes severed himself from all his old Dutch colleagues and became more of a party leader. Meanwhile Kruger watched the breach, assured himself of Dutch support, made no concessions to the Uitlanders, repelled all overtures from Mr. Chamberlain, and steered straight for war. Rhodes, despite his knowledge of the Dutch, made the mistake of believing up to the last moment that Kruger would give way and not fight; but, when the war broke out in 1899, he went up to Kimberley to take his share of the work and the danger. The siege lasted about four months, and Rhodes, though he failed to work harmoniously with the military commandant, rendered many services to the town, thanks to his wealth, influence, and knowledge of the place. When the town was relieved in February 1900, he went to Rhodesia and spent many months there. Though he was urged by his followers to return to politics, Cape Town saw little of him; when he was not in the north, he was mostly at his seaside cottage at Muizenberg, half-way between the capital and the Cape of Good Hope. The heart complaint, from which he had suffered intermittently all his life, had rapidly grown worse; his last year was one of great suffering, and in March 1902 he breathed his last at Muizenberg with Jameson and a few of his dearest friends around him. He was buried in the place which he had himself chosen amid the Matoppo hills. On a bare hill-top seven gigantic boulders keep guard round the simple tombstone on which his name is engraved. After the English service was over, the natives celebrated in their own fashion the passing of the great chief who had already been enshrined in their imagination.

At Kimberley, at Cape Town, in the Matoppos, his work was done before the nineteenth century was finished, and he had earned his rest. The complete union of the European races for which he laboured in Parliament is yet to come. The vast wealth which he won in Kimberley is fulfilling a noble purpose. By his will he founded scholarships at Oxford for scholars from the Dominions and Colonies, from the United States and from Germany—his faith in the Anglo-Saxon race being extended to our Teutonic kinsmen. He regarded a common education and common ideals as the surest cement of Empire. But above all else his name will be preserved among his countrymen by the provinces which he added to the British dominions. Kimberley and Cape Town have their monuments, their memories of his many successes and his few failures: the Matoppos have his grave. To us the peace and solitude of the hills where he lies may seem to contrast strangely with the stirring activity of his life. But solitude will not reign there always, if Rhodes's ideal is fulfilled. It was here that he had stood with a friend, looking towards the vast horizon northwards, and, in an often-quoted sentence, expressed his dream for the future: 'Homes, more homes, that's what I work for!' So long as our race produces such bold dreamers, such strenuous workers, its future, in Africa and elsewhere, need occasion no doubts or fears.

FOOTNOTES:

[1] Farms near Ecclefechan to which his parents moved in 1814 and 1826.

[2] Emerson, *English Traits*, 'World's Classics' edition, p. 8.

[3] The most famous course, on Hero-Worship, was delivered in May, 1840.

[4] Afterwards Lord and Lady Ashburton.

[5] Froude, *Carlyle, Life in London*, vol. ii, pp. 100 and 217.

[6] Walter Bagehot, *Biographical Studies*, p. 17 (Longmans, 1907).

[7] Sir James Graham, afterwards Home Secretary under Peel in 1841.

[8] Since his father's death, in 1830, Peel had been member for Tamworth.

[9] *Correspondence of Sarah, Lady Lyttelton*, by Maud Wyndham (Murray, 1912).

[10] The Right Hon. C. P. Villiers, M.P. for Wolverhampton, began to advocate repeal in 1837, four years before Cobden entered Parliament.

[11] Morley's *Life of Gladstone*, vol. i, pp. 297-300 (cf. Gladstone's own retirement in 1874).

[12] Ceded to Great Britain in 1815 and given by her in 1864 to Greece.

[13] His first wife, whom he married in 1827, died in 1832. He married again in 1835.

[14] The dual control of British India by the Crown and the East India Company lasted from 1778 to 1858.

[15] To help church work by adding to the number of clergy.

[16] See articles in *D.N.B.* on Michael Thomas Sadler (1780-1835) and on Richard Oastler (1789-1861).

[17] 'Talukdār' in the north-west, 'zamīndār' in Bengal.

[18] 'Doāb' = land between two rivers.

[19] Created Lord Napier of Magdala after storming King Theodore's fortress in 1868.

[20] See G. M. Trevelyan, *Life of John Bright*, pp. 384-5.

[21] See Fitzmaurice, *Life of Lord Granville*, vol. i, p. 540.

[22] *Charles Dickens, Social Reformer*, by W. W. Crotch (Chapman & Hall, 1913), p. 53.

[23] *In Memoriam*, c.

[24] Lines written in 1837 and published in the *Manchester Athenæum Album*, 1850.

[25] The portrait of 1838 by Samuel Laurence, of which the original is at Aldworth, speaks for itself.

[26] *Tennyson*, by Stopford Brooke (Isbister, 1894).

[27] *Alfred Lord Tennyson: A Memoir*, by his son, vol. i, p. 209 (Macmillan & Co.).

[28] *Robert Browning*, by Edward Dowden, p. 173 (J. M. Dent & Co.).

[29] See *Memoir*, by Hallam, Lord Tennyson, vol. i, p. 283 (Macmillan).

[30] 'God and the Universe,' from *Death of Oenone*, &c. Macmillan, (1892.)

[31] For a few weeks in 1844 he was curate of Pimperne in Dorset.

[32] See Preface by T. Hughes prefixed to later editions of *Alton Locke*.

[33] Sir Henry Taylor, author of *Philip van Artevelde* and other poems, and a high official of the Colonial Office.

[34] Sir Anthony Panizzi, an Italian political refugee, the most famous of librarians. He served the British Museum from 1831 to 1866.

[35] '"Hure: tête hérissée et en désordre"; se dit d'un homme qui a les cheveux mal peignés, d'un animal, &c.'—Littré.

[36] His allegorical subjects are in the Tate Gallery; his portraits in the National Portrait Gallery.

[37] *Life and Episcopate of G. A. Selwyn*, by H. W. Tucker, 2 vols. (Wells Gardner, 1879).

[38] Melanesia, from Greek μέλας=black, νησος=island.

[39] Bishop Selwyn (Primate), Bishop Abraham of Wellington, and Bishop Hobhouse of Nelson.

[40] This island had lately been colonized by settlers from Pitcairn Island, descended from the mutineers of the *Bounty*, marooned in 1789.

[41] *Life of John Coleridge Patteson*, by Charlotte Yonge, 2 vols. (Macmillan, 1874).

[42] The Latin form in which this epigram was originally couched—*mentiendi causa*—does away with all ambiguity.

[43] The ill-fated Emperor Frederick III, who died of cancer in 1888.

[44] *Memoirs of Sir Robert Morier*, 1826-76, by his daughter, Lady Rosslyn Wemyss, vol. i, p. 303 (Edward Arnold, 1911).

[45] Sir James Hudson, G.C.B., British minister at Turin during the years of Cavour's great ministry; died 1885.

[46] Sir Horace Rumbold, G.C.B., Ambassador at Vienna 1896-1900; died 1913.

[47] W. E. Henley, poet and critic, 1849-1903. His poems, 'In Hospital' include also a very beautiful sonnet on 'The Chief'—Lister himself, which almost calls up his portrait to one who has once seen it: 'His brow spreads large and placid.... Soft lines of tranquil thought.... His face at once benign and proud and shy.... His wise rare smile.'

[48] Professor Volkmann of Halle and Professor von Nussbaum of Munich.

[49] Restricted to thirty German and thirty foreign members.

[50] *Memorials of Edward Burne-Jones*, by G. B.-J., 2 vols. (Macmillan, 1904).

[51] Letter quoted in *Life of Morris*, by J. W. Mackail, vol. i, p. 257 (Longmans, Green & Co., 1911).

[52] Other easily accessible examples are in Christ Church Cathedral, Oxford, and Jesus College Chapel, Cambridge.

[53] *William Morris*, by A. Clutton-Brock (Williams and Norgate, 1914).

[54] *Life of Morris*, by J. W. Mackail, vol. ii, pp. 133-9.

[55] Mr. Hyndman (*Story of an Adventurous Life*, p. 355) describes a visit to the Bodleian Library at Oxford with Morris, and how 'quickly, carefully, and surely' he dated the illuminated manuscripts.

[56] Rev. J. B. Mozley, 1813-78. Canon of Worcester and Regius Professor of Divinity at Oxford: a Tractarian; author of essays on Strafford, Laud, &c.

[57] The first edition of Bryce's *Holy Roman Empire* was published in 1862.

[58] Pragmatic: 'treating facts of history with reference to their practical lessons.' *Concise Oxford Dictionary*.

[59] *Clio and other Essays*, by G. M. Trevelyan, p. 4 (Longmans, Green & Co., 1913).

[60] C. D. Rudd (1844-96), educated at Harrow and Cambridge.

[61] Alfred Beit, born at Hamburg, 1853; died in London, 1906.

[62] Barney Barnato, born in Houndsditch, 1852; died at sea, 1897.

[63] Perhaps the best character sketch of Rhodes is that printed as an appendix to Sir E. T. Cook's *Life of Edmund Garrett* (Edward Arnold, 1909). Garrett's career as journalist and politician in South Africa was terminated by illness in 1899.

[64] General Jacobus Delarey, one of the most successful commanders in the Great Boer War of 1899-1902.

[65] *Cecil Rhodes: a Monograph and a Reminiscence*, by Sir Thomas Fuller (Longmans & Co., 1910)

Milton Keynes UK
Ingram Content Group UK Ltd.
UKHW030904151124
451262UK00006B/1038